THE RIGHT TO SEX

THE RIGHT TO SEX

FEMINISM IN THE TWENTY-FIRST CENTURY

AMIA SRINIVASAN

FARRAR, STRAUS AND GIROUX
New York

Farrar, Straus and Giroux
120 Broadway, New York 10271

Library of Congress Cataloging-in-Publication Data
Names: Srinivasan, Amia, 1984– author.
Title: The right to sex : feminism in the twenty-first century / Amia Srinivasan.
Description: New York : Farrar, Straus and Giroux, [2021] | Includes
    bibliographical references and index.
Identifiers: LCCN 2021016449 | ISBN 9780374248529 (hardcover)
Subjects: LCSH: Sexual rights—Philosophy. | Sex—Political aspects. | Sex—
    Philosophy. | Feminism. | Sexual ethics.
Classification: LCC HQ65 .S75 2021 | DDC 305.42—dc23
LC record available at https://lccn.loc.gov/2021016449

Our books may be purchased in bulk for promotional,
educational, or business use. Please contact your local bookseller
or the Macmillan Corporate and Premium Sales Department
at 1-800-221-7945, extension 5442, or by email at
MacmillanSpecialMarkets@macmillan.com.

www.fsgbooks.com
www.twitter.com/fsgbooks • www.facebook.com/fsgbooks

1   3   5   7   9   10   8   6   4   2

For my mother, Chitra

the thing I came for:
the wreck and not the story of the wreck
the thing itself and not the myth

Adrienne Rich, "Diving into the Wreck"

Contents

Preface

Feminism is not a philosophy, or a theory, or even a point of view. It is a political movement to transform the world beyond recognition. It asks: what would it be to end the political, social, sexual, economic, psychological and physical subordination of women? It answers: we do not know; let us try and see.

Feminism begins with a woman's recognition that she is a member of a sex class: that is, a member of a class of people assigned to an inferior social status on the basis of something called "sex"— a thing that is said to be natural, pre-political, an objective material ground on which the world of human culture is built.

We inspect this supposedly natural thing, "sex," only to find that it is already laden with meaning. At birth, bodies are sorted as "male" or "female," though many bodies must be mutilated to fit one category or the other, and many bodies will later protest against the decision that was made. This originary division determines what social purpose a body will be assigned. Some of these bodies are for creating new bodies, for washing and clothing and feeding other bodies (out of love, never duty), for making other bodies feel good and whole and in control, for making other bodies feel free. Sex is, then, a cultural thing posing as a natural one. Sex, which feminists have taught us to distinguish from gender, is itself already gender in disguise.[1]

There is another sense of the word "sex": sex as a thing we do with our sexed bodies. Some bodies are for other bodies to have sex with. Some bodies are for the pleasure, the possession, the consumption, the worshipping, the servicing, the validating of other bodies. "Sex" in this second sense is also said to be a natural thing, a thing that exists outside politics. Feminism shows that this too is a fiction, and a fiction that serves certain interests. Sex, which we think of as the most private of acts, is in reality a public thing. The roles we play, the emotions we feel, who gives, who takes, who demands, who serves, who wants, who is wanted, who benefits, who suffers: the rules for all this were set long before we entered the world.

A famous philosopher once said to me that he objected to feminist critiques of sex because it was only during sex that he felt truly outside politics, that he felt truly free. I asked him what his wife would say to that. (I couldn't ask her myself; she hadn't been invited to the dinner.) This is not to say that sex cannot be free. Feminists have long dreamed of sexual freedom. What they refuse to accept is its simulacrum: sex that is said to be free, not because it is equal, but because it is ubiquitous. In this world, sexual freedom is not a given but something to be achieved, and it is always incomplete. Simone de Beauvoir, dreaming of a freer sex to come, wrote in *The Second Sex*:

> assuredly, women's autonomy, even if it spares men a good number of problems, will also deny them many conveniences; assuredly, there are certain ways of living the sexual adventure that will be lost in the world of tomorrow: but this does not mean that

love, happiness, poetry, and dreams will be banished from it. Let us beware lest our lack of imagination impoverish the future . . . new carnal and affective relations of which we cannot conceive will be born between the sexes . . . It is absurd to contend that . . . vice, ecstasy, and passion would become impossible if man and woman were concretely peers; the contradictions opposing flesh to spirit, instant to time, the vertigo of immanence to the appeal of transcendence, the absolute of pleasure to the nothingness of oblivion will never disappear; tension, suffering, joy, and the failure and triumph of existence will always be materialized in sexuality . . . on the contrary, it is when the slavery of half of humanity is abolished and with it the whole hypocritical system it implies that the . . . human couple will discover its true form.[2]

What would it take for sex really to be free? We do not yet know; let us try and see.

These essays are about the politics and ethics of sex in this world, animated by a hope of a different world. They reach back to an older feminist tradition that was unafraid to think of sex as a political phenomenon, as something squarely within the bounds of social critique. The women in this tradition—from Simone de Beauvoir and Alexandra Kollontai to bell hooks, Audre Lorde, Catharine MacKinnon, and Adrienne Rich—dare us to think about the ethics of sex beyond the narrow parameters of "consent." They compel us to ask what forces lie behind a woman's *yes*; what it reveals about sex that it is something to which consent must be given; how it is that we have come to put so much psychic, cultural, and legal weight on a notion of "consent" that cannot support it. And they ask us to join them in dreaming of a freer sex.

At the same time, these essays seek to remake the political critique of sex for the twenty-first century: to take seriously the complex relationship of sex to race, class, disability, nationality, and caste; to think about what sex has become in the age of the internet;

to ask what it means to invoke the power of the capitalist and carceral state to address the problems of sex.

These essays respond largely to situations in the US and the UK;
I also pay some attention to India. This is partly a reflection of my
own background. But it is also a deliberate choice. These essays
are critical of much mainstream anglophone feminist thought and
practice, which for decades has been the most visible, and materially powerful, form of feminism around the world. (Of course
the feminists working outside of the anglophone mainstream have
never been invisible, or "marginal," to themselves or their communities.) It is good to be able to write that this dominance has,
of late, been receding, not least because the most exhilarating
recent expressions of feminist energies have come from outside
Anglophone contexts. To take just a few examples at the time of
writing: in Poland, where the right-wing coalition government
is implementing further legal restrictions on abortion, feminists
have led a general uprising across the country, with protests in
more than 500 cities and towns; in Argentina, five years of mass
marches by feminists under the slogan "Ni una Menos" ("Not one
woman less") have compelled the Congress to legalize abortion,
while feminists in Brazil, Chile and Colombia, where abortion
remains largely illegal, are organizing to follow suit; in Sudan,
women led the revolutionary protests that brought down the dictatorial regime of Omar al-Bashir, and it was a young Sudanese
feminist in her early twenties, Alaa Salah, who demanded that the
United Nations Security Council ensure that women, resistance
groups, and religious minorities be included on equal terms in
Sudan's transitional government.[3]

On some matters—sex workers' rights, the destructiveness of
carceral politics, the pathologies of contemporary sexuality—these
essays are adamant. But on others they are ambivalent, unwilling to
reduce what is dense and difficult to something easier. Feminism
must be relentlessly truth-telling, not least about itself. (As the
labor historian David Roediger writes, a radical movement "speaking

frankly to itself" is a "far more important activity than 'speaking truth to power.'"[4]) Feminism cannot indulge the fantasy that interests always converge; that our plans will have no unexpected, undesirable consequences; that politics is a place of comfort.

The feminist scholar and activist Bernice Johnson Reagon, speaking in the last century about this one, warned that a truly radical politics—that is, a coalitional politics—cannot be a home to its members:

> Coalition work is not work done in your home. Coalition work has to be done in the streets . . . And you shouldn't look for comfort. Some people will come to a coalition and they rate the success of the coalition on whether or not they feel good when they get there. They're not looking for a coalition; they're looking for a home! They're looking for a bottle with some milk in it and a nipple, which does not happen in a coalition.[5]

For Reagon, it is the belief that politics should be a perfect home—a place of complete belonging, "a womb," as she puts it—which leads to the exclusionary contradictions of much feminism. Feminism envisaged as a "home" insists on commonality before the fact, pushing aside all those who would trouble its domestic idyll. A truly inclusionary politics is an uncomfortable, unsafe politics.

In these essays I attempt to dwell, where necessary, in discomfort and ambivalence. These essays do not offer a home. But I hope they do offer, for some, a place of recognition. I have written them to be read together, or by themselves. They are not intended to convince or persuade anyone of anything, though I would not be unhappy if they did. Instead, they represent my attempt to put into words what many women, and some men, already know. This has always been the way of feminism: women working collectively to articulate the unsaid, the formerly unsayable. At its best, feminist theory is grounded in what women think when they are by themselves, what they say to each other on the picket line and on the assembly line and on the street corner and in the bedroom, what they have tried to say to their husbands and fathers and sons and bosses and elected officials a thousand times over. At its best, feminist theory discloses the possibilities for women's lives that are latent in women's struggles, drawing those possibilities closer. But, too often, feminist theory prescinds from the particulars of women's lives, only to tell them, from on high, what their lives really mean. Most women have little use for such pretensions. They have too much work to do.

Oxford, 2020

THE RIGHT TO SEX

The Conspiracy Against Men

I know two men who were, I am fairly confident, falsely accused of rape. One of them was a wealthy young man accused by a desperate young woman who had stolen some credit cards and was on the run. The rape accusation was just one part of a larger fraud. The man wasn't where she said he had been when the alleged rape took place, there was no evidence of rape beyond her testimony, and much else of what she said turned out to be false. He was never arrested or charged, and from the start the police assured him that all would be well.

The other man is a creep: narcissistic, charming, manipulative, and a liar. He is known to use all sorts of coercive methods to get sex, but not the sort that fall under the legal definition of rape. The women he has sex with (young, precocious, confident) are consenting; indeed, he's the kind of man who makes women feel, at the time, that they are the ones seducing him—that they are the ones with all the agency and power, when in fact they have relatively little of it. ("She seduced *me*" is of course a defense commonly made by rapists—and by pedophiles.) When one of these women, years later—having learned of the man's pattern, and seeing him for what he was—accused him of assault, it seemed to those who knew him that she might well have been seeking a legal remedy for what he put her through: for having been used, manipulated, and lied to. Maybe, on top of all that, he really did assault her. But the evidence suggested otherwise. He was never charged with rape, though he was, because of his reckless, unprofessional behavior, made to resign from his job. From what I hear, the man (now gainfully re-employed) goes on much as he did before, though more carefully and quietly, and with more plausible deniability. These days he self-styles as a feminist.

I know many more than two women who have been raped. This is unsurprising. Many more women are raped than falsely accuse men of rape. With just one exception, none of the women I know pressed criminal charges or made a report to the police. One friend, when we were both in college, called me to tell me that a guy she knew, a friend of a friend, had, during an early evening group outing when they were fooling around on a pool table in an empty dorm social room, forced himself inside her. She had said no, resisted, finally pushed him off. The evening resumed. Neither she nor I considered going to the police. The purpose of the call was simply to acknowledge that this thing—we didn't call it *rape*—had happened.

Some men are falsely accused of rape; there is nothing to be gained by denying it. But false accusations are rare. The most detailed ever study of sexual assault reports, released by the UK Home Office in 2005, estimated that just 3 percent of 2,643 rape reports made over the course of fifteen years were "probably" or "possibly" false.[1] Yet the British police had classified, in the same period, more than twice as many—8 percent—of these reports as false, based on its officers' personal judgment.[2] In 1996, the FBI also reported an 8 percent rate of "unfounded" or "false" forcible rape complaints, aggregated from police departments across the US.[3] In both Britain and the US, the 8 percent figure was largely the result of police officers' susceptibility to rape myths; in both countries, police officers were inclined to consider a report false if there hadn't been a physical struggle, if no weapon had been involved, or if the accuser had had a prior relationship with the accused.[4] In 2014, according to figures published in India, 53 percent of rape reports in Delhi from the previous year had been false, a statistic giddily seized on by Indian men's rights activists. But the definition of "false" reports had been extended to cover all those cases that hadn't reached court, never mind those that didn't meet the legal standard for rape in India[5]—including marital rape, which 6 percent of married Indian women report having experienced.[6]

In the UK Home Office study, the police judged 216 of 2,643 complaints false. In those 216 cases, the complainants had named a total of thirty-nine suspects; six of these suspects were arrested, and charges were brought against two of them; in both cases, the charges were eventually dropped. So, in the final analysis, bearing in mind that the Home Office counted only a third as many false accusations as the police, just 0.23 percent of rape reports led to a false arrest, and only 0.07 percent of rape reports led to a man being falsely charged with rape; none resulted in wrongful conviction.[7]

I am not saying that false rape accusations are something to shrug at. They are not. An innocent man disbelieved, mistrusted, his reality twisted, his reputation stripped, his life potentially ruined by the manipulation of state power: this is a moral scandal. And, notice, it is a moral scandal that has much in common with the experience of rape victims, who in many cases face a conspiracy of disbelief, especially from police. Nonetheless, a false rape accusation, like a plane crash, is an objectively unusual event that occupies an outsized place in the public imagination. Why then does it carry its cultural charge? The answer cannot simply be that its victims are men: the number of men raped—largely by other men—easily overwhelms the number of men falsely accused of rape.[8] Could it be not only that the victims of false rape accusations are usually men, but also that its assumed perpetrators are women?

Except that, very often, it is men who falsely accuse other men of raping women. This is a thing almost universally misunderstood about false rape accusations. When we think of a false rape accusation we picture a scorned or greedy woman, lying to the authorities. But many, perhaps most, wrongful convictions of rape result from false accusations levied against men by other men: by cops and prosecutors, overwhelmingly male, intent on pinning an actual rape on the wrong suspect. In the US, which has the world's highest incarceration rate, 147 men were exonerated for sexual assault on the basis of false accusations or perjury between 1989 and 2020.[9] (In that same period, 755 people—five times as many—were found to have been falsely accused, and wrongly convicted, of murder.[10]) Fewer than half of these men were deliberately framed by their alleged victims. Meanwhile, over half of their cases involved "official misconduct": a category that applies when the police coach false victim or witness identifications, charge a suspect despite the victim's failure to identify him as the attacker, suppress evidence or induce false confessions.

There is no general conspiracy against men. But there is a conspiracy against certain classes of men. Of the 147 men who were exonerated of sexual assault on the basis of a false accusation or perjury in the US between 1989 and 2020, 85 were non-white and 62 white. Of those 85 non-white men, 76 were black, which means that black men make up 52 percent of those convicted of rape on the basis of false accusations or perjury. Yet black men make up only about 14 percent of the US male population, and 27 percent of men convicted of rape.[11] A black man serving time for sexual assault is 3.5 times more likely to be innocent than a white man convicted of sexual assault.[12] He is also very likely to be poor—not just because black people in the US are disproportionately poor, but because most incarcerated Americans, of all races, are poor.[13]

The National Registry of Exonerations, which lists the men and women wrongly imprisoned in the US since 1989, does not detail the long history of false rape accusations against black men which bypassed the legal system altogether. In particular, it does not record the deployment of the false rape accusation in the Jim Crow period as, in Ida B. Wells's words, "an excuse to get rid of Negroes who were acquiring wealth and property and thus keep the race terrorized."[14] It does not take into account the 150 black men who were lynched between 1892 and 1894 for alleged rape or attempted rape of white women—a charge that included known consensual affairs between black men and white women—as chronicled in Wells's remarkable *A Red Record*.[15] It does not mention the case of William Brooks of Galesline, Arkansas, who was lynched on May 23, 1894, for asking a white woman to marry him, or tell us anything about the "unknown Negro" whom Wells reports having been lynched in West Texas earlier that month for the crime of "writing letter to white woman." In 2007, Carolyn Bryant admitted that she had lied, fifty-two years earlier, when she said that a fourteen-year-old black boy named Emmett Till had grabbed and sexually propositioned her—a lie that spurred Bryant's husband, Roy, and his brother to abduct, bludgeon, shoot, and kill Till.[16] Roy Bryant and his brother were acquitted of murder, despite the overwhelming evidence against them; four months later, they were paid $3,000 for the story of how they did it by *Look* magazine. There is no registry that details the uses of false rape accusations as a tactic of colonial rule: in India, in Australia, in South Africa, in Palestine.[17]

It might seem surprising, then, that false rape accusations are, today, a predominantly wealthy white male preoccupation. But it isn't surprising—not really. The anxiety about false rape accusations is purportedly about injustice (innocent people being harmed), but actually it is about gender, about innocent men being harmed by malignant women. It is an anxiety, too, about race and class: about the possibility that the law might treat wealthy white men as it routinely treats poor black and brown men. For poor men, and women, of color, the white woman's false rape accusation is just one element in a matrix of vulnerability to state power.[18] But false rape accusations are a unique instance of middle-class and wealthy white men's vulnerability to the injustices routinely perpetrated by the carceral state against poor people of color. Well-off white men instinctively and correctly trust that the legal justice system will take care of them: will not plant drugs on them, will not gun them down and later claim to have seen a weapon, will not harass them for walking in a neighborhood where they "don't belong," will give them a pass for carrying that gram of cocaine or bag of weed. But in the case of rape, well-off white men worry that the growing demand that women be believed will cut against their right to be shielded from the prejudices of the law.[19]

That representation is, of course, false: even in the case of rape, the state is on the side of wealthy white men. But what matters—in the sense of what is ideologically efficacious—is not the reality, but the misrepresentation. In the false rape accusation, wealthy white men misperceive their vulnerability to women and to the state.

I n 2016, the Santa Clara County Superior Court Judge Aaron Persky sentenced a twenty-year-old Stanford swimmer, Brock Turner, to six months in county jail (of which he served three) on three felony counts of sexual assault against Chanel Miller. In a letter to the judge, Brock Turner's father, Dan A. Turner, wrote:

Brock's life has been deeply altered forever by the events of Jan 17th and 18th. He will never be his happy go lucky self with that easygoing personality and welcoming smile . . . You can see this in his face, the way he walks, his weakened voice, his lack of appetite. Brock always enjoyed certain types of food and is a very good cook himself. I was always excited to buy him a big ribeye steak to grill or to get his favorite snack for him. I had to make sure to hide some of my favorite pretzels or chips because I knew they wouldn't be around long after Brock walked in from a long swim practice. Now he barely consumes any food and eats only to exist. These verdicts have broken and shattered him and our family in so many ways. His life will never be the one that he dreamed about and worked so hard to achieve. That is a steep price to pay for 20 minutes of action out of his 20 plus years of life.[20]

The myopic focus on his son's well-being—wasn't Miller's life also "deeply altered forever"?—is striking. Even more so is the (presumably inadvertent) sexual pun: "20 minutes of action"—healthy, adolescent fun. Should Brock, Dan Turner seems to want to ask, be punished for that? Then there is the food. Brock no longer loves his steak? You no longer have to hide the pretzels or chips from Brock? This is the way one talks about a golden retriever, not an adult human. But in a sense Dan Turner is talking about an animal, a perfectly bred specimen of wealthy white American boyhood: "happy go lucky," "easygoing," sporty, friendly, and endowed with a healthy appetite and glistening coat. And, like an animal, Brock is imagined to exist outside the moral order. These red-blooded, white-skinned, all-American boys—and the all-American girls who date them and marry them (but are never, ever sexually assaulted by them)—are good kids, the best kids, our kids.

That Supreme Court Justice Brett Kavanaugh was one such all-American kid was his ultimate defense against Christine Blasey Ford's allegations that he had sexually assaulted her when they were both in high school. Ford, Kavanaugh said, "did not travel in the same social circles" as he and his friends.[21] In the summer of 1982, Brett—only child of Martha and Everett Edward Kavanaugh Jr.—was spending time with his friends from Georgetown Prep, among the US's most expensive private schools (and alma mater of Neil Gorsuch and two of Robert Kennedy's sons), together with students of the neighboring Catholic girls' schools: Stone Ridge,

Holy Child, Visitation, Immaculata, Holy Cross. The group—Tobin, Mark, P.J., Squi, Bernie, Matt, Becky, Denise, Lori, Jenny, Pat, Amy, Julie, Kristin, Karen, Suzanne, Maura, Megan, Nicki—spent that summer going to the beach, training for football, lifting weights, drinking beers, attending church on Sundays, and generally having the best time of their lives. Sixty-five women who knew Kavanaugh in high school signed a letter defending him after Ford's allegation was made public. "Friends for a lifetime," Kavanaugh said of these women, "built on a foundation of talking through school and life starting at age 14."

Ford was, in an objective sense, part of Kavanaugh's social and economic order. She was white and rich, and—assuming she remembers correctly, and do you believe she doesn't?—she hung out with Brett and his friends at least once. But Ford's allegations make her an exile from the social world of healthy white girls and boys, who occasionally do things (in Kavanaugh's words) that are "goofy" and "embarrassing"—but never criminal. In their senior yearbook, Kavanaugh and his friends used the phrase "Renate Alumnius [sic]" to describe themselves—an allusion to Renate Schroeder, one of the sixty-five "friends for a lifetime" who signed the letter attesting to Kavanaugh's having "always treated women with decency and respect." Questioned about the phrase, Kavanaugh said that it "was clumsily intended to show affection, and that she was one of us," and that it was "not related to sex." Schroeder, who learned of the yearbook smear after signing the letter, said in a statement to the *Times* that it was "horrible, hurtful and simply untrue." "I can't begin to comprehend what goes through the minds of 17-year-old boys who write such things," she said. "I pray their daughters are never treated this way."[22] After Kavanaugh's confirmation, Christine Blasey Ford's father, Ralph, gave a warm handshake to Ed Kavanaugh, Brett Kavanaugh's father, at the Burning Tree Club in Bethesda, where they both play golf. "I'm glad Brett was confirmed," Ralph Blasey apparently said, one Republican dad to another.[23]

What if Brett Kavanaugh hadn't been white? It's a hard coun-terfactual to evaluate, because the world would have to be very different for a black or brown boy to grow up not only with the sort of financial and social privilege Brett had—the wealthy family, elite school, the legacy at Yale—but moreover to have a phalanx of similarly privileged peers who would have his back come hell or high water. The solidarity on show from the people who knew Kavanaugh when young—what Kavanaugh calls "friendship"—was the solidarity of rich white people. We can't imagine a black or brown Kavanaugh without inverting America's racial and economic rules.

For many women of color, the mainstream feminist injunction "Believe women" and its online correlate #IBelieveHer raise more questions than they settle. Whom are we to believe, the white woman who says she was raped, or the black or brown woman who insists that her son is being set up? Carolyn Bryant or Mamie Till?

Defenders of "men's rights" like to say that "Believe women" vio-lates the presumption of innocence. But this is a category error. The presumption of innocence is a legal principle: it answers to our sense that it is worse, all else being equal, for the law to wrongly punish than to wrongly exonerate. It is for this reason that in most legal systems the burden of proof rests with the accuser, not the accused. "Believe women" is not an injunction to abandon this legal principle, at least in most cases, but a political response to what we suspect will be its uneven application. Under the law, people accused of crimes are presumed innocent, but some—we know—are presumed more innocent than others. Against this prejudicial enforcement of the presumption of innocence, "Believe women" operates as a corrective norm, a gesture of support for those people—women—whom the law tends to treat as if they were lying.

The dismissal of "Believe women" as an abandonment of the pre-sumption of innocence is a category error in a second sense. The presumption of innocence does not tell us what to believe. It tells us how guilt is to be established by the law: that is, by a process that deliberately stacks the deck in favor of the accused. Harvey Weinstein had a right to the presumption of innocence when he stood trial. But for those of us not serving on his jury, there was no duty to presume him innocent or to "suspend judgment" before the verdict was in. On the contrary: the evidence, including the compelling, consistent, and detailed accounts of more than a hundred women, made it extremely likely that Weinstein was guilty of assault and harassment. What's more, we know that men who have the kind of power that Weinstein had are all too liable to abuse it. The law must address each individual on a case-by-case basis—it must start from the assumption that Weinstein is no more likely to be an abuser than a ninety-year-old grandmother—but the norms of the law do not set the norms of rational belief. Rational belief is proportionate to the evidence: the strong statistical evidence that men like Weinstein tend to abuse their power, and the compelling testimonial evidence of the women who accused him of doing so. To be sure, new evidence can surface in a trial, and what previously seemed like good evidence can be discredited. (Equally, wealth and power can make good evidence disappear.) But the outcome of a trial does not determine what we should believe. Had Weinstein been acquitted on all charges, should we have concluded that his accusers were lying?

Some commentators, including some feminists,[24] insist that in cases like Weinstein's we can "never really know" whether someone is guilty of a sex crime, even when all the evidence suggests he is. One can, as a philosophical matter, take such a view. But one would have to be consistent in its application. If you can "never really know" whether Weinstein is a criminal or the victim of an elaborate setup, then you likewise cannot know the same about, say, Bernie Madoff. The question, from a feminist perspective, is why sex crimes elicit such selective skepticism. And the answer that feminists should give is that the vast majority of sex crimes are perpetrated by men against women. Sometimes, the injunction to "Believe women" is simply the injunction to form our beliefs in the ordinary way: in accordance with the facts.

That said, "Believe women" is a blunt tool. It carries with it the implicit injunction "Don't believe him." But this zero-sum logic— she's telling the truth, he's lying—presumes that nothing but sex difference is at work in the assessment of rape allegations. Especially when factors other than gender—race, class, religion, immigration status, sexuality—come into play, it is far from clear to whom we owe a gesture of epistemic solidarity. At Colgate University, an elite liberal arts college in upstate New York, only 4.2 percent of the student body was black during the 2013–14 academic year; and yet 50 percent of accusations of sexual violation that year were against black students.[25] Does "Believe women" serve justice at Colgate?

B lack feminists have long tried to complicate white feminist accounts of rape. Shulamith Firestone's hugely ambitious *The Dialectic of Sex* (1970) falters critically in its treatment of race and rape.[26] For Firestone, the rape of white women by black men is the result of a natural Oedipal urge to destroy the white father and take and subjugate what is his. "Whether innocently or consciously," Angela Davis wrote in her 1981 classic *Women, Race & Class*, Firestone's pronouncements "have facilitated the resurrection of the timeworn myth of the Black rapist." What's more, Davis went on,

> The fictional image of the Black man as rapist has always strength-ened its inseparable companion: the image of the Black woman as chronically promiscuous. For once the notion is accepted that Black men harbor irresistible and animal-like sexual urges, the entire race is invested with bestiality.[27]

On the evening of December 16, 2012, in Delhi, a twenty-three-year-old woman named Jyoti Singh, who came to be known to the Indian public as *Nirbhaya* ("fearless one"), was raped and tortured on a bus by six men, including the driver. Thirteen days later she died, having suffered brain damage, pneumonia, cardiac arrest, and complications related to the attack, in which the assailants penetrated her vagina with a rusty iron rod. Soon after the attack, a friend's father brought it up with me at a dinner. "But Indians are such civilized people," he said. I wanted to tell him that there is no civilization under patriarchy.

Non-Indian commentators, looking on, tended to see Singh's murder as a symptom of a failed culture: of India's sexual repression, its illiteracy, its conservatism. It is undeniable that the specificities of history and culture inflect how a society regulates sexual violence. The realities of caste, religion and poverty, and too the long legacy of British colonialism, shape India's regime of sexual violence, just as the realities of racial and class inequality, together with the legacies of chattel slavery and empire, shape the corresponding regimes in the US or UK. But the brutality of the attack on Jyoti Singh was cited by non-Indians as a way of disavowing any commonality between the sexual cultures of India and their own countries. Soon after the murder, the British journalist Libby Purves explained that "murderous, hyena-like male contempt [for women] is a norm" in India.[28] A first question: why is it that when white men rape they are violating a norm, but when brown men rape they are conforming to one? A second question: if Indian men are hyenas, what does that make Indian women?

B rown and black women in places of white domination have often been considered, owing to their supposed hypersexuality, unrapeable.[29] Their rape complaints are therefore discredited *a priori*. In 1850 in the British-ruled Cape Colony, in present-day South Africa, an eighteen-year-old laborer, Damon Booysen, was sentenced to death after confessing to raping his boss's wife, Anna Simpson. Days after sentencing, William Menzies, the judge in the case, wrote to the governor of Cape Colony to say he had made a terrible mistake. He had assumed Anna Simpson was white, but a group of "respectable" inhabitants of her town had since informed him that "the woman and her husband are Bastard coloured persons." Menzies urged the governor to commute Booysen's death sentence, and the governor obliged.[30] In 1859, a judge in Mississippi overturned the conviction of an enslaved adult man who had raped an enslaved girl; the defense had argued that the "crime of rape does not exist in this State between African slaves . . . [because] their intercourse is promiscuous." The girl was less than ten at the time.[31] In 1918 the Florida Supreme Court said that white women should be presumed chaste—and their rape accusations therefore presumed true—but that this rule should not be applied to "another race that is largely immoral [and] constitutes an appreciable part of the population."[32] A study conducted by the Center on Poverty and Inequality at Georgetown Law found that Americans of all races tend to see black girls as more sexually knowing and in less need of nurture, protection, and support than white girls of the same age.[33] In 2008, R. Kelly, the self-styled "Pied Piper of R&B," was tried on child pornography charges for making a sex tape of himself with a fourteen-year-old girl. In dream hampton's documentary, *Surviving R. Kelly* (2019), one of the trial jurors, a white man, explained the jury's decision to acquit: "I just didn't believe them, the women . . . The way they dress, the way they act—I didn't like them. I voted against. I disregarded all of what they had to say."[34]

The reality is that black girls and women, in the contemporary US and as compared with white women, are particularly susceptible to certain forms of interpersonal violence.[35] The political theorist Shatema Threadcraft writes about the tight focus, in black American politics, on the spectacle of the black male corpse—the lynched black body, the black body gunned down by police—and the way it obscures forms of state violence that are commonly perpetrated against black women. While black women were also lynched in the South during Reconstruction, and black women are murdered by the police today, these "spectacular" forms of violence are not the forms most commonly visited on them by the state. Black women suffer disproportionately from police harassment and sexual assault, forced separation from their children, and routine disbelief and abuse when reporting domestic violence.[36] The susceptibility of black women to intimate-partner violence is itself an effect of state power: higher unemployment rates among black men account for the higher rates at which black women are killed by their partners.[37] "What," Threadcraft asks, "will motivate people to rally around the bodies of our black female dead?"[38]

There is a disturbing genius at work in the white mythology about black sexuality. By portraying black men as rapists and black women as unrapeable—two sides, as Angela Davis says, of the coin of black hypersexuality—the white mythos produces a tension between black men's quest to exonerate themselves and black women's need to speak out against sexual violence, including the violence perpetrated against them by black men. The result is the doubled sexual subordination of black women. Black women who speak out against black male violence are blamed for reinforcing negative stereotypes of their community and for calling on a racist state to protect them. At the same time, the internalization of the sexually precocious black girl stereotype means that black girls and women are seen by some black men as asking for their abuse. Responding in 2018 to decades of well-documented allegations of rape and abuse, R. Kelly's team issued a statement saying that they would "vigorously resist this attempted public lynching of a black man who has made extraordinary contributions to our culture."[39] Kelly's team did not address the fact that almost all his accusers were black.[40]

In February 2019, two women, both black, made public and credible accusations against the black lieutenant governor of Virginia, Justin Fairfax. Fairfax was poised to take over as governor from Ralph Northam, who was being called on to resign for allegedly having appeared in a photo wearing blackface.[41] Vanessa Tyson, a politics professor at Scripps College, accused Fairfax of forcing her to perform oral sex on him at a hotel in 2004, during the Democratic National Convention. Days later, Meredith Watson came forward to say that Fairfax had raped her in 2000, when they were both under-graduates at Duke. In an unplanned speech on the State Senate floor, days after his accusers indicated their willingness to testify publicly, Fairfax compared himself to the historical victims of lynching:

> I have heard much about anti-lynching on the floor of this very Senate, where people were not given any due process whatso-ever, and we rue that … And yet we stand here in a rush to judg-ment with nothing but accusations and no facts, and we decide that we are willing to do the same thing.

Fairfax did not note the irony of comparing black women to a white lynch mob.[42] Neither did Clarence Thomas, for that matter, when he accused Anita Hill in 1991 of triggering a "high-tech lynching." The very logic that made the lynching of black men possible—the logic of black hypersexuality—is repurposed, at the level of meta-phor, to falsely indict black women as the true oppressors.

Jyoti Singh's gang rape and murder prompted a burst of grief and anger across India. But it did not prompt a full reckoning with the meaning of rape. Marital rape—criminalized in the UK only in 1991 and all fifty states of the US in 1993—remains, in India, a legal contradiction in terms. The Armed Forces Special Powers Act, which originates from a colonial law introduced by the British in 1942 to suppress the freedom struggle, still grants the Indian mili-tary impunity to rape women in "disturbed areas," including Assam and Kashmir. In 2004, a young woman from Manipur, Thangjam Manorama, was abducted, tortured, raped, and murdered by mem-bers of the 17th Assam Rifles unit of the Indian Army, who claimed that she was a member of a separatist group. Days later, a group of twelve middle-aged women staged a protest outside the Kangla

Fort, where the Assam Rifles were stationed; they stripped off their clothes and, naked, chanted: *Rape us, kill us! Rape us, kill us!*[43]

In India, as in the world over, some rapes count more than others. Jyoti Singh was a high-caste, educated, urban woman: these were the sociological conditions of her post-mortem elevation as "India's daughter." In 2016, the body of a twenty-nine-year-old Dalit law student named Jisha was found disemboweled and slashed more than thirty times in the southern state of Kerala; examiners concluded that she had been murdered after struggling against being raped. That same year, the body of a seventeen-year-old Dalit woman named Delta Meghwal was found in the water tank of her school in Rajasthan. The day before she was murdered, Meghwal told her parents that she had been raped by a teacher. The attention given to these two dead women did not compare with the furor prompted by the rape and murder of Jyoti Singh. Much like black women in the US and other white-dominated societies, Dalit and "low-caste" women in India are figured as sexually promiscuous and thus unrapeable.[44] No one has been put on trial for Delta Meghwal's rape and murder, and neither she nor Jisha have been given honorific titles by a grieving nation. In September 2020, a nineteen-year-old Dalit woman in Uttar Pradesh died in the hospital after reporting to the police that she had been gang-raped by four upper-caste neighbors. The police, who denied the report, burned the young woman's body in the middle of the night over the protests of her family.[45]

Punita Devi, the wife of one of the men sentenced to death for raping and murdering Jyoti Singh, asked: "Where will I live? What will my child eat?"[46] Devi is from Bihar, one of India's very poorest states. Up until the day of her husband's execution she continued to insist on his innocence. Perhaps she was in denial. Or maybe she was alert to the susceptibility of poor men to false allegations of rape. In any case Punita Devi saw one thing clearly. The law of rape—not the law as it is explicitly codified in statutes, but the unspoken law that governs the way rape is actually treated—does not care about women like her. Had Devi's husband raped not Jyoti Singh but his own wife, or a low-caste woman, he would very likely be alive today. Her husband now dead, the Indian state is indifferent to the matter of how Punita Devi or her child will survive. "Why are the politicians not thinking about me?" Devi asked. "I am a woman too."[47]

Intersectionality"—a term coined by Kimberlé Crenshaw to name an idea first articulated by an older generation of feminists from Claudia Jones to Frances M. Beal, the Combahee River Collective, Selma James, Angela Davis, bell hooks, Enriqueta Longeaux y Vásquez, and Cherríe Moraga—is often reduced, in common understanding, to a due consideration of the various axes of oppression and privilege: race, class, sexuality, disability, and so on.[48] But to reduce intersectionality to a mere attention to difference is to forgo its power as a theoretical and practical orientation. The central insight of intersectionality is that any liberation movement—feminism, anti-racism, the labor movement—that focuses only on what all members of the relevant group (women, people of color, the working class) have in common is a movement that will best serve those members of the group who are least oppressed. Thus a feminism that deals only with "pure" cases of patriarchal oppression—cases that are "uncomplicated" by factors of caste, race, or class—will end up serving the needs of rich white or high-caste women. Likewise, an anti-racist movement that deals only with "pure" cases of racist oppression will end up primarily serving the needs of rich men of color. Both of these movements will, in turn, produce an assimilationist politics, aimed at securing for the best-off women and men of color the right to be treated on equal terms with rich white men.

The politics of "Believe women," in its current form, collides with the demands of intersectionality. It is the common lot of women to be disbelieved when they make credible accusations of sexual violence, at least against certain men. It is to this reality that "Believe women" is offered as a political remedy. Yet black women in particular suffer from the stigmatization of black male sexuality to which the injunction "Believe women" too readily gives cover, just as Dalit women suffer specifically from the sexual stigmatization of Dalit men. When we are too quick to believe a white woman's accusation against a black man, or a Brahmin woman's accusation against a Dalit man, it is black and Dalit women who are rendered more vulnerable to sexual violence. Their ability to speak out against the violence they face from men of their race or caste is stifled, and their status as counterpart to the oversexed black or Dalit male is entrenched.[49] In that paradox of female sexuality, such women are rendered unrapeable, and thus more rapeable. Ida B. Wells patiently documented the lynchings of black men on trumped-up claims of raping white women. But she also recorded the many rapes of black women that inspired no lynch mobs, and of which little notice was taken. One such case was that of Maggie Reese, an eight-year-old girl raped by a white man in Nashville, Tennessee: "The outrage upon helpless childhood needed no avenging in this case; she was black."[50]

In the #MeToo era, the discourse around false accusations has evolved an unusual feature. Many of the men who are widely seen, by themselves and by other men, as being wrongly punished don't deny doing what their alleged victims claim they did. There are of course men who have protested their innocence: Harvey Weinstein, Woody Allen, R. Kelly, James Franco, Garrison Keillor, John Travolta. But just as often, high-profile men—Louis C.K., Jian Ghomeshi, John Hockenberry, Dustin Hoffman, Kevin Spacey, Matt Lauer, Charlie Rose—have conceded their bad behavior, only to demand soon after, like a child growing weary of a timeout, to be let back in to play. One month after the *Times* reported the open secret that Louis C.K. had a habit of masturbating in front of women without their consent, Matt Damon said: "I imagine that the price that he's paid at this point is so beyond anything."[51] A year after admitting the allegations were true, C.K. got a standing ovation as he walked onstage for a surprise return performance at New York's Comedy

Cellar. Soon after, in another set, he made fun of Asian men ("women [with] really big clits"), a "Jewish fag" and "a trans retarded boy."[52] Noticing some discomfort in the audience, he said: "Fuck it, what are you going to take away, my birthday? My life is over, I don't give a shit." C.K.'s shows continue to sell out within hours.[53] Charlie Rose, who was accused of sexual harassment by more than thirty women and was a close personal friend of Jeffrey Epstein, backed away from his initial admission of wrongdoing; his lawyer called his actions "routine workplace interactions and banter."[54] John Hockenberry, the public radio star accused of sexually harassing and bullying several women colleagues, wrote a piece in *Harper's* titled "Exile":

> Being a misguided romantic, or being born at the wrong time, or taking the wrong cues from the sexual revolution of the Sixties, or having a disability that leaves one impotent at the age of nineteen—none of this is a justification for offensive behavior toward women. But is a life sentence of unemployment without possibility of furlough, the suffering of my children, and financial ruin an appropriate consequence? Does my being expunged from the profession in which I have worked for decades constitute a step on the road to true gender equality?[55]

Kevin Spacey, who has been accused of sexual harassment and assault by over thirty men, some of whom were minors at the time, initially responded with a "sincerest apology" to his first accuser, Anthony Rapp.[56] A year later he posted a video on YouTube, "Let Me Be Frank," in which he told his viewers, in the persona of his *House of Cards* character Frank Underwood:

> I know what you want . . . I showed you exactly what people are capable of. I shocked you with my honesty, but mostly I challenged you and made you think. And you trusted me even though you knew you shouldn't. So we're not done no matter what anyone says and besides I know what you want. You want me back.

The video has been viewed more than 12 million times, and has over 280,000 likes.[57]

These men do not deny the truth of the allegations against them, nor even the harm they caused. What they deny is that they deserve to be punished. In a *New York Times* op-ed, the columnist Michelle Goldberg confesses that she "feel[s] bad for a lot of the men caught out by the #MeToo movement." Not, she explains, the really egregious men like Harvey Weinstein, but "the slightly less powerful, less overtly predatory schmoes whose gross behavior was tacitly accepted by those around them until, suddenly, it wasn't." "I can only imagine," Goldberg writes, "how disorienting it must be to have the rules change on you so fast."[58]

This idea—that the rules have suddenly changed on men, so that they now face punishment for behavior that was once routinely permitted—has become a #MeToo commonplace. The implication seems to be that, until very recently, men had been subject to a totalizing patriarchal ideology, one that made it impossible for many of them to tell the difference between flirtation and harassment, coquettishness and refusal, sex and rape. Some feminists have advocated something close to this view. Thirty years ago, Catharine MacKinnon wrote that women are "violated every day by men who have no idea of the meaning of their acts to the women. To them it is sex."[59] In 1976, a British man name John Cogan was acquitted of raping the wife of his friend, Michael Leak.[60] Leak, who had beaten his wife the night before for refusing to give him money when he came home drunk, told Cogan in the pub that she wanted to have sex with him. They left the pub for Leak's house, where Leak told his wife—"a slightly built young woman in her early 20s"—that Cogan was going to have sex with her and warned her not to struggle. Leak then stripped her, laid her on the bed, and invited Cogan in. Cogan watched as Leak had sex with his wife, then had sex with her himself. After Cogan was finished, Leak had sex with his wife once more. The men then returned to the pub. The court ruled that, since Cogan genuinely believed Leak's wife had consented, he did not meet the *mens rea* (guilty mind) requirement for rape.[61]

#MeToo is often seen as having produced a generalized version of the situation in which John Cogan found himself. Patriarchy has lied to men about what is and is not okay, in sex and in gender relations as a whole. Men are now being caught out and unfairly punished for their innocent mistakes, as women enforce a new set of rules. Perhaps these new rules are the correct ones; and, doubtless, the old ones caused a lot of harm. But how were men to have known any better? In their minds they weren't guilty, so don't they too have grounds for acquittal?

How many men are truly unable to distinguish between wanted and unwanted sex, between welcome and "gross" behavior, between decency and degradation? Was Cogan himself unable to draw this distinction? He admitted to the court that Leak's wife had sobbed and tried to turn away from him when he was on top of her. Did he think to ask, either before or during the sexual encounter, if this was really what she wanted? Was there nothing in his history, his life, his conscience, that spoke to him in that moment, that told him the cries of the scared woman on the bed were real and called for a response? Did Louis C.K. have no reason to think that the women in front of whom he masturbated were unhappy about it? Why, then, when he asked another woman if he could masturbate in front of her and she refused, did he flush red and feel compelled to explain to her that he "had issues"?[62]

It is true that women have always lived in a world created by men and governed by men's rules. But it is also true that men have always lived alongside women who have contested these rules. For much of human history their dissent has been private and unsystematic: flinching, struggling, leaving, quitting. More recently it has been public and organized. Those who insist that men aren't in a position to know better are in denial of what men have seen and heard. Men have chosen not to listen because it has suited them not to do so, because the norms of masculinity dictate that their pleasure takes priority, because all around them other men have been doing the same. The rules that have really changed, and are still changing, do not so much concern what is right or wrong in sex: women have been telling men the truth about that, one way or another, for a very long time. The rules that have really changed for men like Louis C.K., Charlie Rose, John Hockenberry, and many others like them is that they can no longer be confident that when they ignore the shouts and silences of the women they demean, no consequences will follow.

W hat consequences should follow?
There are fraught questions for feminists to ask, and together to try and answer, about the proper treatment of sexual abusers: whether such men must be punished, and if so, which of them, and by what means; or, alternatively, whether non-punitive models of reconciliation and repair might be better. Many women, understandably, have an urge to see abusers cowed, stripped, and scared—a reckoning with the behavior not just of these men, per- haps, but generations of men before them. Writing in the *New York Times* about the Shitty Media Men list, leaked by BuzzFeed in 2017, Jenna Wortham wrote:

> During the initial hours after the list's publication, when it still felt secret, for women only, I moved through the world differ- ently. The energy in the air felt charged . . . A friend compared the feeling to the final scenes of *V for Vendetta*. She liked seeing women as digital vigilantes, knowing that men were scared. I did, too. I wanted every single man put on notice, to know that they, too, were vulnerable because women were talking.[63]

When the power of the carceral state is not available—when the statute of limitations has passed, or the evidence consists only in women's testimony, or the behavior does not pass the threshold for criminality, or the man's power makes him effectively untouchable— women turn to the more diffuse punitive power afforded by social media. Some women seem to deny that this is power worth the name: that calling out an alleged harasser or enabler online is just a form of speech, and one of the few forms of speech available to the relatively powerless.

This is not true, as Wortham's reference to "digital vigilantes" makes clear. Tweeting about someone or circulating a spreadsheet with his name on it or publishing an account of a date gone bad may not be the same as calling the cops on him, but in a world in which people can and do get fired not for their actions but for the public outrage they cause, these things cannot be regarded as mere speech. (Of course, some women know this, and welcome the implications.) Nor are the discrete contributions of thousands of individuals mere speech when they aggregate into a collective voice that has the power to expose, shame, and humiliate. For most of us, a single tweet is a drop in the ocean, a negligible addition to a cacophony of opinion, trollery, and cat memes. Sometimes, though, in retrospect, it turns out that we were part of—or even that we instigated—something larger, something with significant psychic and material consequences, and not always ones we anticipated or planned or even wanted.[64] Is it enough to say that these consequences weren't intended, that yours was just one contribution among many, that what you say cannot be treated as the cause of whatever happens to follow? Should it be of any concern to us, as feminists, that this has long been the defense of pornographers, when accused by feminists not merely of depicting the sexual subordination of women, but socially licensing it? Should feminists, of all people, subscribe to the notion that words do no harm, or that the harm they cause is of no ethical or political consequence? Should feminists, of all people, deny that powerless voices joined together can enact great power?

I do not mean to overstate the issue. More than enough men have been called out online for bad or even criminal behavior without serious repercussion. Many more, presumably, are never called out at all. Of the seventeen men accused of sexual violence by multiple anonymous women on the Shitty Media Men list, only a handful appear to have faced formal professional sanctions, forced to resign from their jobs or banned from contributing to particular publications. None are in hiding. Apparently one of them has had a standing lunch date with Woody Allen, during which they discussed their respective victimization by feminists. Harvey Weinstein was sentenced to twenty-three years in prison, a cause for rejoicing on feminist Twitter, yet it had taken a Pulitzer Prize–winning journalistic investigation, a viral social movement, more than a hundred women coming forward and six of them taking the stand, and at the end of it all Weinstein was convicted on just two counts: rape in the third degree and criminal sexual assault in the first.

And yet, if the aim is not merely to punish male sexual domination but to end it, feminism must address questions that many feminists would rather avoid: whether a carceral approach that systemically harms poor people and people of color can serve sexual justice; whether the notion of due process—and perhaps too the presumption of innocence—should apply to social media and public accusations; whether punishment produces social change. What does it really take to alter the mind of patriarchy?

In 2014, Kwadwo Bonsu, a junior at the University of Massachusetts at Amherst, was accused of sexually assaulting a fellow student at an off-campus Halloween frat party. According to the alleged victim, she and Bonsu were hanging out, talking and smoking weed, and eventually they started kissing. Here is what, on her account, happened next:

> It got more intense until finally I shifted so that I was straddling him. I realized through my highness that he could be expecting to have sex, so I told him "I don't want to have sex" and he said "We don't have to have sex." I started to move my hand down his chest and into his pants when he asked me that I turn off the light. I tried to stand up to move the four feet to the light switch but

couldn't move my body to do so. He did it instead and we went back to making out . . . He got up and moved to sit on the bed, so I followed. I got on my knees and started to give him a blow job when I felt a wart [on] my tongue. I removed my mouth but kept going with my hand and realized just how high I was. I said "I'm . . . uncomfortable." He didn't really say anything, and I felt like I was waiting for him to give me permission to leave because I had felt bad for working him up and then backing out. I slowed my hand and said again something like "Yeah, I'm uncomfortable . . . I'm really high and uncomfortable. I think I need to leave" . . . He sat back down and we kissed a little bit more. I stood myself up and muttered again "Yeah, I want to leave." He said something to the effect of "Yeah, you said that. But I think I should get the next two minutes to convince you otherwise." I laughed it off, he stood up, and we kissed a little bit more . . . I finally moved with intention to leave, and he playfully grabbed my arm to pull me back into a kiss. I just kept making sounds that to me held the sentiment . . . he pulled me back to kiss him a few times. I was fixing my clothes which had never been removed when he asked to exchange numbers. We did so, then I went out into the hall.[65]

"As my RA training kicked in," she continued—she was a resident adviser in her dorm, tasked with counseling other students—"I realized I'd been sexually assaulted." She explained that while she knew she could leave at any time, "UMass Student Culture dictates that when women become sexually involved with men they owe it to them to follow through." She went on: "I want to fully own my participation in what happened but at the same time recognize that I felt violated and that I owe it to myself and others to hold him accountable for something I felt in my bones wasn't right."[66]

Soon after, the student filed a complaint against Bonsu for sexual assault with the UMass dean of students and the Amherst police. The police investigated and declined to press charges. Notes taken at a meeting between an assistant dean and the alleged victim record that

Bonsu "didn't ask for a blowjob nor did he initiate, but [the alleged victim] assumed it was supposed to happen."[67] The university scheduled a hearing for the case, and informed Bonsu that he was subject meanwhile to "interim restrictions," including a prohibition on contacting the complainant, visiting dorms other than his own, eating in all but one of the dining halls, and entering the student union. A month later, the student reported to the administration that Bonsu had attempted to friend her on Facebook. The university banned Bonsu from university housing and the campus except to attend classes. Suffering from stress-induced pneumonia and a mental breakdown, Bonsu moved back in with his parents, Ghanaian immigrants, in Maryland. The university hearing took place without him. He was found not guilty of the assault, but guilty of sending the student a Facebook request. He was suspended until after his graduation date, permanently banned from living on campus, and required to get counseling. Bonsu left UMass, and later sued the school for "federal civil rights violations . . . resulting from [the university's] arbitrary, unfair, wrongful, deliberate, discriminatory, and otherwise outrageous decision to suspend Mr Bonsu . . . as a result of false allegations."[68] The lawsuit was settled in 2016 for an undisclosed amount.

Bonsu's lawsuit stated that the allegations brought against him were "false." This is in one sense misleading: by Bonsu's own admission, what she said happened did in fact happen. But, at least so far as UMass and the state of Massachusetts were concerned, these details did not add up to rape.[69] For her part, the alleged victim insisted that Bonsu did not force her to do anything, that he listened when she said no, that she initiated all the sex acts, that she was not afraid of him, that she knew she could have stopped and walked out the door, that she gave multiple indications of wanting to proceed. Nonetheless, something had happened to her that she "felt in [her] bones wasn't right." She had been "violated."[70]

Feminist critics of Title IX, the federal law which prohibits sex discrimination on US college campuses—including Janet Halley,

Laura Kipnis, and Jeannie Suk Gersen—point to cases like Bonsu's as evidence that quotidian sexual interactions are now subject to hysterical moralism and to the regulatory overreach of what Suk Gersen and her husband, Jacob Gersen, have called the "sex bureaucracy."[71] Gersen and Gersen write:

> Eroding procedural protections and expanding the idea of non-consent in tandem means that the bureaucracy will investigate and discipline sexual conduct that women and men experience as consensual (if nonideal) sex. What results is not a sexual violence or sexual harassment bureaucracy. It is a sex bureaucracy, focused on conduct that differs substantially from the actual wrongs and harms that motivated its growth . . . The sex bureaucracy regulates *ordinary* sex, to the detriment of actually addressing sexual violence, and unfortunately erodes the legitimacy of efforts to fight sexual violence.[72]

It is true that US universities have, in recent decades, developed elaborate infrastructures for the management of student sex. These are not designed primarily to protect students from sexual violence, but to protect universities from lawsuits, reputational damage, and the withdrawal of federal funding. It's no surprise that the failures of university sex bureaucracies are so numerous. Many women students who are sexually assaulted are encouraged not to go to the police, only to find that the in-house process fails to hold their perpetrators accountable. On other occasions, men are presumptively punished, as in Bonsu's case, without due process protections.[73]

But by presenting what happened at UMass as a case of "ordinary" sex—sex that is merely "ambivalent, undesirable, unpleasant, unsober, or regretted"[74]—the critics of Title IX make things too easy for themselves. The woman who gave Bonsu a handjob didn't really want to—or, she wanted to at first, and then she stopped wanting to. She kept going for the reason that so many girls and women keep going: because women who sexually excite men are supposed to finish the job. It doesn't matter whether Bonsu himself had this expectation, because it is an expectation already internalized by many women. A woman going on with a sex act she no longer wants to perform, knowing she can get up and walk away but knowing at the same time that this will make her a blue-balling tease, an object of male contempt: there is more going on here than mere ambivalence, unpleasantness and regret. There is also a kind of coercion: not directly by Bonsu, perhaps, but by the informal regulatory system of gendered sexual expectations. Sometimes the price for violating these expectations is steep, even fatal. That is why there is a connection between these episodes of "ordinary" sex and the "actual wrongs and harms" of sexual assault. What happened at UMass may well be "ordinary" in the statistical sense—as in what happens every day—but it isn't "ordinary" in the ethical sense, as in what we should pass over without comment. In that sense it is an extraordinary phenomenon with which we are all too familiar.

B ut whom would it help to call sex of this sort, as many feminists would call it, "rape"?[75] In 2014, California's governor, Jerry Brown, with the backing of feminist campaigners, signed into law SB 967, known as the "Yes Means Yes" bill.[76] It mandated that all colleges and universities that receive state funding for student financial aid adopt an "affirmative consent" standard for judging whether a sex act is consensual. The bill reads:

> "Affirmative consent" means affirmative, conscious, and volun-
> tary agreement to engage in sexual activity. It is the responsibil-
> ity of each person involved in the sexual activity to ensure that
> he or she has the affirmative consent of the other or others to
> engage in the sexual activity. Lack of protest or resistance does

not mean consent, nor does silence mean consent. Affirmative consent must be ongoing throughout a sexual activity and can be revoked at any time. The existence of a dating relationship between the persons involved, or the fact of past sexual relations between them, should never by itself be assumed to be an indicator of consent.

After it became law, Ezra Klein wrote in *Vox* that SB 967 would throw "everyday sexual practice into doubt" and create "a haze of fear and confusion over what counts as consent." But, he said, "everyday sexual practices on college campuses need to be upended, and men need to feel a cold spike of fear when they begin a sexual encounter . . . Ugly problems don't always have pretty solutions."[77]

Would SB 967 have solved problems at UMass? It depends on precisely what you think "the problem" is. If it's men having sex with women without first securing an active "yes," then an affirmative consent law is perhaps an effective, if "unpretty," solution. But if the problem is something deeper, to do with the psychosocial structures that make men want to have sex with women who don't really want it, or make them feel that it's their job to overcome a woman's resistance, and that make women feel they must have sex with men when they don't want to, it's far less clear what a law like SB 967 achieves. As Catharine MacKinnon has pointed out, affirmative consent laws simply shift the goalposts on what constitutes legally acceptable sex: whereas previously men had to stop when women said no, now they just have to get women to say yes.[78] How do we formulate a regulation that prohibits the sort of sex that is produced by patriarchy? Could the reason that this question is so hard to answer be that the law is simply the wrong tool for the job?

Suppose laws like SB 967, by making examples of certain men, were capable of changing how other men had sex. Even so: should feminists

embrace that possibility? Had UMass had an affirmative consent standard, Kwadwo Bonsu would have been found guilty by the university's
Title IX office of sexual assault, and presumably expelled. Had he been
in one of the states—like New Jersey, Oklahoma or Wisconsin—that
have adopted an affirmative consent standard in their rape statutes, he
might have been charged, arrested, convicted, and imprisoned.[79] As a
black man accused by a white woman, this would be disproportionately likely to happen. Already, the quasi-legal machinery of the university dismantled Bonsu's life. This was an outcome that the alleged
victim herself did not appear to want. In her statement to the university, she wrote that Bonsu's punishment should be as "moderate as
possible given the shades of grey this incident is colored with."[80] But
suppose she had wanted it—suppose that she would have felt safer,
somehow made whole, by his imprisonment. Is this a cost feminists
should be willing to bear?

I am not saying that feminism has no business asking better of
men—indeed, asking them to be better men. But a feminism worth
having must find ways of doing so that avoid rote reenactment of
the old form of crime and punishment, with its fleeting satisfactions and predictable costs. I am saying that a feminism worth having must, not for the first time, expect women to be better—not
just fairer, but more imaginative—than men have been.

But it is not up to women alone. Indeed, what is striking about
the high-profile men exposed by #MeToo is just how uninterested they are, on the whole, in being better men. Early on in his
Harper's piece, John Hockenberry says that, even while he does not
"support the zealotry" with which he has "been dismantled," and
denies being "some officer or agent of the patriarchy," he "whole-
heartedly endorse[s] the higher cause of gender equality." At the
same time, he bemoans the end of "traditional romance," characterizes his verbal and physical harassment of his employees as "some
improper, failed, and awkward attempts at courtship," blames

America's "contradictory fusion of sexual puritanism" and "social progressivism," compares #MeToo to the Reign of Terror, laments that "there has been no public defense of . . . someone who spent a lifetime devoted to serving the public," speculates as to whether Andrea Dworkin would be his friend ("Would she embrace me as her penis-less paraplegic male buddy?"), and identifies himself with the fictional character Lolita, a twelve-year-old victim of rape. But he does not find the space, in that great expanse of textual real estate, to consider what his actions did to the women who suffered them. The words "damage" and "harm" do not appear. The words "pain," "painful" or "painfully" appear six times, all in reference to Hockenberry's own experiences, or those of his children.

In his own contribution to the genre that Jia Tolentino calls "My Year of Being Held Responsible for My Own Behavior," Jian Ghomeshi, the Canadian radio host accused of violent sexual assault or harassment by more than twenty women, wrote in the *New York Review of Books* of the "crash course in empathy" he had received since his public shaming.[81] But the empathy wasn't for the women he assaulted and harassed. Instead, it was for other men like him: "I have a new unwavering antipathy toward schadenfreude . . . I now have a different way of seeing anyone who is being attacked in the public sphere, even those with whom I may profoundly disagree."[82] "I feel sorry for a lot of these men," Michelle Goldberg writes, "but I don't think they feel sorry for women, or think about women's experience much at all."[83]

These disgraced but loved, ruined but rich, never to be employed again until they are employed again, prodigal sons of #MeToo: they and their defenders are not, for all their protestations of innocence and accusations of lynching, outraged by the falsity of women's accusations. They are outraged by the truth of those accusations. They are outraged, most of all, that saying sorry doesn't make it all better: that women expect them, together with the world that brought them to power, to change. But why should they? Don't you know who the fuck they are?

Talking to My Students About Porn

D id porn kill feminism? That's one way of telling the story of the US women's liberation movement, which exploded with such joyous fury and seriousness of purpose in the late 1960s, yet within the space of a generation had become a fractured and worn thing. Debates about porn—is it a tool of patriarchy or a counter to sexual repression? A technique of subordination or an exercise of free speech?—came to preoccupy the women's liberation movement in the US, and to some degree the UK and Australia, and then to tear it apart.

In April 1982, the Barnard Sex Conference (as it came to be known)[1] was held in New York. Its theme was "women's sexual pleasure, choice and autonomy." In the conference's concept paper, "Towards a Politics of Sexuality," Carole Vance called for an acknowledgment of sex as "simultaneously a domain of restriction, repression, and danger as well as a domain of exploration, pleasure, and agency."[2] About 800 feminist scholars, students, and activists[3] attended talks and workshops including "Pornography and the construction of a female subject," "Politically correct, politically incorrect sexuality," and "The forbidden: eroticism and taboo." As one of the organizers wrote in *Diary of a Conference on Sexuality*— a punk zine of critical essays, witty reflections, reading suggestions, and sexually explicit images to be handed out to participants—the conference was intended to be "a coming out party for feminists who [had] been appalled by the intellectual dishonesty and dreariness of the anti-pornography movement."[4] With a week to go before it began, anti-porn feminists began inundating Barnard's administrators and trustees with phone calls, complaining that the conference had been planned by "sexual perverts."[5] The president of Barnard, Ellen Futter, allowed the conference to go ahead, but not before interrogating the organizers and confiscating all 1,500 copies of the *Diary*, which she declared was a piece of pornography.[6]

At the conference itself, anti-porn feminists, wearing T-shirts emblazoned with "For a Feminist Sexuality" on the front and "Against S/M" on the back, handed out leaflets accusing the conference of supporting not just pornography and sadomasochism but also patriarchy and child abuse.[7] (The last charge wasn't entirely baseless. The same organizer who called the conference a "coming out party" also wrote in the *Diary*: "I understand the advanced position on porn, on s and m, but I can't understand the argument for pederasty!"[8]) When the *Diary* was finally reprinted, Andrea Dworkin sent out photocopies of it with a cover letter declaring it "perniciously anti-woman and anti-feminist." The feminist publication *off our backs*, "the closest thing to a newspaper of record of the feminist movement," devoted much of its June 1982 issue to lambasting the conference, triggering an "avalanche" of enraged replies.[9]

The Barnard organizers recalled "a McCarthyite atmosphere of witch-hunting and purges"[10] in the wake of the conference, and the Barnard Women's Center lost its sponsor for the conference series. One British feminist, observing events from across the Atlantic, ruefully noted that Barnard and its fallout had "deepened the already scarring divisions in the American movement."[11] In 1986, a conference at Mount Holyoke on "Feminism, Sexuality, and Power" descended into a "pitched battle," at which, one of its organizers recalled, some "speakers refused to be moved off the issues of pornography and S/M and . . . were downright nasty to their sisters."[12] In 1993, a group of anti-porn feminists wrote a letter to the vice chancellor of the Australian National University demanding that an invitation to US pro-sex feminists, including Gayle Rubin and Carole Vance, be rescinded. One of the signatories was Sheila Jeffreys, a central figure on the "revolutionary feminist" wing of the British women's liberation movement, which insisted—contrary to the then dominant socialist feminist position—that male sexual violence, rather than capitalism, was the foundation of women's oppression. In recent years Jeffreys has decried the "vilification" and "censoring" of feminists who, like her, are trans-exclusionary.[13] Jeffreys apparently does not recognize the irony in objecting to the same tactics that she and other anti-porn feminists pioneered forty years ago. In 2011 Gayle Rubin, who ran a workshop at the Barnard conference, wrote that she still nursed "the horror of having been there."[14]

A ll this can seem odd, even quaint, to us now. All this fuss over porn? At a practical and technological level, albeit not a philosophical one, the internet has settled the "porn question" for us. It was one thing to entertain the possibility of abolishing porn when porn meant top-shelf magazines and seedy movie theaters: when porn had a physical location and was, in principle, containable. But in the era of ubiquitous, instantaneously available porn, it is another thing altogether.[15]

The intensity of the "porn wars" is more understandable when you bear in mind that porn came to serve, for feminists of an earlier generation, as a metonym for "problematic" sex in general: for sex that took no account of women's pleasure, for sadomasochistic sex, for prostitution, for rape fantasies, for sex without love, for sex across power differentials, for sex with men. Pornography thus became not just one contested question among many in a new politics of the personal, but a lightning rod for two conflicting views of sex. The "anti-sex" view was that sex as we know it is a patriarchal construct—an eroticization of gender inequality—from which there can be no true liberation without a revolution in relations between men and women. Short of this, separatism, lesbianism, or abstinence were (at best) the only emancipatory options. On the "pro-sex" view, women's freedom required a guarantee of women's right to have sex when, how, and (subject to the other party's consent) with whom they liked, without stigma or shame. (Of course, many feminists found themselves somewhere between these two poles—wanting, for example, to fiercely oppose what they saw as a widespread rape culture, facilitated by porn, while distinguishing rape from "wanted" sex.) While contemporary feminism—in its insistence on women's right to sexual pleasure, and consent as the sole boundary of permissible sex—has largely taken up the pro-sex perspective, many feminists still feel the pull of an older, more circumspect approach to sex. To them, sex once more appears to be in need of revolutionary transformation. In this sense, the worries that animated the porn wars are still with us.

But the porn wars, though they were about sex as a totality, were also very much about porn itself: about top-shelf magazines and private shops and the movies shown in XXX theaters. Second-wave feminists began protesting against pornography in the late 1960s. In the spring of 1969, record companies, under pressure from the FBI, began pulling advertising from underground newspapers. In need of funds, these papers began publishing pornographic ads and supplements instead.[16] That these organs of the New Left were capitalizing on sexism did not come as a surprise to feminists of the period; the women's liberation movement was in large part formed in reaction to the misogyny of their supposedly radical comrades. In 1970, thirty women occupied the executive office of the alternative publishing house Grove Press, whose owner, Barney Rosset (tagged "The Old Smut Peddler" by *Life* magazine), had moved on from aggressively defending his legal right to publish "obscene" literature by D. H. Lawrence and Henry Miller to become a major distributor of pornographic films. (Rosset was also a union-buster; Robin Morgan was among the nine employees fired for attempting to unionize Grove.[17])

By the mid-1970s, amid a growing cultural backlash against feminism, feminists began to identify porn as the lynchpin of patriarchy. "Pornography is the theory, and rape the practice," Robin Morgan declared in 1974.[18] In 1976, the first feminist anti-porn group, Women Against Violence in Pornography and Media, was founded in the San Francisco Bay Area; its aim was to "put an end to all portrayals of women being bound, raped, tortured, mutilated, abused, or degraded in any way for sexual or erotic stimulation."[19] That same year, Andrea Dworkin, together with other radical feminists, organized a picket of a movie theater in New York showing the film *Snuff*, which depicted supposedly real footage of a pregnant woman being murdered and dismembered by a film crew in Argentina. (*Snuff*'s tagline was: "The film that could only be made in South America . . . where Life is CHEAP!") The group went on to form Women Against Pornography (WAP), and began running biweekly "tours" of Times Square sex shops, peep shows, and topless bars. A *New York Times* reporter who went on one of the tours, led by Susan Brownmiller, described the consciousness-raising slideshow that preceded it: "A dozen women stared frozen-faced in the tiny storefront, as images of women being bound, beaten and abused flashed across the screen."[20] (Some feminists later admitted to having been aroused by WAP's slideshows.) WAP's headquarters on Ninth Avenue had been given to the group, rent-free, by the mayor's Midtown Enforcement Project, which had closed down the "soul food restaurant and gathering place for transvestites and prostitutes" that had previously occupied the space. (Carl Weisbrod, the director of the Enforcement Project, commented: "Obviously the issue of pornography is a matter of concern to both the city and the feminists."[21]) In Los Angeles in 1976, Women Against Violence

Against Women (WAVAW) protested against the billboard for the Rolling Stones album *Black and Blue*, which depicted a bound and bruised woman with the caption "I'm 'Black and Blue' from The Rolling Stones—and I love it!" Chapters of WAVAW sprang up across the US and UK. In 1986, the British Campaign Against Pornography was launched to lobby against topless "page three girls" in tabloid newspapers. In New Zealand, Women Against Pornography called for the resignation of the country's chief censor, who had given a pass to a horror film, *I Spit on Your Grave* (1978), that featured a half-hour-long gang-rape scene.

For anti-porn feminists of this era, porn wasn't merely the misogynistic depiction of women and sex. It was "propaganda, no more and no less."[22] It was the ideological scaffold of patriarchy: eroticizing, inciting, and legitimating male violence against women—and reinforcing the broader social and political subordination of women by men. As Catharine MacKinnon put it in her anti-porn manifesto *Only Words* (1993):

> The message of these materials . . . is "get her," pointing at all women, to the perpetrators' benefit of ten billion dollars a year and counting. This message is addressed directly to the penis, delivered through an erection, and taken out on women in the real world. The content of this message is not unique to pornography. It is the function of pornography in effectuating it that is unique.[23]

To say that it is porn's function to *effectuate* its message is to see porn as a mechanism not just for depicting the world, but for making it. Porn, for MacKinnon and other anti-porn feminists, was a machine for the production and reproduction of an ideology which, by eroticizing women's subordination, thereby made it real.

This analysis, uncompromising in its insistence on porn's world-making power, was, in the hands of black feminists of this period, historicized and racialized. They identified the template for mainstream pornography in the historical display of black women's bodies in the contexts of colonialism and slavery: Sarah Baartman, for example, the "Hottentot Venus," whose near-naked body was exhibited across Europe as a specimen of African female hypersexuality; and the countless enslaved women who were stripped, prodded, and sold at auction. Thus Alice Walker wrote that the "ancient roots of modern pornography are to be found in the almost always pornographic treatment of black women who, from the moment they entered slavery . . . were subjected to rape as the 'logical' convergence of sex and violence."[24] In her classic *Black Feminist Thought* (1990), Patricia Hill Collins identified a precursor to the white female pornographic object in the mixed-race slave women who were specifically "bred" to be indistinguishable from white women. These women "approximated the images of beauty, asexuality, and chastity forced on white women," Collins wrote, but "inside was a highly sexual whore, a 'slave mistress' ready to cater to her owner's pleasure."[25] It is from this racialized and gendered practice, Collins suggested, that mainstream porn got its canonical female persona: the demure slut. If porn represented an attack on the status of white women, this was doubly true for women of color, whose objectification under the racist and patriarchal gaze off the screen was the original model for the treatment of all women's bodies on it.

Were anti-porn feminists being hysterical? Censorious prudes? In the age of internet porn, DVDs and video cassettes, let alone centerfolds and seedy theaters, can be joked about as nostalgic throwbacks. It may seem to some, looking back, that feminist anti-porn campaigners must have been overtaken by anxiety about a mass culture that was becoming more open about sex, and that was quite capable of separating fantasy from fact. Feminists anxious about sex under patriarchy found it easier, a group of pro-porn feminists wrote in 1983, "to attack the picture of what oppresses us than the mysterious, elusive . . . thing itself."[26] The implication is that anti-porn feminists were overestimating the power of porn: they had lost perspective. But what if the true significance of the perspective of anti-porn feminists lay not in what they were paying attention to, but when? What if they weren't hysterical, but prescient?

It was my students who first led me to think about this question. Discussing the "porn question" is more or less mandatory in an introductory class on feminist theory. But my heart wasn't really in it. I imagined that the students would find the anti-porn position prudish and passé, just as I was trying hard to make them see the relevance of the history of feminism to the contemporary moment. I needn't have worried. They were riveted. Could it be that pornography doesn't merely depict the subordination of women, but actually makes it real, I asked? Yes, they said. Does porn silence women, making it harder for them to protest against unwanted sex, and harder for men to hear those protests? Yes, they said. Does porn bear responsibility for the objectification of women, for the marginalization of women, for sexual violence against women? Yes, they said, yes to all of it.

It wasn't just the women students talking; the men were saying yes as well, in some cases even more emphatically. One young woman pushed back, citing the example of feminist porn. "But we don't watch that," the men said. What they watched was the hardcore stuff, the aggressive stuff—what is now, on the internet, the free stuff. My male students complained about the routines they were expected to perform in sex; one of them asked whether it was too utopian to imagine sex that was loving and mutual and not about domination and submission. My women students talked about the neglect of women's pleasure in the pornographic script, and wondered whether it had something to do with the absence of pleasure in their own lives. "But if it weren't for pornography," one woman said, "how would we ever learn to have sex?"

Porn meant so much to my students; they *cared* so much about it. Like the anti-porn feminists of forty years ago, they had a heightened sense of porn's power, a strong conviction that porn did things in the world. Talking with my graduate teaching assistant after that seminar (she was a handful of years younger than me), I realized what should have been obvious from the start. My students belonged to the first generation truly to be raised on internet pornography. Almost every man in that class would have had his first sexual experience the moment he first wanted it, or didn't want it, in front of a screen. And almost every woman in the class would have had her first sexual experience, if not in front of a screen, then with a boy whose first sexual experience had been. In that sense, her experience too would have been mediated by a screen: by what the screen instructed him to do. While almost all of us today live in a world where porn is ubiquitous, my students, born in the final years of the last century, were the first to have come of age sexually in that world.

My students would not have stolen or passed around magazines or videos, or gathered glimpses here and there. For them sex was there, fully formed, fully interpreted, fully categorized—*teen*, *gangbang*, *MILF*, *stepdaughter*—waiting on the screen. By the time my students got around to sex IRL—later, it should be noted, than teenagers of previous generations—there was, at least for the straight boys and girls, a script in place that dictated not only the physical moves and gestures and sounds to make and demand, but also the appropriate affect, the appropriate desires, the appropriate distribution of power. The psyches of my students are products of pornography. In them, the warnings of the anti-porn feminists seem to have been belatedly realized: sex for my students is what porn says it is.

After that first time I taught a seminar on porn, one of the students visited me in office hours. "It helped me understand the sex I've been having," she said. Her ex-boyfriend had always told her she was doing it wrong. "I see now he wanted me to be like those women"—the women in porn. She wasn't like that, didn't know how to be like that, so he dumped her.

My student, like the anti-porn feminists of the 1970s, traced a straight line from the consumption of porn to the negative treatment of women by men. "Sooner or later," MacKinnon wrote in *Only Words*:

> the consumers want to live out the pornography further in three dimensions . . . As pornography consumers, teachers may become epistemically incapable of seeing their women students as their potential equals . . . Doctors may molest anaesthetised women, enjoy watching and inflicting pain during childbirth . . . Some consumers write on bathroom walls. Some undoubtedly write judicial opinions. Some . . . presumably serve on juries, sit on the Senate Judiciary Committee, answer police calls reporting domestic violence . . . and produce mainstream films . . . Some sexually harass their employees and clients, molest their daughters, batter their wives, and use prostitutes . . . Some gang rape women in fraternities and at rest stops on highways . . . Some become serial rapists and sex murderers—using and making pornography is inextricable to these acts.[27]

It's a startling image: porn as a virtual training ground for male sexual aggression. Could it be true? Or is this image itself a kind of sexual fantasy, which reduces misogyny to a single origin, and its many, diverse agents to a single subject: the porn watcher?

In a scathing review of *Only Words*, the political philosopher Ronald Dworkin (no relation to Andrea) claimed that porn viewing simply wasn't pervasive enough to have the widespread negative effects that MacKinnon and other anti-porn feminists claimed for it. If anything in mass culture was an obstacle to sexual equality, Dworkin wrote, it was soap operas and advertising. That may have been true in 1993, but it's less plausible now. In 2018, the five biggest porn sites—PornHub, XVideos, BongaCams, xMaster, and xnxx— got a total of more than six billion visits per month. PornHub alone claimed that it had 28.5 billion visits in 2017.[28]

A 2010 meta-analysis concluded that there is a "significant over-all relationship between pornography consumption and attitudes supporting violence against women."[29] The association was "significantly stronger" in the case of pornography classed as "violent," but was still statistically significant in the case of "non-violent" pornography.[30] (MacKinnon and others would want to know: where do we draw the line between "violent" and "non-violent" porn? Is it violent if he smacks her? If he calls her a bitch? If he ejaculates on her face? If he tells her that she likes it, that she wants it? If her "No" finally becomes a "Yes"?) Studies have found that men who watch porn frequently are less likely to support affirmative action for women[31] and to empathize with rape victims;[32] they are also more likely to report an intent to rape,[33] and more likely to commit sexual assault.[34] Meanwhile, in one study of sorority members, the women who watched porn were less likely to intervene when they saw other women being sexually assaulted.[35]

Critics question the strength of these correlations: they cite their own favored studies, and insist on adults' capacity to distinguish fantasy from fact. They remind us that women watch porn too: according to PornHub, 32 percent of all its users are women. (Then again, who said women can't be misogynists?) Most important, they remind us that correlation isn't causation: maybe men are more likely to watch porn if they are already disposed to sexual violence and derogatory attitudes toward women.

Measuring the ideological effects of porn is also made difficult by the absence of reliable data on young people's porn habits. Most of the sources are either Christian anti-porn advocacy groups—keen to tell you that your child is, right now, uploading a pornographic video of herself to the internet—or websites like PornHub, which have a strong interest in denying that under-eighteens are accessing their content. A 2012 University of Sydney study of 800 regular porn users found that 43 percent of them started watching porn between the ages of eleven and thirteen.[36] In a study from 2007 of students aged thirteen to fourteen in Alberta, Canada, 90 percent of boys reported accessing sexually explicit media; 35 percent said they had viewed porn "too many times to count."[37] Lisa Ann, one of the world's most popular porn stars, is forty-eight years old, a veteran of the MILF genre. On *The Butterfly Effect*, Jon Ronson's podcast about the porn industry in the age of the internet, Lisa Ann tells Ronson that in the 1990s she was only ever recognized on the street by adults. Now she has "twelve-, thirteen-, fourteen-year-olds coming up . . . [saying] 'Can we fuck?'" "I just say to them, listen, what you see on those sites will probably never happen for you, so don't ask a girl to do it and don't think that's what sex is really about."[38] What will the world look like once another generation or two has passed, when every person on earth will have come of age sexually in the pornworld?

You're doing it wrong. What struck me most about what my student said wasn't the causal connection she drew between her ex-boyfriend's porn habit and his humiliating her, but the terms in which he dealt out that humiliation. *You're doing it wrong.* Porn was for this young man the normative standard of sex, against which his girlfriend was measured and found wanting. Porn is not pedagogy, yet it often functions as if it were. Here is a representative sample of what young male students, aged between fourteen and eighteen, interviewed as part of a report for the UK Office of the Children's Commissioner, issued in 2013, had to say about porn:[39]

You learn how to have sex, you're learning new moves.

You get to see the way it's done, and the way people do it . . . you have a kind of idea of how you might be able to do it.

You go on there for . . . entertainment but as you're watching you pick up different things, things you don't really know about. You just pick up things and you learn more things.

The main reason I think people look at pornography is for information, what's doing, how to do stuff.

What is remarkable about these comments is how little the boys talk about using porn to get off. On their own account, they turn to porn to "learn," to "have a kind of idea," to "pick up things," for "information," for "what's doing." Of course they're getting off as well: porn is "for entertainment." But these boys, some of them presumably virgins, are quick to treat porn as an authority on how to have sex. Here is what some of the young women said in the same study:

> I think young people expect sex to be like porn. There's that standard where if it's not like that, then sex isn't good.
>
> It sort of makes boys' fantasies become like real because it's real people. And then they will assume [that's] what it's always like . . . and it can be a bit aggressive, a bit forceful.
>
> It gives [boys] a worse opinion, like, image of a girl. Like all girls should be like that, all girls want to have sex.
>
> I think at this age boys are really quite naive and it's about who [you] can trust and you know if they're watching this kind of stuff, you're not really sure how they will treat you.

These girls don't regard porn as an authority on sex; they really can distinguish fantasy from fiction. But they know that, for boys, porn sets the "standard" for "good" sex, grounds their assumptions about "what it's always like" (that is, "a bit aggressive, a bit forceful"), and produces their "opinions" and "images" of girls.

Porn may tell lies about sex and women—in John Stoltenberg's famous formula, "pornography tells lies about women" but "tells the truth about men"—but so what? Is it porn's responsibility to tell people, especially young people, the truth about sex? In order to hold porn and its makers responsible for what its consumers do, it will not suffice to show that porn has the effect of making men objectify and demean women. For speech often has inadvertent harmful effects. If I say the word "fire" as a punchline to a joke and it makes you spill your tea, this is an effect of what I've said but hardly a harm for which I am responsible. By contrast, if I shout "Fire!" in a crowded theater, I am responsible for the stampede that follows. For the stampede isn't a random or coincidental effect, but the natural result of the speech act I was performing: that is, a warning. Crucial to anti-porn feminism is the thought that porn doesn't just happen to result in women's subordination: it is itself an act of subordinating women. Specifically, pornography performs the speech act of *licensing* the subordination of women, and *conferring* on women an inferior civic status. Like the stampede that follows my shouting "Fire!," porn's effects on women are not just, anti-porn feminists think, the expected result, but moreover the whole point of pornography.

For that to be true, porn must have authority. Otherwise, it will be able to depict women as inferior but not to make them inferior; it will be able to depict women's subordination, but not to license it. The feminist philosopher Rae Langton asks whether porn is more like an umpire vested with the authority to make dispositive verdicts, or a bystander making calls from the sidelines. "If you believe," Langton writes, "that pornographic utterances are made by a powerless minority, a fringe group especially vulnerable to moralistic persecution," then you will answer that porn is like the bystander, issuing calls that may or may not be taken up, but without authority—and so without any responsibility to be accurate. "Not so if you believe . . . that pornography's voice is the voice of the ruling power."[40]

To be sure, pornographers, unlike umpires, were never formally invested with the authority to tell the truth about sex. No one elected or appointed the pornographers. If porn is indeed the voice of the "ruling power," it is not officially so. Whatever authority porn has is granted by those who watch it: by the boys and men who trust porn to tell them "what's doing." Some critics of anti-porn feminism say that this sort of de facto authority isn't enough to hold porn responsible. Just because boys, and presumably some girls, take porn to be an authority on sex, doesn't mean it really is. Whatever power it has was never sought or formally conferred. But this is to draw a sharp distinction between authority and power that belongs, perhaps, to an earlier time. The internet blurs the distinction between power and authority. Platforms for speech—previously allocated by radio stations, TV shows, newspapers, publishing houses—are now overabundant, infinitely available, and practically free. Without any formal grant of authority, individual speakers can amass great power—"influence," as we have learned to call it. To what standard, if any, should we hold those who wield such power?

The porn star Stoya performs in what she describes as "gender-binary-heterosexual-oriented pornography for a production company that aims to have as much mass appeal as possible."[41] In a *New York Times* op-ed, she acknowledged an authority she did not seek out: "I didn't want the responsibility of shaping young minds. And yet thanks to this country's nonfunctional sex education system and the ubiquitous access to porn by anyone with an internet connection, I have that responsibility anyway." "Sometimes," she went on, "it keeps me awake at night."[42]

T he invocation of young people in political discourse often serves reactionary ends. Calls to protect their innocence are based on a fantasy of childhood that does not and never did exist—a childhood untouched by the world of adults and adult desires. The appeal to childhood innocence also tends to draw an implausibly sharp distinction between the way things were and the way things are now, skating over the continuities: between the Rolling Stones and Miley Cyrus, between top-shelf magazines and PornHub, between making out in the back row and the dick pic. What's more, it is arguably the rest of us, and not today's teenagers and young adults, who are under-equipped to deal with the technological renovation of our social world. By this I don't just mean that kids are the ones who most easily grasp the semiotic possibilities of TikTok and Instagram. I also mean that they have a sensitivity to the workings of gendered and racialized power that outstrips anything seen before in the political mainstream. It would be a mistake to assume that they are unable to cope with the pornworld just because we believe that we, as children, couldn't have coped. Like the anti-porn feminists of the second wave, perhaps my students attribute too much power to porn, and have too little faith in their ability to resist it.

Peggy Orenstein's *Girls & Sex: Navigating the Complicated New Landscape* (2016), her bestseller about the sexual reality of young people in the twenty-first century, opens with a description of a "welcome back" school assembly at a large high school in California. After reminders about attendance and warnings against alcohol and drugs, the dean addressed his female students directly: "Ladies, when you go out you need to dress to respect yourself and respect your family . . . This isn't the place for your short shorts or your tank tops or your crop tops. You need to ask yourself: if your grand-mother looks at you, will she be happy with what you're wearing?" The dean then moved on to a discussion of sexual harassment. One of the seniors, a young Latina woman, jumped up and took the mic. "I think what you just said is not okay and is extremely sexist and promoting 'rape culture,'" she said. "If I want to wear a tank top and shorts because it's hot, I should be able to do that and that has no correlation to how much 'respect' I hold for myself. What you're saying is just continuing this cycle of blaming the victim." The rest of the students cheered.[43]

I finished high school in 2003. At the time, girls wore their jeans slung low, pocketless and tight on the ass; shirts and sweaters were cropped to reveal pierced belly buttons and (if you were lucky) jutting hip bones. At a faculty board meeting—I was the student representative—the teachers discussed their alarm at how the girls were dressing. "I don't see how the boys are supposed to learn the quadratic equation," my math teacher complained, "if they're star-ing at a girl's thong." I remember hearing him say the word *thong* made me feel sick. Were the boys really distracted—they seemed fine—or was my teacher projecting? I was furious, but at the time didn't have the conceptual resources—*slut shaming*, *victim blaming*, *rape culture*—to say anything articulate. I think I may have managed something about how schools should be a safe place for students to explore their self-presentation, that it was the boys' responsibility to learn how to do quadratic equations, that no one told the attractive boys to put bags over their heads lest the girls be distracted. But maybe I just thought these things. After the meeting faculty members took it as their right to tell girls to pull down their shirts and pull up their jeans.

The young women Orenstein discusses in *Girls & Sex* would have known, unlike my younger self, exactly what to say. They would not have been ashamed, as I and all my friends were, to call themselves feminists. How should we understand the relation between this raised state of feminist consciousness among young women, and what appear to be their worsening sexual conditions: increased objectification, intensified body expectations, decreasing pleasure, and shrinking options for sex on their terms?[44] Perhaps girls and young women are becoming more feminist because their worsening circumstances demand it. Or perhaps, as Orenstein suggests, feminist consciousness is for many young women a mode of false consciousness, which plays into the hands of the very system of sexual subordination they take themselves to be opposing. Does a discourse of sexual empowerment and autonomy mask something darker and unfree? The feminist philosopher Nancy Bauer writes about asking her women students why they spend "their weekend evenings giving unreciprocated blow jobs to drunken frat boys." "They tell me they enjoy the sense of power it gives them," she writes. "You doll yourself up and get some guy helplessly aroused, at which point you *could* just walk away. But you don't."[45]

I recently interviewed a group of seventeen-year-old girls at a London school about sex. They talked about the importance of sex education and consent training, about queer sexualities, about women's pleasure. They were bright, thoughtful, and funny. They were also, it became clear the longer they spoke, disappointed. One girl described having been outed as gay when a photo of her and her girlfriend was sent around school. They all talked about double standards: boys were allowed to have sex, but the girls who did were sluts. Women's masturbation, they said, was taboo. They talked about boys who were nice online but in person turned out to be mean and sexually aggressive. One of them said, very quietly, that porn led boys to have unrealistic expectations of girls: that it meant they didn't ask what you wanted. The fact that you weren't a virgin, she said, was all the consent they needed.[46]

In a review of *Girls & Sex*, Zoë Heller charged Orenstein with intergenerational hysteria:

> History has taught us to be wary of middle-aged people complaining about the mores of the young. The parents of every era tend to be appalled by the sexual manners of their children . . . There were some in the 1950s who were pretty sure that the decadent new practice of "going steady" augured moral disaster.

While Heller concedes that Orenstein has "grim and arresting information to impart about the lives of American girls," she faults her for failing to avoid "the exaggerations, the simplifications, the whiff of manufactured crisis that we have come to associate with this genre."[47]

There is certainly something in these complaints of maternal alarmism; Orenstein is also the author of a book titled *Cinderella Ate My Daughter*. But the person who told me to read Orenstein's book wasn't an excitable parent with a bad historical memory, but a young woman who had just graduated from university. She and her girlfriends had all read Orenstein's book, and they were all talking about it. The situation Orenstein described was, they said, their own: a life of sex without dating, where girls gave and boys received, and where a discourse of empowerment and body confidence masked a deeper sense of disappointment and shame. This young woman and her friends didn't blame porn, exactly, perhaps because it's hard to blame what seems like a built-in feature of your existence. But they identified in their lives a way of thinking about sex and having sex that felt to them at once inevitable and insufficient, that seemed enforced somehow from the outside, from beyond an unreachable horizon.

W hat is to be done?
      In 1972, for the first time, a pornographic film was given a broad release in mainstream movie theaters. *Deep Throat*, now a cult classic, featured the actress Linda Boreman, stage name Linda Lovelace, in search of an orgasm—something, thanks to an unusually positioned clitoris, she was only able to achieve by performing fellatio. At the time, the film was taken to be a celebration of female sexuality; after its release, Boreman published a pornographic memoir describing the emancipatory experience of making it. The film remains one of the highest-grossing pornographic films of all time; it was released around the world, and screened several times a day in theaters across the US. The *New York Times* reviewer quoted a porn director (a "seriously bearded young man with an interest in Cinema") who said of porn actresses that "They do it because they enjoy it and because it's an easy way to make money— I think in that order. They're also exhibitionists. The camera turns them on."[48]

Eight years later, in 1980, Boreman wrote another memoir, *Ordeal*, in which she revealed that she had been forced into pornography and prostitution, and raped by her husband and manager, Chuck Traynor. Boreman made these charges public at a press conference for the book, alongside Catharine MacKinnon and Andrea Dworkin. Afterward, Dworkin and MacKinnon discussed the possibility of using the law to combat pornography. Rather than invoking traditional arguments against porn—that it was obscene, indecent, and violated community standards—they decided to argue that pornography was a form of sex discrimination, depriving women of their civil rights by undermining their status as equal citizens.

In 1983, MacKinnon and Dworkin were invited to draft an anti-pornography ordinance for Minneapolis. The ordinance gave women, both those who acted in porn and those who didn't, the right to bring civil suits against pornographers for the harm caused to them by porn. The ordinance was passed by the Minneapolis

City Council but ultimately vetoed by the mayor, who cited free speech concerns. A version of the Dworkin-MacKinnon ordinance was passed in Indianapolis in 1984, but was later struck down as unconstitutional by the Seventh Circuit Court of Appeals, a decision affirmed by the US Supreme Court. Judge Easterbrook wrote the opinion for the Seventh Circuit Court. "We accept the premises of this legislation," he said. "Depictions of subordination tend to perpetuate subordination. The subordinate status of women in turn leads to affront and lower pay at work, insult and injury at home, battery and rape on the streets." But this "simply demonstrates the power of pornography *as speech*."[49]

To say that pornography is speech is, in a liberal jurisdiction such as the US, to say that porn is deserving of special protection. Freedom of speech is connected to many things liberal societies value (or claim to): individual autonomy, the democratic accountability of the government, the sanctity of personal conscience, tolerance of difference and disagreement, the pursuit of truth. In the US speech is given unusually strong protection, and the notion itself— "speech"—is interpreted with unusual breadth. In 1992 the Supreme Court, in a unanimous decision, struck down on First Amendment grounds a Minnesota crime ordinance that had been used to charge a white teenager for burning a cross on the lawn of a black family.[50] The St. Paul Bias-Motivated Crime Ordinance had provided that:

> Whoever places on public or private property a symbol, object, appellation, characterization or graffiti, including, but not limited to, a burning cross or Nazi swastika, which one knows or has reasonable grounds to know arouses anger, alarm or resentment in others on the basis of race, color, creed, religion or gender commits disorderly conduct and shall be guilty of a misdemeanor.[51]

What troubled Justice Scalia, who wrote the majority opinion of the Court, was that the ordinance proscribed certain "speech" (e.g., cross burning) on the basis of the views it expressed (e.g., the inferiority of black people). While this viewpoint might be abhorrent, Scalia reasoned, it was still a viewpoint, whose expression must therefore be protected. The only permissible restrictions on speech were grounded, Scalia insisted, on the *form* that speech took—for example, knowingly false speech (libel, defamation), or speech that involved the criminal abuse of children for its production (child pornography). Racist or sexist speech could not be prohibited or suppressed on the grounds of its content, for then the state would be intervening in the free marketplace of ideas. The Court concluded that "St. Paul has no . . . authority to license one side of a debate to fight freestyle, while requiring the other to follow [Marquess] of Queensberry Rules," alluding to the first boxing regulations that required the wearing of gloves. In other words, in the "debate" between white supremacists and black people over racial equality, the state couldn't take sides.

A similar argument was mobilized by judges and legal scholars against the Dworkin-MacKinnon anti-porn ordinances. The legislation, they argued, violated the right of mainstream pornographers to express their viewpoint that women were objects for the sexual use of men. Since the Dworkin-MacKinnon ordinances did not target all pornographic material, but only pornographic material that subordinated women by presenting them as dehumanized sexual objects, it discriminated on the basis of content rather than form. In the debate between misogynists and feminists over women's equality, the state couldn't take sides.

MacKinnon, in *Only Words*, rejected this argument, for two reasons. First, porn's "contribution" to the debate about women's status precludes the possibility of women's entering the debate on equal terms. Porn "silences" women, MacKinnon said, taking away their ability to testify to their own sexual experiences. Porn teaches men to hear "Yes" when women say "No"; to disbelieve women who say they were harassed or raped; to see resistance as coyness, and coyness as invitation. The exercise of pornographers' right to free speech undermines women's own right to free speech.

Second, MacKinnon argued, pornography doesn't merely express the view that women are to be subordinated—it is not "only words." By training our attention on porn and its worldly effects, we can come to see it as an act of subordination, whose function is to enforce the second-class status of all women in relation to men. The very fact that judges, lawyers, and philosophers insist on treating porn as a question of free speech—as a question of what porn says rather than what it does—betrays their implicitly male perspective, their failure to see porn as many women see it. For, MacKinnon writes, "social life is full of words that are legally treated as the acts they constitute without so much as a whimper from the First Amendment."[52] Consider, MacKinnon says, someone shouting "Kill!" to a trained attack dog. The law does not treat this as the mere expression of a viewpoint: "I want you dead." Instead, the law treats it as a criminal act: ordering an attack. When the dog's owner is arrested, is his freedom of speech being violated? If not, MacKinnon asks, why are things different for men who, by creating porn, order attacks on women? MacKinnon's answer to her own question is that the law is a male institution, made by and for men. "Free speech," which poses as a merely formal principle of adjudication, is in fact, MacKinnon suggests, an ideological tool selectively deployed to protect the freedoms of the dominant class. (This is something that the feminist philosophers who have sought to elaborate and defend MacKinnon's argument generally miss: the issue, for MacKinnon, is not that pornography *really is*, metaphysically speaking, an action rather than mere speech, but that the very distinction between speech and action is political all the way down.)

There is a lot in this. The Supreme Court's decision on cross burning, like its decision in *Citizens United v. Federal Election Commission* (2010) that political spending is protected speech, shows just how easily "free speech" can function ideologically to buttress existing regimes of power. But there are reasons, apart from an indifference to social equality, to be cautious about imposing legal restrictions on porn. In its 1992 decision in *R. v. Butler*,

Canada's Supreme Court expanded the country's obscenity laws to criminalize pornography that depicts violence, as well as non-violent porn that is "degrading or dehumanising."[53] In justifying its decision, the Court said that porn of this kind subordinated women and violated their right to equality, invoking the very rationale that Dworkin and MacKinnon were pressing in the US: "This was not big bad state power jumping on poor powerless individual citizen," MacKinnon wrote, "but a law passed to stand behind a comparatively powerless group in its social fight for equality."[54] Within months, Canadian police seized from Toronto's Glad Day Bookshop copies of *Bad Attitude,* a magazine of lesbian erotic fiction that "contained sexually explicit materials with bondage and violence . . . and not what Canadians would abide other Canadians seeing." The Ontario Superior Court, citing *Butler,* found Glad Day—Canada's first gay and lesbian bookstore—guilty of criminal obscenity.[55] MacKinnon was right that the *Butler* decision was intended to help "a comparatively powerless group in its social fight for equality." But in practice it was used as cover for attacking sexual minorities, leaving mainstream pornographers untouched. In the two years after *Butler,* Randy Jorgensen, the owner of Canada's then (and the world's) largest adult video emporium, built twenty new stores, unimpeded by the law.[56]

The standard division of feminists into "anti-porn" and "pro-porn" camps is misleading. While some second-wave feminists defended mainstream porn as a healthy expression of human sexuality (Ellen Willis wrote in 1979 that "in rejecting sexual repression and hypocrisy" porn "expresses a radical impulse"[57]), most pro-porn feminists took the view not exactly that porn was good, but that it was a bad idea to legislate against it. The early feminist campaigns against porn in the 1960s took direct action against the makers and sellers of porn in the form of boycotts and protests. By contrast, the anti-porn campaigners of the early 1980s called on the power of the state. This, by their own admission, meant appealing to an entity that was fundamentally male in its outlook. Should it have come as a surprise when the state, under the cover of feminism, acted to further the subordination of women and sexual minorities?

This question had a particular significance in the late 1970s and early 1980s, when the US anti-porn feminists were campaigning. The decision of the US Supreme Court in *Roe v. Wade* (1973) to legalize abortion represented a significant victory for feminism, but also led to an organized right-wing backlash which united, to determining and lasting effect, religious conservatives with proponents of neoliberal economics. Central to the New Right's ideological program was a reversal of feminist achievements: not just the legalization of abortion, but also the availability of contraception and birth control, sex education, gay and lesbian rights, and women's mass entry into the workforce. In this climate, radical feminist critiques of pornography dovetailed with a conservative ideology which made a distinction between "bad" women (sex workers, "welfare queens") who must be disciplined by the state and "good" women who needed its protection, and which saw men as naturally rapacious and in need of taming by the institutions of monogamous marriage and the nuclear family. When a version of the Dworkin-MacKinnon ordinance was debated in Suffolk County, New York, it was amended to describe pornography as a primary cause of "sodomy" and "a serious threat to the health, safety, morals and general welfare" of citizens.[58] (MacKinnon called the Suffolk ordinance "bastardized" and fought to defeat it.) It was Ronald Reagan, the lodestar of the New Right, who as president ordered his attorney general to conduct an investigation into the harms of pornography, to which MacKinnon and Dworkin gave expert testimony. The resulting 1,960-page report of the Meese Commission repeated, without attribution, Robin Morgan's declaration that "pornography is the theory, and rape the practice."[59] But the report did not repeat Morgan's warning, from the same essay, about the futility of turning to the law for help:

I'm aware . . . that a phallocentric culture is more likely to begin its censorship purges with books on pelvic self-examination for women, or books containing lyrical paeans to lesbianism than with "*See Him Tear and Kill Her*" . . . Nor do I place much trust in a male-run judiciary . . . I feel that censorship often boils down to some male judges sitting up on their benches, getting to read a lot of dirty books with one hand.[60]

In 2014, the British government passed a law that effectively prohibits the following sex acts from featuring in porn produced in the UK:

Spanking
Caning
Aggressive whipping
Penetration by any object "associated with violence"
Physical or verbal abuse (regardless of if consensual)
Urolagnia (known as "water sports")
Role-playing as non-adults
Physical restraint
Humiliation
Female ejaculation
Strangulation
Facesitting
Fisting[61]

At first glance the list is oddly disjunctive. It includes sex acts that you might assume involve women's subordination—spanking, caning, aggressive whipping, physical or verbal abuse, physical restraint, humiliation—but are in fact characteristic of femdom porn, in which women subject men to physical pain and psychic shame. The list features an act that is emblematic of women's pleasure and almost never features in mainstream porn: female ejaculation. There's also an act that doesn't seem problematic apart from being, to many, abject: water sports. There's "penetration by any object 'associated with violence.'" Does a man's penis count? Presumably not. Strangulation and facesitting (also associated with femdom porn) are included apparently because they are potentially "life-endangering," though it is unclear how many men have died from women sitting on their faces.

The UK's list of prohibited sex acts makes sense only when you see what it leaves out: good old-fashioned straight "strip-blow-fuck-cum" porn—the sort of porn that Stoya describes making, the kind where hot blondes suck dicks, get fucked hard, told that they like it, and end up with semen on their face. This sort of porn conveys the message that women are there to be fucked, and that they love it: that tying women up, hitting them or overpowering their refusals is generally unnecessary. Only one of the UK's listed restrictions—"role-playing as non-adults"—features heavily in mainstream porn, in the ubiquitous "teen" category. Otherwise, what is officially sanctioned here, by virtue of being left off the list, is the most mainstream porn, the porn that turns most people on. But the whole point of the feminist critiques of porn was to disrupt the logic of the mainstream: to suggest that what turns most people on is not thereby okay. To prohibit only what is marginal in sex is to reinforce the hegemony of mainstream sexuality: to reinforce mainstream misogyny.

Itziar Bilbao Urrutia, a London-based, balaclava-clad, gun-wielding and skateboard-riding femdom who runs a fetish site called the Urban Chick Supremacy Cell, has so far managed to escape the 2014 law via a loophole. Urrutia and her team berate men for their complicity in capitalist patriarchy, while restraining, pegging, and bleeding them (consensually, and for a fee, or "femdom tax"). Sometimes the men are made to recite feminist texts. In most femdom fetish porn, men are humiliated for failing to meet the demands of heteromasculinity: for being "sissies." In Urrutia's pornworld, men who are rich, successful, and dominant are objects of contempt; the sissies might be saved. (It's all very Valerie Solanas.) When the UK's ban on non-normative pornographic acts was introduced in 2014, Urrutia said: "It's the corporate shopping chain crushing independent shops on the high street by piling it high and marketing it to the dumbest common denominator. In five years' time we may only have one-size-fits-all porn, peddled by the porn equivalent of Primark."[62]

In 2013, Iceland (which ranked best in the 2012 Global Gender Gap Report) considered a proposal to extend its ban on the production and sale of pornography to include "violent and hateful" porn on the internet. The Ministry of the Interior, which came up with the proposal, cited the finding that Icelandic children first view porn, on average, at the age of eleven. An adviser to the minister said: "We are a progressive, liberal society when it comes to nudity, to sexual relations, so our approach is not anti-sex but anti-violence. This is about children and gender equality, not about limiting free speech."[63] A parliamentary election in 2013 stalled the legislation, but the plan included web filters, blocking sites, and criminalizing the use of Icelandic credit cards to pay for porn sites. The proposal, explicitly motivated by gender considerations, distinguished between "violent and hateful" porn and the rest. The Urban Chick Supremacy Cell would be out. Would *Deep Throat* stay?

In 2011, Chinese police arrested thirty-two authors of *yaoi* slash fiction, which riffs on a pornographic genre imported from Japan (where most of Southeast Asia's porn comes from). *Yaoi* depicts animated homoerotic fantasies, and is made by women for women.[64]

In 2017 the UK government promised to institute an "age ban" on porn. The proposal, quietly abandoned following widespread criticism that it wouldn't have worked,[65] was to require porn viewers to prove their age by uploading a passport or driving licence, or buying a "porn pass" at their local newsagent. One age verification system that the UK proposed to use, AgeID, was created by MindGeek, the parent company of PornHub, RedTube, and YouPorn.[66] MindGeek has a near-monopoly on online porn.

Australia's Guidelines for the Classification of Films and Computer Games prohibits porn films that depict fisting, together with other "fetishes such as body piercing, application of substances such as candle wax, 'golden showers,' bondage, spanking." If fisting isn't allowed, the crip theorist Ryan Thorneycroft asked recently in the academic journal *Porn Studies*, what does that mean for the practice of "stumping," the insertion of a person's arm or leg stump into a vagina or anus?[67]

In 2018, Nepal banned digital porn in response to protests against an increase in sexual assaults against women. The list of 24,000 banned websites included those encouraging sex positivity, sex education, and queer platforms.[68]

In 2007, the then prime minister of Australia John Howard launched an "emergency" intervention in response to a report, commissioned by the Northern Territory Government, which found a high incidence of child abuse in Aboriginal communities. The report called for increased provision of social services and for greater sensitivity to the way a history of colonial violence and dispossession had shaped contemporary Aboriginal culture. Instead, Howard staged a military occupation of the Northern Territories, and introduced a total ban on the possession and dissemination of porn. Australia, where Aboriginal people make up only 3 percent of the total population, is the ninth-biggest consumer of porn on PornHub. Australians view videos tagged with "rough sex" 88 percent more often than the rest of the world on average.[69] There is no ban on the consumption of pornography by white Australians.

Attempts to legislate against porn—like attempts to legislate against sex work generally—invariably harm the women who financially depend on it the most. Free sites like PornHub are driven by pirated content uploaded by users. While porn production houses can request removal of pirated material, in practice they can never keep up with the rate at which it is uploaded. In turn, professional porn producers are watching their margins shrink; free porn sites pull an estimated two billion dollars out of the industry each year.[70] The cost of the shift of money and power away from porn production toward techno-piracy has been borne largely by women performers. Today, a porn actress in California's San Fernando Valley, the center of the world's largest porn industry, stays in the business for an average of four to six months, and graduates to higher-paying hard-core sex acts, like anal, much more quickly than performers of earlier generations.[71]

In 2020, mass unemployment caused by the COVID-19 pandemic brought tens of thousands of new performers into the porn industry via cam sites, where "models" of all sexes offer live-streamed sex performances (and a lot of talking therapy) for individual paying clients. In March 2020, CamSoda reported a 37 percent increase in new model sign-ups; ManyVids reported a 69 percent increase.[72] OnlyFans reported that 60,000 new models had signed up in the first two weeks of March alone.[73] Typically, camgirls and boys keep only about half of the revenue they generate. The LA-based cam site IsMyGirl offered McDonald's employees, who were set to be fired without sick pay, a special deal: "an exclusive offer to earn 90 percent of their proceeds (after credit card processing)." Evan Seinfeld, the founder of IsMyGirl, said: "Of course, it's up to them to make good content and to know how to engage with their fans. We have great stories from women who were living out of their cars who are making $10,000 a month."[74]

Former McDonald's employees, like workers everywhere, would be better off if they had access to adequate unemployment benefits, health care that wasn't attached to employment, and secure housing that didn't require them to work out of their cars. Not to mention employers who didn't skim 50 percent of the revenue they generate as profit. But would the tens of thousands of recently unemployed, homeless women with no health insurance who have turned to porn be better off if they were also breaking the law?

Whatever the law says, porn is going to be made bought, and sold. What should matter most to feminists is not what the law says about porn, but what the law does for and to the women who work in it.

N ot one of my students, in the now several years I have been teaching seminars on porn, has suggested using legislation to mitigate its effects. This isn't because my students are free speech fanatics. It's because they are pragmatists. They instinctively know that the internet cannot be contained, and that blocking access to it may work on members of older, less savvy generations, but not on theirs. They know that they aren't just the consumers but also increasingly the producers of porn: that the de facto target of such legislation won't be Larry Flynt but young people for whom uploading a sex video is on a continuum with taking a selfie. They are wary of the criminalization of sex work, not because they condone the men who buy sex, but because they know that the ones hurt most by criminalizing the sale of sex are the women who already exist at the margins of society.

When it comes to porn, my students think bad speech must be battled with better speech. Like Stoya, they blame inadequate sex education for the authority that porn wields over them and their lives. In their view, porn has the power to teach them the truth about sex not because the state has failed to legislate, but because the state has failed in its basic responsibility to educate.

I n one sense they are plainly right. Only 25 percent of young Britons report having had sex education that was "good" or "very good."[75] Meanwhile just 41 percent of British teachers say they have received adequate training in ways to teach about sex.[76] As of September 2020, the British mandatory curriculum broadened to include same-sex relationships, sexual assault and "porn literacy," and parents will no longer be able to opt-out their children once they reach the age of fifteen. A petition with more than 118,000 signatures protested against the change, insisting that it was parents' "fundamental right to teach their child" about sex.[77] What these parents are missing is that their children are already being taught about sex, and not by them.

In the US, only thirty of the fifty states mandate sex ed. Even in those states, individual school districts often decide what will be taught and what won't.[78] This includes whether or not the students will be made aware of any sexual option other than abstinence; twenty-six states require that there must be a stress on abstinence whenever sex education is taught.[79] Girls who have abstinence education are more likely to have sex for the first time with a significantly older partner, and more likely to describe their first time having sex as unwanted.[80] In the thirty-seven countries with available data between 2011 and 2016, only 36 percent of men and 30 percent of women aged fifteen to twenty-four had learned about HIV-prevention.[81]

We need more, and better, sex education. But the appeal to education, like the appeal to the law, is often based on a misguided view of its transformative power. Where education is understood as Plato understood it—as the sum total of words and images and signs and tropes to which we are exposed from birth—it is true that the problem of porn is a problem of education. But when "sex education" is understood as it typically is—as a formal program of teaching conducted by schools—it is less clear that it can counter the ideological force of porn. Who teaches the teachers? If teachers are anything like ordinary people, a lot of them watch porn, including most of the men. (Recall MacKinnon's comment about porn rendering male teachers "incapable of seeing their women students as their potential equals." Recall the noticed thong.) Are we surprised when teachers have difficulty talking about the patriarchal construction of sex? Will any amount of "teacher training"—short of full feminist consciousness-raising—change that? And which state is going to pay for *that*?

Unlike porn, formal sex education really is speech, as a matter of fact rather than legal fiction. It is speech spoken by teachers, designed to convey information and to persuade students. Insofar as sex education works on young people, it does so by appealing to their intellects—by asking them to deliberate, question, and understand. In this, sex education, traditionally conceived, does not propose to meet porn on its own ground. For porn does not inform, or persuade, or debate. Porn trains. It etches deep grooves in the psyche, forming powerful associations between arousal and selected stimuli, bypassing that part of us which pauses, considers, thinks. Those associations, strengthened through repetition, reinforce and reproduce the social meaning assigned by patriarchy to sexual difference. This is especially true of filmed pornography, which harnesses the power of the most ideologically potent entertainment apparatus of all: the moving picture. The movie (pornographic or not), unlike the still image or book or audio recording, needs nothing from us— no input, no elaboration. It requires only our enthralled attention, which we are compelled to give, and give willingly. In front of the porn film, the imagination halts and gives way, overtaken by its simulacrum of reality. The browser window is transformed into a window onto the world, the pornworld, in which slick bodies fuck and are fucked for their own pleasure. Any arousal the viewer experiences, and any use of the film the viewer makes in masturbation, is incidental to what unfolds in that world. The pleasures afforded by the porn film *as* a film are those afforded by any other: the pleasures of looking and listening.

Except that, in reality, there is no pornworld and no window onto it, and there is nothing incidental about the pleasures we take from porn. Porn is an elaborate construction designed to get the viewer off. That the sex in it might be real, and that the pleasure sometimes is too, doesn't change this. Obviously, mainstream porn offers the pleasures of looking at the woman's body on display, its orifices, one by one, awaiting penetration: mouth, vagina, anus. But, more than this, it offers the pleasures of ego-identification. For mainstream porn depicts a very particular kind of sexual schema— in which, on the whole, women are hungry for the assertion of male sexual power—and then assigns to the viewer a particular focus of identification within it. Mainstream porn is made for men, not merely in the sense that it is overwhelmingly men who consume porn, but in the sense that its visual logic compels the viewer to project himself onto what Laura Mulvey, in her groundbreaking essay from 1975, "Visual Pleasure and Narrative Cinema," calls "his screen surrogate": the male actor.[82] The civil libertarians who say that porn expresses a viewpoint are more correct than they know. The camera in porn doesn't linger on the man's face, if it's shown at all; very often the camera is positioned so as to replicate his point of view. Where the male body is pictured, it is an active body, the agent of the film's action, the source of its motive desire and narrative progression. The only part of the male body to be given any real screen time is the erect penis—a stand-in for the viewer's own. (Of course, this surrogate penis is larger and harder than the viewer's, a fact that the film enables him to forget, at least for its duration. As Mulvey writes: "A male movie star's glamorous characteristics are . . . not those of the erotic object of the gaze, but those of the more perfect, more complete, more powerful ideal ego.") Canonically and near-invariably, the porn film ends with the penis ejaculating— "If you don't have the come shots, you don't have a porno picture," instructed the *Film Maker's Guide to Pornography* (1977)[83]—onto the woman's body, which is pinned by the camera's gaze. If the viewer times things right—online, unlike in the cinema, one can always pause, fast-forward, rewind—it becomes his semen on her face and breasts.

W here is the woman viewer in all this? The defenders of mainstream porn like to remind us that many consumers of mainstream porn are women. But that doesn't tell us what porn does or doesn't do for the women who watch it. We can assume they get off on it. But who or what are they identifying with? Most obviously, women who watch mainstream porn identify with the women they see on-screen, the ones whose sexual pleasure is mediated through the display of male desire and its satisfaction through physical and psychic dominance: through ordering, demanding, shoving, pounding. These viewers "take it in the eye," as Carol Clover puts it.[84] But women viewers of porn can also identify with the men on-screen, becoming the ones, for once, doing the ordering, demanding, shoving, and pounding. Ellen Willis asks: "When a woman is aroused by a rape fantasy, is she perhaps identifying with the rapist as well as the victim?"[85] Willis's "perhaps" is too weak: this form of sex-inverted identification is presumably very common, perhaps just as common as the conventional form. The woman's identification as a viewer might oscillate between male agent and female object.[86] It is easy to see why many women—and not just the ones dealing with a history of sexual trauma—might find something salutary in a phantasmic role reversal. So too there might be something salutary in identifying, in the case of rape porn, with the actress who willingly consents to a performance of non-consensual sex.

Likewise, there may be salutary possibilities in sexual objectification. Jennifer Nash argues that feminists like Alice Walker and Patricia Hill Collins have been too quick to condemn mainstream porn featuring black women for its contribution to black women's racial and sexual subordination. For, Nash says, such depictions can "represent blackness as a locus of pleasure and sexual arousal" for both the white male and black female viewer.[87] (Absence from porn might be as much a sign of oppression as presence: is the fact that there is relatively little porn fetishizing Native American, Aboriginal, or Dalit women evidence that they are *not* oppressed?) Nash's argument echoes the legal philosopher Leslie Green's discussion of mainstream gay male porn. Although much of it recycles tropes of masc domination and fem submission from straight porn, Green argues that it can nonetheless give gay men—for whom being denied the status of sexually desirable objects is a "motif experience"—"a robust sense of their own *objectivity*." Without such a sense, Green says, a male "gay sexuality still can be spiritual, political or intellectual. What it cannot be is hot, wet or fun."[88]

This is all surely right. Anti-porn feminists are too confident in their assumption that images of sexual and racial domination on-screen can do nothing but exacerbate sexual and racial domination off the screen. The simplicity of this picture is undone, not least, by the notoriously unruly unconscious: who can be sure what it will make of what the conscious mind deems "good" and "bad"? That said, it is interesting how few if any pro-porn theorists suggest that men who watch rape porn identify with the raped woman, or that white men who watch interracial porn identify with the black woman.

Still we can ask: why does the woman viewer have to become a man to exert power? Why does the fem gay man or black woman need to watch someone who looks like them be bent over and fucked to know that they, in their femness or blackness, are desirable? I am not saying the need is not real, or that sexist and racist porn cannot be repurposed to serve it. I am asking why the need exists in the first place, and what it tells us about how far the power of porn can be subverted or diverted. I am asking that we do not confuse the necessities of negotiation under oppression with the signs of emancipation.

I am also asking that we don't discount the power of the pornographic mainstream. The internet meme "Rule 34" states "If it exists, there is porn of it. No exceptions." It's true, near enough. Even on the biggest porn sites one can find things to suit recherché or even politically refreshing tastes: porn with elderly performers or performers with visible disabilities, porn where women peg men, balloon porn, *Star Trek* porn. But that doesn't mean that the porn-world is a place of free idiosyncratic desire and personal kink. Porn, like all cultural forms, has strong trends and through-lines. Of the top twenty most popular stars on PornHub in 2017, all but two were white, and all were slim, able-bodied, fem, cis, and waxed to pre-pubescent hairlessness.[89] Piper Perri, ranked number seventeen, is ninety pounds and 4'10", the same height—coincidentally?—as Nabokov's Lolita. She has braces on her perfectly straight teeth, and looks no older than fourteen. (A proposal for Rule 35: Whatever's ugly in our sexual politics, it's wildly popular in porn.)

But free online porn doesn't just reflect preexisting sexual tastes. Sites like PornHub are driven by sophisticated algorithms, built on the same logic that powers YouTube and Amazon. These algorithms learn and then shape users' preferences based on the data they collect: not just search histories, but also their location, gender, and the times of day they're most likely to be online. In turn, the algorithm gives users what others in their demographic like to watch, bringing their sexual tastes into conformity. What's more, the algorithm teaches users to think about sex itself in prescribed categories. As Shira Tarrant, author of *The Pornography Industry*, observes: "If you are interested in something like double oral, and you put that into a browser, you're going to get two women giving one guy a blowjob . . . you're not likely to get two men or two people giving a woman oral sex." She adds: "Online-porn users don't necessarily realize that their porn-use patterns are largely molded by a corporation."[90] Thanks to PornHub's algorithmic categories, porn actresses who are too old to feature in the "teen" category and too young for "MILF"—that is, actresses between twenty-three and thirty—now find it extremely difficult to get booked for shoots.

P orn is powerful. The hope that it can be neutered through education doesn't take seriously enough the power it has—not as speech, but as film. The creators of feminist and indie queer porn tacitly know this. What they offer, in a sense, is an alternative form of sex education, which seeks to reveal, and revel in, the sexiness of bodies, acts, and distributions of power that do not conform to heterosexist, racist, and ableist erotic standards. In 1984, Candida Royalle set up Femme Productions, the first feminist porn production house. Royalle avoided money shots ("as an actress, I had asked, 'Why are they in there?' They said: 'To prove it's really happening'"[91]), and having consulted sex therapists on ways to avoid reinforcing rape myths, contextualized scenes of coercive sex with conversations about consent between the actors.

Following Royalle's lead, today a new generation of porn producers and performers seek to make porn that resists hegemonic understandings of which bodies and acts are arousing and whose pleasure matters. (It's easy to forget, but in almost all mainstream porn men have real orgasms and women fake it.) Erika Lust, a feminist porn director and producer based in Barcelona, credits her move into indie porn to Linda Williams's academic treatise on pornographic film, *Hard Core: Power, Pleasure, and the "Frenzy of the Visible"* (1989).[92] Lust's films are beautiful to look at, narratively and emotionally complex, and driven by an egalitarian ethos of pleasure-seeking. To see the trailers, you'd think they were arthouse movies, which in a way is exactly what they are.

Shine Louise Houston is a black queer porn director with a film degree from the San Francisco Art Institute, whose film *The Crash Pad* (2005) is a "dyke porn" cult classic. Houston is known for her representation of queer and non-white sexual agency. Her actors decide what it is they want to do together instead of following a script, and each is paid the same flat fee regardless of the sex acts they perform, bucking a market that normally enforces a strict financial hierarchy: anal over vaginal penetration, double penetration over single, and straight over lesbian sex. The actors in Houston's online series, CrashPadSeries.com, describe themselves variously as non-binary butch femmes, witches, trans lesbians, transdykes, "non-human women," bears, genderqueer unicorns, butch futch trans girl enby dykes, sex nerds, and ftM sadist sexual omnivores. The episodes are accompanied by content warnings (in the case of "consensual non-consensual sex") and "behind the scenes" footage in which the actors debrief after shooting.

The porn industry in Japan—among the largest in the world—has suffered (as it has everywhere else) from the availability of free and uncensored porn.[93] But there is a huge appetite for woman-directed, if not self-consciously feminist, porn for women.[94]

The problem, simply put, is that feminist and indie porn movies are rarely free. And even if they were—say, if states subsidized their directors and actors as part of a program of gender and racial equality—it would hardly fly as formal sex education. Indeed, in many jurisdictions, it would be illegal to show anyone under eighteen this material, or even encourage them to watch it. (This is also a serious problem for any attempt to teach "porn literacy" in schools: how do you teach people to read texts you can't show them?) Among my own students, all of them over eighteen, the prospect of a different kind of porn is greeted by some with enthusiasm. But many feel that it's too late for them, that they are already too old to reconfigure their desires. Children of the internet, with its infinite variety, somehow they find all but one possibility foreclosed.

The argument that what young people need is better and more diverse representations of sex is, with the rise of internet porn, heard increasingly often. Beyond the difficulties of delivering such a thing, there is a more principled reservation. The demand for better representation leaves in place the logic of the screen, according to which sex must be mediated; and the imagination is limited to imitation, riffing on what it has already absorbed. Perhaps, today, the logic of the screen is inescapable. If that is so, then "better representation" is indeed the best we can hope for.

But something is lost here. While filmed sex seemingly opens up a world of sexual possibility, all too often it shuts down the sexual imagination, making it weak, dependent, lazy, codified. The sexual imagination is transformed into a mimesis-machine, incapable of generating its own novelty. In *Intercourse* (1987) Andrea Dworkin warned of just this:

> Imagination is not a synonym for sexual fantasy, which is only—
> pathetically—a programmed tape loop repeating repeating in the
> narcoleptic mind. Imagination finds new meanings, new forms;

complex and empathetic values and acts. The person with imagination is pushed forward by it into a world of possibility and risk,
a distinct world of meaning and choice; not into a nearly bare
junkyard of symbols manipulated to evoke rote responses.[95]

If sex education sought to endow young people not just with better "rote responses" but with an emboldened sexual imagination—
the capacity to bring forth "new meanings, new forms"—it would
have to be, I think, a kind of negative education. It wouldn't assert
its authority to tell the truth about sex, but rather remind young
people that the authority on what sex is, and could become, lies
with them. Sex can, if they choose, remain as generations before
them have chosen: violent, selfish, and unequal. Or sex can—if they
choose—be something more joyful, more equal, freer. How such a
negative education is to be achieved is unclear. There are no laws to
draft, no easy curriculums to roll out. Rather than more speech or
more images, it is their onslaught that would have to be arrested.
Perhaps then the sexual imagination could be coaxed, even briefly,
to recall its lost power.

The Right to Sex

On May 23, 2014, Elliot Rodger, a twenty-two-year-old college dropout, became the world's most famous incel. The term— short for "involuntary celibate"—can, in theory, be applied to both men and women, but in practice it picks out not sexless men in general, but a certain kind of sexless man: the kind who is convinced he is owed sex, and is enraged by the women who deprive him of it. Rodger stabbed to death his two housemates, Weihan Wang and Cheng Hong, and their friend, George Chen, as they entered his apartment on Seville Road in Isla Vista, California. A few hours later he drove to the Alpha Phi sorority house near the campus of UC Santa Barbara. He shot three women outside, killing two of them, Katherine Cooper and Veronika Weiss. Rodger then went on a drive-by shooting spree through Isla Vista, killing Christopher Michaels-Martinez, also a student at UCSB, with a single bullet to the chest inside a deli, and wounding fourteen others. He eventually crashed his BMW coupé into a parked car, after shooting himself in the head. He was found dead by the police.

In the hours between murdering three men in his apartment and driving to Alpha Phi, Rodger went to Starbucks, ordered coffee, and uploaded a video, "Elliot Rodger's Retribution," to his YouTube channel. He also emailed a 107,000-word memoir-manifesto, "My Twisted World: The Story of Elliot Rodger," to a group of people including his parents and his therapist. Together these two documents detail the massacre to come and Rodger's motivations. "All I ever wanted was to fit in and live a happy life," he explains at the beginning of "My Twisted World," "but I was cast out and rejected, forced to endure an existence of loneliness and insignificance, all because the females of the human species were incapable of seeing the value in me."

He goes on to describe his privileged and happy early childhood in England—Rodger was the son of a successful British filmmaker—followed by his privileged and unhappy adolescence in Los Angeles as a short, bad-at-sports, shy, weird, friendless kid, desperate to be cool. He writes of dyeing his hair blond (Rodger was half white and half Malaysian Chinese; blond people were "so much more beautiful"); of finding "sanctuary" in Halo and World of Warcraft; being shoved by a pretty girl at summer camp ("That was the first experience of female cruelty I endured, and it traumatized me to no end"); becoming incensed by the sex lives of his peers ("How could an inferior, ugly black boy be able to get a white girl and not me? I am beautiful, and I am half white myself. I am descended from British aristocracy. *He* is descended from slaves"); dropping out of successive schools and then community college; and fantasizing about a political order in which he ruled the world and sex was outlawed ("All women must be quarantined like the plague they are"). The necessary result of all this, Rodger said, was his "War on Women," in the course of which he would "punish all females" for the crime of depriving him of sex. He would target the Alpha Phi sorority, "the hottest sorority of UCSB," because it contained "the very girls who represent everything I hate in the female gender . . . hot, beautiful blonde girls . . . spoiled, heartless, wicked bitches." He would show everyone that he was "the superior one."

Late in 2017, the online discussion forum Reddit closed down its 40,000-member "Incel" support group, for those "who lack romantic relationships and sex." Reddit took the action after introducing a new policy of prohibiting content that "encourages, glorifies, incites or calls for violence." What had started out as a support group for the lonely and sexually isolated had become a forum whose users not only raged against women and the "noncels" and "normies" who got to sleep with them, but also frequently advocated rape. A second incel Reddit group, "Truecels," was also banned following the site's policy change. Its sidebar had read: "No encouraging or inciting violence, or other illegal activities such as rape. But of course it is okay to say, for example, that rape should have a lighter punishment or even that it should be legalized and that slutty women deserve rape."

Soon after Rodger's killings, incels took to the manosphere to explain that women (and feminism) were in the end responsible for what had happened. Had one of those "wicked bitches" just fucked Elliot Rodger he wouldn't have had to kill anyone. Feminist commentators were quick to point out what should have been obvious: that no woman was obliged to have sex with Rodger; that his sense of sexual entitlement was a case study in patriarchal ideology; that his actions were a predictable if extreme response to the thwarting of that entitlement. They could have added that feminism, far from being Rodger's enemy, may well be the primary force resisting the very system that made him feel—as a short, clumsy, effeminate, interracial boy—inadequate. His manifesto reveals that it was overwhelmingly boys, not girls, who bullied him: who pushed him into lockers, called him a loser, made fun of him for his virginity. But it was the girls who deprived him of sex, and the girls, therefore, who had to be destroyed.

Could it also be said that Rodger's unfuckability was a symptom of the internalization of patriarchal norms of male sexual attractiveness on the part of women? The answer to that question is complicated by two things. First, Rodger was a creep, and it was at least partly his insistence on his own aesthetic, moral and racial superiority, and whatever it was in him that made him capable of stabbing his housemates and their friend a total of 134 times, not his failure to meet the demands of heteromasculinity, that kept women away. Second, plenty of non-homicidal nerdy guys get laid. Indeed, part of the injustice of patriarchy, something unnoticed by incels and other "men's rights activists," is the way it makes even supposedly unattractive categories of men attractive: geeks, nerds, effete men, old men, men with "dad bods." Meanwhile there are sexy schoolgirls and sexy teachers, manic pixie dream girls and MILFs, but they're all taut-bodied and hot, minor variations on the same normative paradigm. (Can we imagine *GQ* carrying an article celebrating "mom bod"?)

That said, it's true that the kind of women Rodger wanted to have sex with—hot sorority blondes—don't as a rule date men like Rodger, even the non-creepy, non-homicidal ones, at least not until they make their fortune in Silicon Valley. It's also true that this has something to do with the rigid gender norms enforced by patriarchy: alpha females want alpha males. And it's true that Rodger's desires—his erotic fixation on the "spoiled, stuck-up, blonde slut"—are themselves a function of patriarchy, as is the way the "hot blonde slut" becomes a metonym for all women. (Many in the manosphere gleefully pointed out that Rodger didn't even succeed in killing the women he lusted after, as if in final confirmation of his "omega" sexual status: Katherine Cooper and Veronika Weiss were non "hot blondes" from Delta Delta Delta who just happened to be passing by the Alpha Phi house.) Feminist commentary on Elliot Rodger and the incel phenomenon more broadly has said much about male sexual entitlement, objectification, and violence. But so far it has said little about desire: men's desire, women's desire, and the ideological shaping of both.

It used to be the case that if you wanted a political critique of desire, feminism was where you would turn. A few decades ago feminists were nearly alone in thinking about the way sexual desire—its objects and expressions, fetishes and fantasies—is shaped by oppression. The radical feminists of the late 1960s and 1970s demanded that we abandon the Freudian view that held sexual desire to be, in the words of Catharine MacKinnon, "an innate primary natural prepolitical unconditioned drive divided along the biological gender line."[1] Instead, they urged, we must recognize that it is patriarchy that makes sex, as we know it, what it is: a practice marked by male domination and female submission, whose constitutive emotions are, in MacKinnon's formulation, "hostility and contempt, or arousal of master to slave, together with awe and vulnerability, or arousal of slave to master."[2] For so-called "anti-sex" feminists, that there were women who seemed capable of achieving pleasure under these conditions was a sign of how bad things were. For many of them, the solution lay in refusing sex and marriage with men. This was true, for example, of The Feminists, a women's liberation group founded by Ti-Grace Atkinson in New York in 1969, which implemented a rule allowing no more than a third of its membership to be married to or living with a man. This quota represented The Feminists' conviction that feminism "must not only deal with what women want" but moreover "*change* what women want."[3] Cell 16, a Boston-based group founded in 1968, practiced sex separatism, celibacy, and karate. Its first order of business was to read Valerie Solanas's *SCUM Manifesto*, which declared that the

> female can easily—far more easily than she may think—condition away her sex drive, leaving her completely cool and cerebral and free . . . when the female transcends her body . . . the male, whose ego consists of his cock, will disappear.[4]

Echoing Solanas, Cell 16's founder Roxanne Dunbar-Ortiz observed that the "person who had been through the whole sex-scene, and then becomes by choice and revulsion, a celibate, is the most lucid person."[5]

While all radical feminists of the late 1960s and early 1970s saw sex as a construction of patriarchy, some pushed back, from the beginning, against the idea that women's desires had to be brought into line with their politics. As Alice Echols details in *Daring to be Bad* (1989), her study of radical feminism in the US, self-proclaimed "pro-woman" feminists saw sex and marriage with men as both a legitimate desire and a strategic necessity for most women—a means of acquiring political power or just surviving—rather than a symptom of patriarchal indoctrination. What women needed wasn't liberation from the deluded desire for heterosexual marriage, but that heterosexual marriage be reconceived on more equal terms.[6] The manifesto of the radical feminist group Redstockings, founded in 1969 by Shulamith Firestone and Ellen Willis, insisted that "women's submission is not the result of brainwashing, stupidity, or mental illness but of continual, daily pressure from men. We do not need to change ourselves, but to change men."[7] It followed, for the Redstockings and other pro-woman feminists, that "personal solutionism"—the idea that revolutionary possibilities were contained in the separatist practices of groups like Cell 16 and The Feminists—should be rejected. For pro-woman feminists, such militancy presupposed a false dichotomy between "true" feminist women and the benighted women who, in their relations with men, betrayed the revolutionary cause. In the view of pro-woman feminists, all women were engaged in acts of negotiation and accommodation; real liberation required structural, not personal, transformation. One prominent Redstocking is reported to have declared at a meeting: "We won't get off the plantation until the revolution!"[8] (As the choice of metaphor might suggest, the Redstockings were, like most radical feminist groups, overwhelmingly white.)

Pro-woman feminists likewise worried that anti-sex feminists, in their zeal to exorcise patriarchy, were colluding in the denial of women's sexuality. They were not without grounds. Ellen Willis remembers Ti-Grace Atkinson attending a Redstockings meeting and saying "very patronizingly" that sexual desire "was all in my head."[9] But despite their insistence on the reality of women's sexual desires, pro-woman feminists on the whole had little interest in defending the legitimacy of desires beyond the confines of heterosexuality. They saw straight marriage as both pragmatically necessary and intrinsically desirable, and accused lesbians of retreating from the "sexual battlefield" and alienating mainstream women. One gay woman who quit the Redstockings noted that the group "was not too pro-woman when it came to Lesbians."[10]

In their tendency toward homophobia, pro-woman feminists were, unusually, allied with anti-sex feminists, many of whom saw lesbians as "male-identified" sexual threats to other women. When lesbian feminists began vociferously arguing for the compatibility of their sexual identities with their politics, they did so by framing lesbianism as a matter of political solidarity rather than innate sexual orientation. The Furies, a radical lesbian collective founded in Washington, DC, in 1971, declared that "lesbianism is not a matter of sexual preference, but rather one of political choice which every woman must make if she is to . . . end male supremacy."[11] The anti-sex feminist case for celibacy was thus repurposed as an argument for lesbianism, albeit of a very particular kind. As political lesbians began to be seen as the vanguard of the women's liberation movement, pro-woman feminists accused them, as they had anti-sex feminists before, of being more interested in personal transformation than political confrontation. In response, political lesbians accused pro-woman feminists of propping up male power.

In the UK a similar pattern played out. The inaugural National Women's Liberation Movement Conference took place at Ruskin College in Oxford in 1970. From the beginning, the British second wave was intellectually and politically dominated by socialist feminists like Juliet Mitchell, Sally Alexander, and Sheila Rowbotham, who regarded the fight against capitalist exploitation as central to women's emancipation, and male leftists as important (if imperfect) allies. Some feminists dissented, setting up separatist women's houses and groups. But it wasn't until 1977 that a decisive rift emerged between socialist feminists and those feminists who saw men, not capitalism, as the fundamental enemy. At the ninth Women's Liberation Movement Conference, this time held in London,

Sheila Jeffreys gave a paper titled "The Need for Revolutionary Feminism," in which she took socialist feminists to task for not recognizing that male violence rather than capitalist exploitation lay at the foundation of women's oppression, and for making "reformist" demands like socialized childcare.[12] "The women's liberation movement is, and should be seen to be, a threat," Jeffreys said, "and I cannot see that it serves a useful purpose to represent it as mixed Tupperware party with men doing the coffee."[13] A vocal minority of English feminists rallied around Jeffreys, forming separatist groups like the Leeds Revolutionary Feminist Group, famous for its pamphlet "Political Lesbianism: The Case against Heterosexuality." At the following year's conference in Birmingham, revolutionary feminists submitted a proposal to abolish the six demands that the WLM had committed to at previous conferences, on the grounds that "it is ridiculous for us to demand anything from a patriarchal state—from men—who are the enemy."[14] The proposal was left off the plenary agenda—deliberately, claimed the revolutionary feminists. When it was finally read aloud it was met with fierce opposition by socialist feminists, in turn leading the revolutionary feminists to protest by disrupting other speakers and singing. The two factions went on to wrangle bitterly over whether male sexual violence was a symptom of "male supremacy" or of other social ills such as class oppression, and whether lesbian sexuality should be afforded special protection by feminists. As the session wore on, little could be heard over the shouting; microphones were wrenched from speakers' hands; many women left in frustration and disgust. The Birmingham conference was the tenth and last of the National Women's Liberation Movement conferences.[15]

As the women's liberation movement unfolded through the 1970s and into the 1980s, these battle lines hardened. From the mid-1970s onward, anti-sex feminists in the US, and to a lesser extent revolutionary feminists in the UK, became increasingly focused on the issue of pornography, which came to symbolize for some feminists the whole of patriarchy. (In keeping with the theme of feminist homophobia, anti-porn feminists were, on the whole, also virulently opposed to lesbian sadomasochism, which they thought recapitulated patriarchal dynamics.) Many feminists, most notably Ellen Willis, found the preoccupation with porn troubling for the same reasons that pro-woman feminists had objected to militant celibacy: namely, that it colluded in the repression of women's sexuality. But many feminists also wanted to distance themselves from the pro-woman line that the ideal state for most women was monogamous heterosexual marriage. Threading between the poles of pro-woman and anti-sex feminism, Willis led the way in the development of what came to be called "pro-sex" or "sex-positive" feminism. In her classic essay from 1981, "Lust Horizons: Is the Women's Movement Pro-Sex?," Willis argued that both pro-woman and anti-sex feminism reinforced the conservative idea that men desire sex while women merely put up with it, an idea whose "chief social function" was to curtail women's autonomy in areas outside the bedroom (or the alleyway). Both forms of feminism, Willis wrote, asked "women to accept a spurious moral superiority as a substitute for sexual pleasure, and curbs on men's sexual freedom as a substitute for real power."[16] Drawing inspiration from the contemporaneous LGBT rights movement, Willis and other pro-sex feminists insisted that women were sexual subjects in their own right, whose acts of consent—saying yes and saying no—were morally dispositive.

Since Willis, the case for pro-sex feminism has been buttressed by feminism's turn toward intersectionality. Thinking about the ways patriarchal oppression is inflected by race and class has made feminists reluctant to make universal prescriptions, including universal sexual policies. The demand for equal access to the workplace will be more resonant for white, middle-class women who have been expected to stay home than it will be for the black and working-class women who have always been expected to labor alongside men. Similarly, sexual self-objectification may mean one thing for a woman who, by virtue of her whiteness, already conforms to the paradigm of female beauty, but quite another thing for a black or brown woman, or a trans woman. The turn toward intersectionality has also deepened feminist discomfort with thinking in terms of false consciousness: that's to say, with the idea that women who have sex with and marry men have internalized the patriarchy. The important thing now, it is broadly thought, is to take women at their word. If a woman says she enjoys working in porn, or being paid to have sex with men, or engaging in rape fantasies, or wearing stilettos—and even that she doesn't just enjoy these things but finds them emancipatory, part of her feminist praxis—then we are required, many feminists think, to trust her. This is not merely an epistemic claim: that a woman's saying something about her own experience gives us strong, though perhaps not indefeasible, reason to think it true. It is also, or perhaps primarily, an ethical claim: a feminism that trades too freely in notions of self-deception is a feminism that risks dominating the subjects it presumes to liberate.

The case made by Willis in "Lust Horizons" has so far proved the enduring one. Since the 1980s, the wind has been behind a feminism which does not moralize about women's sexual desires, and which insists that acting on those desires is morally constrained only by the boundaries of consent. Sex is no longer morally problematic or unproblematic: it is instead merely wanted or unwanted. In this sense, the norms of sex are like the norms of capitalist free exchange. What matters is not what conditions give rise to the dynamics of supply and demand—why some people need to sell their labor while others buy it—but only that both buyer and seller have agreed to the transfer. It would be too easy, though, to say that sex positivity represents the co-option of feminism by liberalism. Generations of feminists and gay and lesbian activists have fought hard to free sex from shame, stigma, coercion, abuse, and unwanted pain. It has been essential to this project to stress that there are limits to what can be understood about sex from the outside, that sexual acts can have private meanings which cannot be grasped from a public perspective, that there are times when we must take it on trust that a particular instance of sex is okay, even when we can't imagine any way it could be. Thus feminism finds itself not only questioning the liberal distinction between the public and the private, but also insisting on it.

Yet it would be disingenuous to make nothing of the convergence, however unintentional, between sex positivity and liberalism in their shared reluctance to interrogate the formation of our desires. Third-wave feminists are right to say, for example, that sex work is work, and can be better work than the menial labor undertaken by most women. And they are right to say that what sex workers need are legal and material protections, safety and security, not rescue or rehabilitation. But to understand what sort of work sex work is—just what physical and psychical acts are being bought and sold, and why it is overwhelmingly women who do it, and overwhelmingly men who pay for it—surely we have to say something about the political formation of male desire. And surely there will be related things to say about other forms of women's work: teaching, nursing, caring, mothering. To say that sex work is "just work" is to forget that all work—men's work, women's work—is never just work: it is also sexed.

Willis concludes "Lust Horizons" by saying that for her it is "axiomatic that consenting partners have a right to their sexual proclivities, and that authoritarian moralism has no place" in feminism. And yet, she goes on, "a truly radical movement must look . . . beyond the right to choose, and keep focusing on the fundamental questions. Why do we choose what we choose? What would we choose if we had a real choice?" This may seem an extraordinary reversal on Willis's part. After laying out the ethical case for taking our sexual preferences, whatever they may be, as fixed points, protected from moral inquisition, Willis tells us that a "truly radical" feminism would ask precisely the question that gives rise to "authoritarian moralism": what would women's sexual choices look like if they were really free? One might feel that Willis has given with one hand

and taken away with the other. But perhaps she has given with both. Here, she tells us, is a task for feminism: to treat as axiomatic our free sexual choices, while also seeing why, as "anti-sex" and lesbian feminists have always said, such choices, under patriarchy, are rarely free. What I am suggesting is that, in our rush to do the former, feminists risk forgetting to do the latter.

When we see consent as the sole constraint on ethically okay sex, we are pushed toward a naturalization of sexual preference in which the rape fantasy becomes a primordial rather than a political fact. But not only the rape fantasy. Consider the supreme fuckability of "hot blonde sluts" and East Asian women, the comparative unfuckability of black women and Asian men, the fetishization and fear of black male sexuality, the sexual disgust expressed toward disabled, trans, and fat bodies. These facts about "fuckability"—not whose bodies are seen as sexually available (in that sense black women, trans women, and disabled women are all *too* fuckable), but whose bodies confer status on those who have sex with them—are political facts. They are facts that a truly intersectional feminism should demand we take seriously. But the sex-positive gaze, unmoored from Willis's call to ambivalence, threatens to neutralize these facts, treating them as pre-political givens. In other words, the sex-positive gaze risks covering not only for misogyny, but for racism, ableism, transphobia, and every other oppressive system that makes its way into the bedroom through the seemingly innocuous mechanism of "personal preference."

The beautiful torsos on Grindr are mostly Asian men hiding their faces," a gay friend of mine says. The next day I see on Facebook that Grindr has started a web series called "What the Flip?" In its first three-minute episode, a beautiful, blue-haired East Asian guy and a well-groomed, good-looking white guy trade Grindr profiles. The results are predictably grim. The white guy, now using the

Asian guy's profile, is hardly approached, and when he is it's by men announcing that they're "Rice Queens" and like Asian men for being "good at bottoming." When he ignores their messages, abuse is hurled at him. The Asian guy's inbox, meanwhile, is inundated with admirers. Talking about it afterward, the white guy expresses his shock, the Asian guy cheerful resignation. "You're not everybody's cup of tea, but you're going to be somebody's," the white guy offers, feebly, before they hug it out. In the next episode, a ripped Ryan Gosling–type switches profiles with a pretty-faced chubby guy. In another episode a fem guy trades with a masc guy. The results are as one would expect.[17]

The obvious irony of "What the Flip?" is that Grindr, by its nature, encourages its users to divide the world into those who are and those who are not viable sexual objects according to crude markers of identity—to think in terms of sexual "deal-breakers" and "require-ments." In so doing, Grindr simply deepens the discriminatory grooves along which our sexual desires already move. But online dat-ing—and especially the abstracted interfaces of Tinder and Grindr, which distill attraction down to the essentials: face, height, weight, age, race, witty tagline—has arguably taken what is worst about the current state of sexuality and institutionalized it on our screens.[18]

A presupposition of "What the Flip?" is that this is a peculiarly gay problem: that the gay male community is too superficial, too body-fascist, too judgy. The gay men in my life say this sort of thing all the time; they all feel bad about it, perpetrators and victims alike (most see themselves as both). I'm unconvinced. Can we imagine predominantly straight dating apps like Bumble or Tinder creating a web series that encouraged the straight "community" to confront its sexual racism or fatphobia? If that is an unlikely prospect, it's hardly because straight people aren't body fascists or sexual racists. It's because straight people—or, I should say, white, able-bodied cis straight people—aren't much in the habit of thinking there's anything wrong with how they have sex. By contrast, gay men—even the beautiful, white, rich, able-bodied ones—know that who we have sex with, and how, is a political question.

There are of course real risks associated with subjecting our sexual preferences to political scrutiny. We want feminism to be able to interrogate the grounds of desire, but without slut shaming, prudery or self-denial: without telling individual women that they don't really know what they want, or can't enjoy what they do in fact want, within the bounds of consent. Some feminists think this is impossible, since any openness to desire-critique will inevitably lead to authoritarian moralism. (We can think of such feminists as making the case for a kind of "sex positivity of fear," just as Judith Shklar once made the case for a "liberalism of fear"—that is, a liberalism motivated by a fear of authoritarian alternatives.[19]) But there is a risk too that repoliticizing desire will encourage a discourse of sexual entitlement. Talk of people who are unjustly sexually marginalized or excluded can pave the way to the thought that these people have a right to sex, a right that is being violated by those who refuse to have sex with them. That view is galling: no one is under an obligation to have sex with anyone else. This too is axiomatic. And this, of course, is what Elliot Rodger, like the legions of angry incels who celebrate him as a martyr, refused to see. On the now defunct Reddit group, a post titled "It should be legal for incels to rape women" explained that "No starving man should have to go to prison for stealing food, and no sexually starved man should have to go to prison for raping a woman." It is a sickening false equivalence, which reveals the violent misconception at the heart of patriarchy. Some men are excluded from the sexual sphere for politically suspect reasons—including, perhaps, some of the men driven to vent their despair on anonymous forums—but the moment their unhappiness is transmuted into a rage at the women "denying" them sex, rather than at the systems that shape desire (their own and others'), they have crossed a line into something morally ugly and confused.

In her shrewd essay "Men Explain *Lolita* to Me," Rebecca Solnit reminds us that "you don't get to have sex with someone unless they want to have sex with you," just as "you don't get to share someone's sandwich unless they want to share their sandwich with you."[20] Not getting a bite of someone's sandwich is "not a form of oppression either," Solnit says. But the analogy complicates as much as it elucidates. Suppose your child came home from primary school and told you that the other children share their sandwiches with each other, but not with her. And suppose further that your child is brown, or fat, or disabled, or doesn't speak English very well, and that you suspect this is the reason for her exclusion from the sandwich-sharing. Suddenly it hardly seems sufficient to say that none of the other children is obliged to share with your child, true as that might be.

Sex is not a sandwich. While your child does not want to be shared with out of pity—just as no one really wants a mercy fuck, and certainly not from a racist or a transphobe—we wouldn't think it coercive were the teacher to encourage the other students to share with your daughter, or were they to institute an equal sharing policy. But a state that made analogous interventions in the sexual preference and practices of its citizens—that encouraged us to "share" sex equally—would probably be thought grossly authoritarian. (The utopian socialist Charles Fourier proposed a guaranteed "sexual minimum," akin to a guaranteed basic income, for every man and woman, regardless of age or infirmity; only once sexual deprivation has been eliminated, Fourier thought, could romantic relationships be truly free. This social service would be provided by an "amorous nobility" who, Fourier said, "know how to subordinate love to the dictates of honour."[21]) Of course, it matters just what those interventions would look like: disability activists, for example, have long called for more inclusive sex education in schools, and many would welcome regulation that ensured diversity in advertising and the media. But to think that such measures would be enough to alter our sexual desires, to free them entirely from the grooves of discrimination, is naive. And whereas you can quite reasonably demand that a group of children share their sandwiches inclusively, you just can't do the same with sex. What works in one case will not work in the other. Sex isn't a sandwich, and it isn't really like anything else either. There is nothing else so riven with politics and yet so inviolably personal. For better or worse, we must find a way to take sex on its own terms.

Within contemporary feminism, these issues are much discussed in relation to trans women, who often face sexual exclusion from lesbian cis women who at the same time claim to take them seriously as women. This phenomenon was named the "cotton ceiling"—"cotton" as in underwear—by the trans porn actress and activist Drew DeVeaux. As many trans women have noted, the phrase is deeply unfortunate. While the "glass ceiling" implies the violation of a woman's right to advance on the basis of her work, the "cotton ceiling" describes a lack of access to what no one is obligated to give. Yet simply to say to a trans woman, or a disabled woman, or an Asian man, "No one is required to have sex with you," is to skate over something crucial. There is no entitlement to sex, and everyone is entitled to want what they want, but personal preferences—NO DICKS, NO FEMS, NO FATS, NO BLACKS, NO ARABS, NO RICE, NO SPICE, MASC-FOR-MASC—are rarely just personal.

In a piece for *n+1* in 2018, the feminist and trans theorist Andrea Long Chu argued that the trans experience, contrary to how we have become accustomed to think of it, "expresses not the truth of an identity but the force of a desire." Being trans, she says, is "a matter not of who one *is*, but of what one *wants*." She goes on:

I transitioned for gossip and compliments, lipstick and mascara, for crying at the movies, for being someone's girlfriend, for letting her pay the check or carry my bags, for the benevolent chauvinism of bank tellers and cable guys, for the telephonic intimacy of long-distance female friendship, for fixing my make-up in the bathroom flanked like Christ by a sinner on each side, for sex toys, for feeling hot, for getting hit on by butches, for that secret knowledge of which dykes to watch out for, for Daisy Dukes, bikini tops, and all the dresses, and, my god, *for the breasts*. But now you begin to see the problem with desire: we rarely want the things we should.[22]

This declaration, as Chu is well aware, threatens to bolster the argument made by anti-trans feminists: that trans women equate, and conflate, womanhood with the trappings of traditional femininity, thereby strengthening the hand of patriarchy. Many trans women respond to this accusation by insisting that being trans is about identity rather than desire: about already being a woman, rather than wanting to become a woman. (Once one recognizes trans women as simply women, complaints that they reinforce gender stereotypes begin to look invidious, since one hears far fewer complaints about the "excessive femininity" of cis women.) Chu's response, by contrast, is to insist that trans women are constituted by a desire to have something they currently lack: not just some abstract membership in the metaphysical category "woman," but the specific trappings of a culturally constructed, and oppressive, femininity—Daisy Dukes, bikini tops, and "benevolent chauvinism." The right of trans women to have their identifications not only respected but also materially supported rests, for Chu, on the premise that "nothing good comes of forcing desire to conform to political principle." This is, she says, "the true lesson of political lesbianism as a failed project."[23] What a truly liberatory feminism needs, in other words, is to fully exorcise the radical feminist ambition to stage a political critique of desire.

The argument cuts both ways. If all desire must be insulated from political critique, then so must the desires that exclude and marginalize trans women: not just erotic desires for certain kinds of body, but the desire not to share womanhood itself with the "wrong" kinds of women. The dichotomy between identity and desire, as Chu suggests, is surely a false one; and in any case the rights of trans people should not rest on it, any more than the rights of gay people should rest on the idea that homosexuality is innate rather than chosen (a matter of who gay people are rather than what they want). But a feminism that totally abjures the political critique of desire is a feminism with little to say about the injustices of exclusion and misrecognition suffered by the women who arguably need feminism the most.

The question, then, is how to dwell in the ambivalent place where we acknowledge that no one is obliged to desire anyone else, that no one has a right to be desired, but also that who is desired and who isn't is a political question, a question often answered by more general patterns of domination and exclusion. It is striking, though unsurprising, that while men tend to respond to sexual marginalization with a sense of entitlement to women's bodies, those women who protest against their sexual marginalization typically do so with talk not of entitlement but empowerment. Or, insofar as they do speak of entitlement, it is entitlement to respect, not to other people's bodies. That said, the radical self-love movements among black, fat, and disabled women do ask us to treat our sexual preferences as less than perfectly fixed. "Black is beautiful" and "Big is beautiful" are not just slogans of empowerment, but proposals for a reevaluation of our values. Lindy West describes studying photographs of fat women and asking herself what it would be to see these bodies—bodies that previously filled her with shame and self-loathing—as objectively beautiful. This, she says, isn't a theoretical issue, but a perceptual one: a way of looking at certain bodies—one's own and others'—sidelong, inviting and coaxing a gestalt shift from revulsion to admiration.[24] The question posed by radical self-love movements is not whether there is a right to sex (there isn't), but whether there is a duty to transfigure, as best we can, our desires.[25]

To take this question seriously requires that we recognize that the very idea of fixed sexual preference is political, not metaphysical. As a matter of good politics, we treat the preferences of others as sacred: we are rightly wary of speaking of what people really want, or what some idealized version of them would want. That way, we know, authoritarianism lies. This is true, most of all, in sex, where invocations of real or ideal desires have long been used as a cover for the rape of women and gay men. But the fact is that our sexual preferences can and do alter, sometimes under the operation of our own wills—not automatically, but not impossibly either. What's more, sexual desire doesn't always neatly conform to our own sense of it, as generations of gay men and women can attest. Desire can take us by surprise, leading us somewhere we hadn't imagined we would ever go, or toward someone we never thought we would lust after, or love. In the very best cases, the cases that perhaps ground our best hope, desire can cut against what politics has chosen for us, and choose for itself.[26]

Coda: The Politics of Desire

1. I began writing the essay that would eventually become "The Right to Sex" in the summer of 2014, after Elliot Rodger's manifesto appeared on the internet. I was struck, as were others who read it, by its peculiar blend of narcissistic rage, misogynistic and class-driven entitlement, and racialized self-loathing. My idea at first was to simply offer a close reading of the manifesto, as a document of intersecting and compounding political pathologies: misogyny, classism, racism. But what came to interest me most, as the commentaries piled in, was the way in which other feminists read it, and the way they interpreted the Rodger phenomenon more generally.

2. The most common feminist take was that Rodger was the embodiment of misogynistic entitlement: specifically, the embodiment of the violence that inevitably erupts when that entitlement is thwarted. This was surely correct, and worth saying, given that

many mainstream commentators refused to see Rodger as a misogynist. (How could he hate women, they asked, if he was desperate to be loved by them? And how could his killing spree be an act of misogynistic violence if he ended up killing more men than women? Didn't Rodger hate the Chads as much as the Stacys? And so on.) Still, what struck me about this response was its apparent disinterest concerning Rodger's claims to having been sexually and romantically marginalized on the basis of his race, introversion, and lack of stereotypical masculinity. This self-diagnosis was no doubt mistaken—at the very least, Rodger's grandiosity and homicidal rage should tell us that his social marginalization was overdetermined. It was also deeply self-serving: while lamenting his own loneliness, Rodger was happy to enforce a strict hierarchy of female desirability—to fetishize the "hot blonde slut"—as well as a strict racial hierarchy, according to which he was more deserving of sex than black men. But the kind of diagnosis Rodger offered, in which racism and the norms of heteromasculinity placed him beyond desirability, need not in principle be wrong. Racism and heteronormativity do extend into the sphere of romance and sex; indeed it is in this intimate sphere, protected by the logic of "personal preference," that they sink some of their deepest roots. Did feminists not have anything to say about this?

3. One thing a feminist might say is that even to contemplate this question is to risk thinking like a rapist. After the original publication of my "Right to Sex" essay, one feminist tweeted: "Could we please stop discussing whether or not there is a right to sex? Of course there is not. There is a right not to be raped. Enough handwringing. The end." As a "small addendum" she added: "The observation that the extent to which one gets what one wants out of life, in any domain, is often largely a matter of luck and happenstance and privilege and characteristics you don't have control over is about as banal as it gets."[1]

4. There is no right to sex. (To think otherwise *is* to think like a rapist.) But is it "as banal as it gets" to observe that what is ugliest about our social realities—racism, classism, ableism, heteronormativity—shapes whom we do and do not desire and love, and who does and does not desire and love us?

5. That would be news to the people of color and the working-class, queer, and disabled people who have drawn a clear connection between the more obvious, public dimensions of their oppression and the more hidden, private mechanisms that enable and partly constitute it, including the mechanisms of the club, the dating app, the bedroom, the school dance.

6. I have a friend who explains that because she is black, and despite being beautiful and otherwise popular, she was simply "off the table" when it came to dating in her predominantly white prep school.

7. It would also be news to the feminists who have long demanded that we see sex, as we know it, not as some primordial, pre-political given, but as an effect of politics, all too easily and falsely naturalized. The task was to liberate sex from the distortions of oppression, not simply to divide it into the consensual (unproblematic) and non-consensual (problematic).

8. Indeed, what is male sexual entitlement—the false conviction that men have a right to sex, a right that they can coercively enforce—if not a paradigm of how politics shapes sexual desire? Can we position ourselves against male sexual entitlement to women's bodies in general, and against the misogynistic fetishization of the hot blond slut or sexy East Asian doll or the vulnerable child's body, without opening ourselves to a political critique of sex?

9. To liberate sex from the distortions of oppression is not the same as just saying everyone can desire whatever or whomever they want. The first is a radical demand; the second is a liberal one. Like many liberal demands, the second is often fueled by an individualist suspicion of the coercive power of the community. If my desire must be disciplined, who will do the disciplining? And if my desire refuses to be disciplined, what will happen to me then?

10. I am not saying such worries are ungrounded. It is not perverse to want to be left alone.

11. Except, properly understood, the radical demand that we liberate sex from the distortions of oppression is not about disciplining desire at all. When I wrote that "desire can cut against what politics has chosen for us, and choose for itself," I was not imagining a desire regulated by the demands of justice, but a desire set free from the binds of injustice. I am asking what might happen if we were to look at bodies, our own and others', and allow ourselves to feel admiration, appreciation, want, where politics tells us we should not. There is a kind of discipline here, in that it requires us to quiet the voices that have spoken to us since birth, the voices that tell us which bodies and ways of being in the world are worthy and which are unworthy. What is disciplined here isn't desire itself, but the political forces that presume to instruct it.

12. After my piece was published, a gay man wrote to me about his husband of fourteen years—a large, fat man, he explained, whom he loves deeply, and with whom he has a satisfying sex life. And yet he has "had to work, deliberately and consciously, to let him be sexy, if that makes sense." He went on: "while we cannot alter what does and does not turn us on, we can on the one hand displace what

might be getting in the way of erotic excitement and on the other teach ourselves to eroticize what is happening in front of us during sex."

13. Is this an act of discipline, or of love?

14. In her classic essay from 1980, "Compulsory Heterosexuality and Lesbian Existence," the poet and feminist theorist Adrienne Rich takes aim at the idea—accepted, she says, by most feminists—that heterosexuality is the default form of human life, and lesbianism at best a mere sexual preference, at worst a deviant species of sexuality.[2] Rich's point is that heterosexuality is a political institution that compels even "straight" women—through its psychic internalization, yes, but also through its violent enforcement—to regulate their intimacies, affinities, and relations in ways that often betray what it is they really want. Rich wants straight women to think of the moments of closeness and complicity they have experienced with other women, and to reflect on the felt necessity of setting these aside—as immature, less than sufficient—for men. Think back, she asks straight women, to the first time you betrayed your best friend for male attention. Was that natural? Inevitable? Or something demanded of you by the infrastructure of male domination, which fears most of all the absence of female desire, and with it the end of men's presumed access to women's bodies, labor, minds, hearts?

15. What if the envy you feel for another woman's body, her face, her charm, her ease, her brilliance, were not envy at all—but desire?

16. To ask yourself such questions is, I wrote, to "treat our sexual preferences as less than perfectly fixed." But perhaps it would be better to say that it requires us to question their status as "preferences" altogether.

17. Adrienne Rich writes: "To acknowledge that for women heterosexuality may not be a 'preference' at all but something that has had to be imposed, managed, organized, propagandized, and maintained by force is an immense step to take if you consider yourself freely and 'innately' heterosexual. Yet the failure to examine heterosexuality as an institution is like failing to admit that . . . capitalism or the caste system of racism is maintained by a variety of forces including both physical violence and false consciousness. To take the step of questioning heterosexuality as a 'preference' or 'choice' for women—and to do the intellectual and emotional work that follows—will call for a special quality of courage in heterosexually identified feminists."[3]

18. Asserting the innateness and sovereignty of preference has its political uses. Consider how important the idea of being "born this way" has been to the gay rights movement, or of being "trapped in the wrong body" to the trans rights movement. Both ways of thinking grate against the constructivist, anti-essentialist tendencies of feminism—and the experiences of many gay and trans people—yet both have been politically vital in a world in which blame is associated with choice but with not natural endowment. Political claims are often dialectical, best understood as responses to the normative terrain as it stands in the moment they are made, not in some hoped-for future.

19. But the ideology of innate preference also has its limits. In 2012 the actress (now turned politician) Cynthia Nixon got into trouble with gay and lesbian activists when she said that, for her, being gay was a choice. "I've been straight and I've been gay," she said, "and gay is better." Perhaps this talk of "choice" played, plays still, into the hands of anti-gay crusaders. But does Nixon's choice to be gay—to set aside men and heterosexuality in favor of a lesbianism that she finds more valuable, more livable—make her un-gay? (In *Ambiguity and Sexuality*, William Wilkerson writes: "Even though we

think that our feelings were always there before coming out, we forget, in the very process of this remembering, that our memory reconstructs the previous feelings in light of what they become."[4]) There are many women for whom men are no option at all: women who would feel permanently thwarted if forced into a life of heterosexuality. But what straight woman feels none of this thwartedness? Silvia Federici, noting the price of "isolation and exclusion" paid by gay women, asks on behalf of straight women: "But can we really afford relations with men?"[5]

20. Taking Rich and Federici seriously requires that we rethink the well-worn feminist distinction between "political" lesbianism and "real" lesbianism. (A lesbian philosopher recently wrote to me to say that while she "acknowledge[s] the phenomenon of … political lesbianism" she would "differentiate between it and a desire-based lesbianism.") It is of course true that many feminists in the 1970s and 1980s took up lesbian forms of life for self-consciously political reasons. But how often is there a lesbian relationship that is not in some important sense political—that is not at a deep level about honoring what women, outside the script of heterosexual male domination, can have and be together? (This is not to say that relationships between women can ever fully exist outside that script.) Misogynists like to say that lesbians have just given up on men. What of it?

21. If this is right, in what sense is political lesbianism, as Andrea Long Chu insists, a failed project?

22. In an interview Chu responded at length to "The Right to Sex." She acknowledges the phenomenon with which I am concerned: "Obviously something like 'no fats, no femmes, no Asians' is a desire that has a history, and has a politics, that can be described by reference to political processes: imperialism, white supremacy, and also, like, the world-historical defeat of the female sex." But she adamantly resists the idea that we can or should do anything about

it. "I can't *stand* body positivity," she says, alluding to my discussion of Lindy West. "I *cannot* stand it. It is just *anathema* to me. It's moralizing. It's really fucking hard to figure out a way to tell people to change their desires that isn't moralistic."[6]

23. Is there no difference between "telling people to change their desires" and asking ourselves what we want, why we want it, and what it is we want to want? Must the transformation of desire be a disciplinary project (willfully altering our desires in line with our politics)—or can it be an emancipatory one (setting our desires free from politics)?

24. In 1978 Audre Lorde wrote: "We have been raised to fear the *yes* within ourselves, our deepest cravings. But, once recognized, those which do not enhance our future lose their power and can be altered. The fear of our desires keeps them suspect and indiscriminately powerful, for to suppress any truth is to give it strength beyond endurance. The fear that we cannot grow beyond whatever distortions we may find within ourselves keeps us docile and loyal and obedient, externally defined."[7]

25. Where does speaking about morality end and moralizing begin? To say that we are moralizing is to say that we have overstepped the proper bounds of the moral, wrongly imposing our "personal" choices and ways of seeing onto others. Does ethics never belong in the bedroom? How about the club, the dating app, the school dance? As Sandra Lee Bartky writes in *Femininity and Domination* (1990), to presuppose that politics does not belong in these places is to give "essentially a *liberal* response to a *radical* critique of sexuality and, as such, it fails entirely to engage this critique."[8]

26. Chu identifies her main point of disagreement with me as follows: "My worry [is] that moralism about the desires of the

oppressor can be a shell corporation for moralism about the desires of the oppressed." She means, I take it, that a political critique of desire can too easily be mobilized against those who are themselves marginalized: gay men who refuse to sleep with non-white men, black men who only want to date light-skinned black women, trans women (Chu's example) who want all the trappings of patriarchal femininity. But this is to presuppose a false dichotomy between oppressor and oppressed, as if being oppressed along one dimension exonerates us from the possibility we might oppress anyone else. Are black women not entitled to hold black men to account for their sexual racism—and, indeed, to expect more of black men than they do of white men? Should these black women be accused of moralizing?

27. Is my talk of transforming desire moralizing in a different sense, in that it focuses too much on personal responsibility? Racism, classism, ableism, heteronormativity: these are structural problems and—as we have learned to say—they demand structural solutions. That is surely right. It is also surely right that a myopic focus on individual action is characteristic of a bourgeois morality whose ideological function is to distract from the broader systems of injustice in which we participate. (To use Chu's phrase, individualistic morality can be a shell corporation for systemic injustice.) But to say that a problem is structural does not absolve us from thinking about how we, as individuals, are implicated in it, or what we should do about it.

28. This is something that earlier feminists knew well. Radical feminists did not rethink their ways of working, child-rearing, arguing, decision-making, living, and loving because they were bourgeois moralists.[9] They were not confused about the structural nature of what it was they wanted, or about the demands it placed on them as women. It is true they were often divided on the question of

how much of the "personal" to make "political": whether feminism required separatism, lesbianism, communal property, collective child-rearing, the dissolution of family relations, the end of femininity. And it is true that, taken too far, a prefigurative politics—a politics that insists individuals act as if they were already in the world to come—not only alienates those who do not conform, but also becomes an end in itself for those who do. At its worst, prefigurative politics allows its practitioners to substitute individual personal transformation for collective political transfiguration. It becomes, in other words, a liberal politics. But the same is true of a politics that refuses prefiguration. What does it mean to say that we want to transform the political world—but that we ourselves will remain unchanged?

29. Here, then, is the real question: how do we engage in a political critique of sex without slipping into the misogynistic logic of sexual entitlement ("the right to sex") or into a moral authoritarianism that disciplines rather than emancipates? How do we address our desires without fear, as Lorde puts it, of the distortions we may find within ourselves? And how do we do so without turning inward, without replacing a political project with a personal one? The answer to the question, I take it, is a practical one—a matter, as philosophers like to say, not of knowing-*that*, but of knowing-*how*. Know-how is to be found not through theoretical investigation but through experiments of living.[10]

30. In "The Right to Sex" I talk about "the supreme fuckability of 'hot blonde sluts' and East Asian women, the comparative unfuckability of black women and Asian men." On Twitter, one reader, a black woman, took me to task for this: "You wrote abt the unfuckability of black women as a political fact—i'm wondering on what basis this fact is defensible? seems like you're conflating fuckability, generally, with the range of differences in

how society rewards you for fucking blondes v black women, specifically."[11]

31. By talking about "fuckability" and "unfuckability" I am not speaking about some pre-political, innate desirability. I am talking about desirability as constructed by our sexual politics, which enforces a racialized hierarchy that places the white woman above the brown or black woman, the light-skinned brown or black woman above the dark-skinned brown or black woman, and so on. Fuckability (like Catharine MacKinnon's "rapeability") is precisely a product of the "differences in how society rewards you for fucking blondes v black women." There is no "fuckability, generally," if this means some kind of pre-political, pre-social desirability. Similarly, there is no "rapeability, generally": certain women's bodies are rapeable, and certain women's bodies fuckable, because they are assigned that status by the dominant cultural norms. The fuckable body, like the rapeable body, is in this sense irreducibly a construction.

32. Even so—and I think this is what the tweet was correctly getting at—there is something reductive about the notion of "fuckability." The bodies of brown and black women—especially when they belong to women who are also poor, incarcerated, or undocumented—are in an important sense supremely fuckable, much more so than the bodies of white women. For these bodies can be violated with impunity and without consequence. Black women's bodies are coded as hypersexual, inviting, and demanding men's sexual attention, while conferring on the men who have access to them less social status than they gain by having access to the supposedly chaste and innocent bodies of white women. (The flip side of this is that violations of black women's bodies are rarely, socially speaking, fully violations. The serial rapist police officer Daniel Holtzclaw knew what he was doing when he chose a string of poor black women as his

victims.) The truth is that all women's bodies are supremely fuck-able, in one way or another.

33. Fuckability is not some good that should be distributed more fairly. It isn't a good at all. Katherine Cross, a sociologist and gam-ing critic, writes: "To some white men, Asian women top their hier-archies of desirability. But what do those women get out of that? Suffocating stereotypes of docility; discrimination; abuse. These are the wages of being in someone *else's* hierarchy."[12]

34. One of the more arresting emails I got about "The Right to Sex" was from a man from Sydney—a multicultural city in a country notorious for its racism. Originally from Sri Lanka, he was adopted by two white parents. "I reassure you," he said, "that I'm no psycho-path like that mixed-race kid who underpins your thesis and massa-cred those poor souls after rejection based allegedly on his race. I'm rational enough to accept my fate and try and make the best of my short existence." He said that it was heartbreakingly difficult to date as a non-white man. He said that dating profiles, including those of Asian women, list "Caucasian," "white guys only," and "no Indians" as their preferences. He said that he had once posted a critical com-ment on a YouTube video called "Why Filipinas like White Guys," and that a white woman had replied "Suck it up, the truth hurts." He said he was profoundly lonely, as were his other Asian friends, and that he had taken up various hobbies "to stymie the spectre of undesirability." He said that many "white-guy-ethnic-girl rela-tionships must be love" but asked whether some were not "a re-enactment of colonial conquest and rescue." "And if it is?" he said. "Well that's their right. It's consensual. Us ethnic guys just have to suck it up. Besides, if we were good enough they'd stay with us. Love is immune from scrutiny, even when it's political." He said, "I certainly don't feel the right to Sex, nor do I feel the right to Love. But that doesn't mean it doesn't hurt." He said, "I suppose I have the right to feel hurt." He said, "I haven't come across many women,

ethnic or otherwise, that acknowledge what us Ethnomen face. They just think we're all backward. Sophistication is a province only found in Caucasia."

35. In 2018, Yowei Shaw, a co-host of NPR's *Invisibilia* podcast, put out a source call for a "possible story about white male asian female couples and their families."[13] Shaw was interested, she said, "in exploring the idea of internalized white supremacy among asian women . . . Looking at questions like: how does the culture-at-large leave a fingerprint on something so intimate and seemingly automatic as desire? How does power shape our relationships? Is it possible to reprogram your sexual desire? How do you do it? Is this something we should even ask people to do?" Shaw noted that this topic was "extremely sensitive and must be approached with care and nuance." She faced an immediate backlash from Asian American women. "Holy cow," tweeted Heather Chin, a journalist, "it's like the story angle came straight from the reddit, 4chan and other AAPI [Asian American/Pacific Islander] male incel message boards."[14] Chin was referring to the rise of "MRAsians": Asian men who, under the banner of anti-racism (taking a page from the playbook of angry white men), spew misogynistic vitriol at Asian women who date and marry white men.

36. In 2018, the novelist Celeste Ng wrote a piece for *The Cut* titled "When Asian Women Are Harassed for Marrying Non-Asian Men."[15] The piece begins with an email Ng had received. Its subject line was "I'm a huge fan," but the rest continued: "of watching your son develop mental illness because of your internalized self hate. Your Asian looking son will grow up knowing his mom thinks he's ugly, and his dad won't be able to relate." After Ng shared the email on Twitter, other women who had been targeted for being in a "WMAF" (white male/Asian female) relationship came forward. The writer Christine Tan had received an email which promised to "kill a whole lot of white motherfuckers and their asian sell out bitches . . . to get

their kids heads and smash them into the concrete pavement." Some of the Asian women Ng spoke to had been told that their mixed-race sons would turn out to be the next Elliot Rodger.

37. The subreddit r/AZNidentity—a "Pan Asian community … against all forms of anti-Asianism" with tens of thousands of members—is the source of much of this anti-WMAF cyber-bullying. In a moderator's post from 2016, AZNidentity told its users to mind the distinction between "calling out the wrong kind of AF—the self-hating, white worshiping kind AND hurling invective constantly against AF in general."[16] "If you want to critique AF," it went on, "discourage their errant behavior, take a fuller perspective of social dynamics and what can be done about them—that's perfectly fine … There are a few individuals however, who keep taking this too far." But the community, the post said, would not "go out of way to appease AF. Nor will we self-censor to protect their feelings or anyone else's … We can critique AF. We can point out their follies. Their succumbing to white brainwashing … Our vision [is] for a better life for Asians."

38. There is much that is striking here, not least the admission that a "Pan Asian" forum is really a forum for Asian men. Also taken for granted is the thesis that Asian women—as enactors of white supremacy—are in every way the dominant Asian class, and that Asian men are their victims. It is perhaps true that in the white imagination—which is much of the world's imagination—Asian men are less than fully men. But that does not stop Asian men, like men of all races, controlling, exploiting, thwarting, beating, and raping Asian women.

39. It is on the whole black women who hold to task black men for sexual racism: for their preference for white or light-skinned black women. Here we have a relatively subordinate group (black

women) holding to account a relatively dominant group (black men). This inverts the general pattern among Asians, where it is the relatively dominant (Asian men) who take to task the relatively subordinate (Asian women). The fight against sexual racism in the black community is rarely if ever a cover for sexual entitlement. Black women know how to talk about the political formation of desire without demanding to be desired. For straight men, including straight Asian men, the temptation to misogyny, to entitlement, to the enforcement of mythic "rights," is always live.

40. In a justly celebrated essay in *n+1*, Wesley Yang describes looking at a photograph of Seung-Hui Cho, the twenty-three-year-old Virginia Tech mass murderer: "You see a face that looks like yours. You know that there's an existential knowledge you have in common with that face. Both of you know what it's like to have a cultural code superimposed atop your face, and if it's a code that abashes, nullifies, and unmans you, then you confront every visible reflection of that code with a feeling of mingled curiosity and wariness . . . Seung-Hui Cho's face. A perfectly unremarkable Korean face— beady-eyed, brown-toned, a small plump-lipped mouth, eyebrows high off his eyelids, with crooked glasses perched on his nose. It's not an ugly face, exactly: it's not a badly made face. It's just a face that has nothing to do with the desires of women in this country."[17] On April 16, 2007, Seung-Hui Cho, armed with two semiautomatic pistols, killed thirty-two people and wounded seventeen others, before shooting himself in the head.

41. Ten years later, in an *Esquire* profile of Jordan Peterson, the Canadian psychologist and hero of the men's rights movement, Yang defended Peterson against his critics: "The young men who love Jordan Peterson love him for all the reasons that the smart set despises him. He gives them something the culture . . . wants to

deny them. A sense of purpose in a world that increasingly defines their natural predispositions—for risk, adventure, physical challenge, unbridled competition—as maladaptive to the pacified, androgynous ideals of a bureaucratized, post-feminist world."[18] I want to ask Yang: is it not precisely this ideology of a "natural" masculinity—a masculinity that is inherently risk-taking, adventurous, competitive, dominant; a masculinity that is never fully accessible to a skinny, friendless, pimply East Asian boy—that produced Seung-Hui Cho?

42. In the sixth season of *America's Next Top Model*, a Korean American contestant said "there's just not enough Asian models out there" and that she wanted to "break down that barrier." Moments later she announced she was "not into Asian guys." (Tyra Banks was admirably quick to point out the tension: "First you were saying 'I'm Asian, I'm strong, I'm Korean,' and then you're saying 'Screw Korean boys and I want a white boy.'") On an episode of the Australian dating show *Take Me Out*, two Asian women explained their rejection of an Asian "bachelor." "I kinda have a 'No Dating Asians' sort of policy. You kinda look a bit like my brother," one of them said. "I'm sorry, I have a 'No Dating Asians' policy as well," chimed the other: "I don't wanna be mistaken as, like, brother and sister." In May 2018, an Asian woman with a white husband posted on Instagram a photograph of herself and her young baby, with the caption: "I always dreamed of having a blonde blue eyed baby and people told me who am I kidding, I'm Chinese through and through! Well suck it people I have a white baby complete with a set of blue eyes too." On Yowei Shaw's *Invisibilia* podcast "A Very Offensive Rom-Com," a young Asian American man describes overhearing, as a twelve-year-old, his sister telling his mother that she would never date an Asian guy because they're unattractive.[19] In 2015, Celeste Ng tweeted: "To be honest, I do not often find Asian men attractive. (They remind me of my cousins.)"[20] Ng later apologized, explaining that the tweet was intended as self-exposure, not an expression of self-hatred: since

the only Asian men she knew were her cousins, she hadn't developed an attraction to Asian men.[21]

43. In an opinion piece for the *New York Times*, Audrea Lim details the strangely prevalent phenomenon of alt-right men who date and marry Asian American women.[22] Discussing a photo of Tila Tequila, a Vietnamese American media personality, giving a Nazi salute at a dinner before a white supremacist conference hosted by Richard Spencer, Lim writes that the photo "conjured up my memories of being a fourteen-year-old Asian girl in an overwhelmingly white school who wanted to be interesting, self-possessed and liked. Instinctively, I knew it meant distancing myself from the other Asian kids, especially the nerdy and studious ones. I knew I had succeeded when a friend remarked that I wasn't really Asian, I was white, 'because you're cool.'"

44. I also have friends who joke that I am "basically white." Maybe it isn't a joke.

45. I know many East and South Asian women, living in western countries, who don't want to marry the sort of men our mothers, our grandmothers, and our aunts married. Sometimes when we say that Asian men remind us of our cousins, we are saying: we know too much about how these boys and men are raised. One question is: aren't Asian women within their rights to make such choices? Another question is: why think that white boys and men are raised any better? *Is sophistication to be found only in Caucasia?*

46. My "Right to Sex" piece received a barrage of furious tweets from "gender critical" lesbian feminists who have accused me of endorsing the logic of the "cotton ceiling." I find a small irony in this, given that I diagnosed the notion of the "cotton ceiling" as part of a logic of sexual entitlement that must be rejected. I wrote that "the 'cotton ceiling' describes a lack of access to what no one is

obligated to give." What is required, I said, is a discourse not of entitlement but of empowerment and respect.

47. It is clear that some lesbian feminists want to resist any possible analogy between the white person who as a matter of policy doesn't sleep with black people, and the cis lesbian who as a matter of policy doesn't sleep with trans women. (Well, some lesbian feminists want to resist this analogy. Others want to argue that there's nothing wrong with the sexual racist, either.) They insist that the essence of lesbianism is being innately attracted to people who were born with female bodies and female genitalia. If so, then there can be no analogy between the sexual racist and the trans-exclusionary lesbian: the former makes a politically suspect choice while the latter acts out of natural, fixed, and thus blameless inclination.

48. I find this reduction of sexual orientation to genitalia—what's more, genitalia *from birth*—puzzling. Is anyone innately attracted to penises or vaginas? Or are we first attracted to ways of being in the world, including bodily ways, which we later learn to associate with certain specific parts of the body?

49. Consider the gay men who express delighted disgust at vaginas. Consider the idea of the "Platinum Star Gay," the gay man who, birthed via a caesarean, never even made bodily contact with his mother's vagina. Is this the expression of an innate, and thus permissible revulsion—or a learned and suspect misogyny?

50. In a recent interview with *The TransAdvocate*, Cristan Williams asks Catharine MacKinnon: "How do you work with people who passionately tell you that in order for women to have liberation, 'woman' needs to first be defined in terms of a discrete biological group?" MacKinnon responds: "Male dominant society has defined women as a discrete biological group forever. If this was going to produce liberation, we'd be free."[23]

51. This is not to say that we can just change at will the sort of sexed bodies we are attracted to. Neither is it to deny that for some women (including some trans women) the penis might be a symbol of male power and violence such that it cannot be, for them, a viable object of desire. The crucial question, in a sense, is whether a sexual aversion to women with penises is best explained by an unjustified transphobia, or a justified wariness of men. But this is precisely the distinction that trans-exclusionary feminists are unwilling to draw.

52. Dylann Roof, who in 2015 gunned down nine people in a Black church in Charleston, South Carolina, after joining their Bible study, announced during the massacre: "I have to do this because y'all are raping our women."

53. On December 7, 2017, William Atchison shot two students at his former high school in New Mexico before killing himself. An autopsy of his body revealed ink markings of a swastika, "SS," "BUILD WALL," and "AMOG"—short for "alpha male of the group." He used the pseudonym "Elliot Rodger" online.

54. On Valentine's Day 2018, Nikolas Cruz shot dead seventeen students and staff members at Marjory Stoneman Douglas High School in Parkland, Florida. A white supremacist and gun fanatic (and Trump supporter) who had fantasized on social media about orchestrating a school shooting, Cruz was also a hater of women. He stalked and harassed an ex-girlfriend, threatening to kill her and her new boyfriend. In a comment on a YouTube video Cruz had vowed that "Elliot rodger will not be forgotten."

55. On April 23, 2018, a month after my essay was originally published, twenty-five-year-old Alek Minassian drove a van onto the sidewalk of a busy Toronto street, killing ten people and injuring sixteen more. Before the attack Minassian had posted on Facebook: "The Incel Rebellion has already begun! We will

overthrow all the Chads and Stacys! All hail the Supreme Gentleman Elliot Rodger!"

56. On June 28, 2018, Jarrod Ramos gunned down five people in the newsroom of *The Capital* in Maryland. Six years earlier he had filed a defamation suit against *The Capital* for reporting that he had pleaded guilty to harassing a former high school classmate. He had friended her on Facebook, asking if she remembered him, which she did not. After a back-and-forth, he evidently began to feel she was responding too slowly to his messages. He told her to kill herself and warned that she was going to need a protective order.

57. On the evening of July 18, 2018, Mollie Tibbetts, a University of Iowa sophomore, went missing while jogging near her home in Brooklyn, Iowa. Surveillance footage later showed a man, Cristhian Bahena Rivera, following Tibbetts in a car. Rivera eventually confessed to murdering Tibbetts, and led police to her body, buried in a field under corn husks. The autopsy recorded the cause of death as "multiple sharp force injuries." Rivera was a Mexican farmworker who had immigrated to the US when he was seventeen. Speaking of the murder of Tibbetts, Donald Trump said: "A person came in from Mexico illegally and killed her. We need the wall, we need our immigration laws changed, we need our border laws changed."

58. Would the wall have prevented the deaths of the thirty-nine people murdered by Elliot Rodger, Nikolas Cruz, William Atchison, Dylann Roof, and Jarrod Ramos?

59. On August 16, 2018, during a high school assembly in Luther, Oklahoma, a fourteen-year-old boy stabbed a girl of the same age, silently and repeatedly, with a four-inch folding knife, wounding her in the arm, upper back, wrist, and head. She had told him that she didn't want to have a romantic relationship with him, saying she "liked him as a friend."

60. On November 2, 2018, forty-year-old Scott Beierle, a military veteran and former teacher in the Anne Arundel County public school system in Maryland, shot six people at a yoga studio in Tallahassee, Florida, killing two women. In a series of YouTube videos, Beierle had complained about being sexually rejected by women, expressed sympathy for Elliot Rodger, and ranted about the evils of interracial relationships. He had been arrested twice, in 2012 and then in 2016, for grabbing women's asses, and was fired from a teaching post for asking a student if she was "ticklish" and touching her stomach below her bra-line.

61. On February 19, 2020, forty-three-year-old Tobias Rathjen shot fourteen people, killing nine, at two shisha bars in Hanau, Germany. He then returned to his flat, where he shot his mother before killing himself. Rathjen's manifesto, uploaded to his personal website, called for the annihilation of immigrants from Muslim-majority countries. An expert on radicalization said that the manifesto revealed "a very wild mixture of conspiracy theories, racism, and incel ideology."

62. On February 24, 2020, an unnamed seventeen-year-old boy attacked three people with a machete in a Toronto massage parlor, fatally wounding one woman. The Canadian authorities connected the suspect with the incel subculture, and charged him with terrorism.

63. On March 16, 2021, eight people, including six women of East Asian descent, were shot and killed during a spree of attacks on massage parlors in Atlanta, Georgia. The shootings were followed by intensive debate about whether the suspect charged with the murders, Robert Aaron Long, was motivated by misogynistic or racial animus. Long himself cited his "sex addiction"—for which he been given "treatment" at an evangelical facility—and explained that he hoped that by targeting the spas he would "help" other men. Those

who infer from this that race was irrelevant to Long's actions miss, we might think, the way in which anti–East Asian racism is entwined with the sexual fetishization of East Asian women.

64. The phrase "involuntary celibate" was coined by Alana, a "nerdy queer woman" who had never been on a date, and who wanted a name for her loneliness and the loneliness of others like her. In the late 1990s, when she was an undergraduate in Ottawa, Canada, Alana created an all-text website called Alana's Involuntary Celibate Project. It was a forum and support community, for women and men, young and old, gay and straight. They referred to themselves as "invcels" until one forum member suggested dropping the "v." They swapped advice on dealing with shyness, awkwardness, depression, and self-hatred. Some of the men talked about women as objects, Alana says, but there was none of the violent entitlement that characterizes today's incel forums. Eventually, Alana got into a relationship and left the forum, handing over the job of moderator to another community member. She didn't find out what had become of the incel movement until nearly twenty years later, when she read an article in *Mother Jones* about Elliot Rodger. Incels today claim that there are no women incels, or "femcels."

65. Alana's story reminds me of Arthur Galston, a plant physiologist who, as a graduate student, found that 2,3,5-triiodobenzoic acid could be used to hasten the growth of soybeans. In a footnote to his dissertation, *Physiology of flowering, with especial reference to floral initiation in soybeans*, published in 1943, Galston noted that excessive amounts of triiodobenzoic acid would cause the soybean plant to shed its leaves. The US military took note, and in 1945 started producing and testing 2,4,5-triiodobenzoic acid for use as an aerial defoliant, with plans to use it in Japan had the Second World War continued. It later became the chemical basis of Agent Orange, used by the US to ravage more than 4.5 million acres of land during the Vietnam War. Galston, on discovering how his research was being

used, began an intensive campaign to end the use of Agent Orange as a military weapon. He eventually convinced Nixon to retire the weapon in 1971.

66. Five days after the Toronto van attack, Alana started a website called Love Not Anger. The project collects and promotes research on how best to support those who are "lonely for love." Alana wrote that it was "the *combination* of loneliness with sexism, misogyny, privilege and entitlement that has led many men to be angry that women are not sexually available to them." The project has been inactive since November 2019; Alana says that "stepping away has improved [her] mental health."

67. A vexed question: when is being sexually or romantically marginalized a facet of oppression, and when is it just a matter of bad luck, one of life's small tragedies? (When I was a first-year undergraduate I had a professor who said, to our grave disappointment, that there would be heartbreak even in the post-capitalist utopia.) Are the un-beautiful an oppressed class? The short? The chronically shy?

68. We might attempt to draw this line—between those causes of undesiredness that are and are not facets of oppression—by distinguishing between good and bad reasons for desiring someone. But what is a good reason for desiring someone? If not her body, then what about her mind? The beauty of her soul? Is the beauty of our souls up to us? Does it matter? Should it?

69. The subreddit r/trufemcels is a support forum for girls and women who want a long-term relationship but can't find one. It is filled with women in their late twenties and thirties who have never been kissed, never had sex, never had a boyfriend. A recurring theme is the hypocrisy of incel men, who claim to be too ugly or socially awkward to find love and sex, but who are explicitly

uninterested in conventionally unattractive or socially awkward women. (Femcels say that such men are not true incels, but volcels—voluntary celibates.) Femcels point out that for most of these men, what they really want is not love or sexual intimacy, but the status that comes with attracting hot white women. I notice that on one incel forum, as members address the question of why incels aren't interested in non-high-status women, someone posts: "You're upset because people don't want to fuck actual filth?"

70. "Female hypergamy" is a central term in the lexicon of incels, MRAs, pickup artists, and Jordan Peterson acolytes. They believe that most of the female population has sex with only a small subset of the male population. (In Peterson's words, "Women mate across and up dominance hierarchies, men mate across and down."[24]) According to one manosphere blogger, the "beta males" who are left behind by runaway hypergamy are "the debt-loaded middle class of the ultrahypergamous sexual market, and the price for entry to the world of slender, chaste, feminine, young White women has sky-rocketed beyond their means." He goes on: "An angry young man revolt is all but assured under these chronically persistent conditions of sexual, romantic, and marital inegalitarianism. Trump's election was the first salvo of this justifiably angry young man revolution. If Trump fails, the next salvos won't be so benign. Shitlibs and pussyhatters will soon know what real anguish is."[25]

71. The analogy between angry incels and the "angry young man" Trump voter is telling. In both cases, the anger is ostensibly about inequality, but in reality it is often about the threatened loss of white male privilege. We now know that the protest of a certain kind of Trump voter was: *Why should whites be doing no better than blacks and Latinos?* Likewise, the protest of the incel is: *Why should white men have to make do with low-status women—women who are not "slender, chaste, feminine, young [and] White"?* There is no protest against

inequality or injustice here, merely a protest at the loss of presumed entitlement.

72. What's more, in both cases—the racially aggrieved Trump voter, the incel—the reality to which they subscribe is a myth. White Americans are not doing worse than black or Latino Americans; the opposite remains true, even as the worst-off whites are in absolute terms doing worse than before—in which respect they have legitimate grounds for serious grievance. (This is the source of the debate, now wearily familiar, over what motivated Trump's low-income white voters: racial antagonism or economic precarity. Whatever the full answer—presumably it should start with a refusal of the neat distinction between racial and economic anxiety—we should remember the rich rural businessmen who formed Trump's donor base, and the high-income voters who voted for him, in the majority, in both 2016 and 2020.[26]) Meanwhile, it is not the case that a few men are absorbing the sexual attention of most women while large swaths of men sexually "starve." As Katherine Cross writes: "Societal hierarchies of desirability structure images of who is and is not sexually attractive. This *does not* strictly correlate with who is and is not having sex."[27]

73. Young people in general—at least in the US, UK, Europe, and Japan—are having less sex than young people were a generation ago.[28] But surveys show that it is women who are significantly likelier to be going without sex than men, and men who are likelier to have had two or more sexual partners in the last year. Only 0.8 percent of American men had more than ten sexual partners in 2016: there are very, very few Chads. The percentage of straight American men over eighteen who have never had sex, and aren't celibate for religious reasons, is about 1.3 percent. Many of these men are young adults who have not yet been in a relationship, indeed have not yet left their parental homes.[29]

74. Again, this should not come as a surprise. Incels' anger is not about inequality of distribution, whatever they claim. It is about a (mis)perceived thwarting of entitlement to sexual status.

75. Of course, the analogy between the incel and the angry white male Trump voter is not only that. There are direct connections between the world of incels, pick-up artists and MRAs, and the far-right movement that helped bring Trump to power.[30] The grievance politics of flailing white masculinity that fuel the manosphere have served as an ideological and material gateway to the more overt grievance politics of ethnonationalism: from Gamergate, Red Pill, and Jordan Peterson to Unite the Right, Proud Boys, and Three Percenters. Two of the men arrested for their involvement in the Capitol riot on January 6, 2021, were Patrick Stedman, a "dating and relationship strategist" and expert in "female psychology," and Samuel Fisher (aka "Brad Holiday"), the owner of a YouTube channel that promises to "help men get high value girls." Two months before storming the Capitol, Stedman tweeted "You don't have a problem with Trump, you have a problem with masculine energy."[31]

76. After the Toronto van attack, Ross Douthat, a conservative Catholic columnist for the *New York Times*, published a piece called "The Redistribution of Sex."[32] It opened by saying that "sometimes the extremists and radicals and weirdos see the world more clearly than the respectable and moderate and sane." One such "brilliant weirdo," Douthat said, was the George Mason University economist Robin Hanson. Soon after the Toronto van attack, Hanson asked on his blog why progressives are preoccupied with redistributing wealth but not with redistributing sex. He was widely decried—a *Slate* headline read, "Is Robin Hanson America's Creepiest Economist?" But Hanson, who is an opponent of wealth redistribution, was charging progressives with hypocrisy. His question was: if wealth inequality is an injustice that demands to be corrected, why isn't sex inequality, too?

77. The idea of "redistributing" sex is problematic for at least two reasons. First, incels, as I have said already, aren't angry about their lack of sex, but about their perceived lack of sexual status. Second, talk of "redistribution" immediately raises the spectre of coercion.

78. Many feminists responded to Hanson by saying that any proposal to redistribute sex is de facto a proposal to rape women. Hanson replied by offering other ways of effecting the redistribution of sex: giving sex-less men money to spend on prostitutes, or encouraging traditional norms of pre-marital celibacy and what Jordan Peterson has called "enforced monogamy." The irony is that these proposals, like rape, are also coercive. Women sell sex, on the whole, because they need money; to give sex-less men money with which to pay for sex presupposes that there are women who need to sell sex to live. As for returning to traditional norms of pre-marital celibacy (for women) and enforced monogamy (for women): how far does this take us from the coercion of rape?

79. Some feminist commentators, including Laurie Penny and Jaclyn Friedman, responded to Douthat and Hanson by saying the very idea of distributing sex is to treat women as a commodity.[33] In turn, these feminists argued, this only underscored a capitalist logic of sex, of which the incel phenomenon was a symptom. As Rebecca Solnit put it: "Sex is a commodity, accumulation of this commodity enhances a man's status, and every man has a right to accumulation, but women are in some mysterious way obstacles to this, and they are therefore the enemy as well as the commodity." Incels, Solnit says, "are furious at their own low status, but don't question the system that allocates status and commodifies us all in ways that are painful and dehumanizing."[34]

80. Solnit is right that incels crave status—the status that having sex with high-status women confers, and the status they see as the price of access to high-status women. At the same time, incels hate the

commodification of sex and want to be released from it. They hate the idea that sex is governed by market relations, that sex with high-status women is not given out to them freely and lovingly. This is the deep contradiction at the heart of the incel phenomenon: incels oppose themselves to a sexual market in which they see themselves as losers, while being wedded to the status hierarchy that structures that market.

81. In this, incels represent a collision of two pathologies. On one hand, there is the pathology of what is sometimes called neoliberalism: an assimilation of an ever-increasing number of domains of life to the logic of the market. On the other, there is the pathology of patriarchy, which has, in capitalist societies, tended to see women and the home as refuges from the market, as sources of freely given care and love. In so doing, patriarchy ignores all the ways that these "spontaneous" acts of devotion have been demanded of women: by gendered training, by the material necessities of marriage, by implicit threat. That these two tendencies are in tension does not mean they do not serve each other, or that they do not form an organic unity. As Selma James, Mariarosa Dalla Costa, and Silvia Federici pointed out in the 1970s, and Nancy Fraser has argued since, the family as a site of feminine care serves capitalism by giving men emotional and sexual compensation for the coercion of market relations.[35] The hidden cost of this is the coercion of the patriarchal home: a cost borne principally by women. Incels' real complaint is that there are no women to offer them respite from the very system that their ideology—in its insistence on women as status-conferring commodities—props up.

82. The other "extremist and radical and weirdo" that Ross Douthat discussed in his *New York Times* op-ed was me. While Douthat grants that, unlike Hanson, I wasn't suggesting that there might be a "right to sex," he sees both our pieces as "responsive to the logic of late-modern sexual life," by which he means a sexual revolution that

"created new winners and losers" and brought in "new hierarchies to replace the old ones." Douthat correctly reads me as offering a utopian feminist response to our current situation, and Hanson as offering a solution more in keeping with the trend toward libertarian techno-commerce—the age of the sex robot and insta-porn. Douthat himself prefers what he calls an "alternative, conservative response . . . namely, that our widespread isolation and unhappiness and sterility might be dealt with by reviving or adapting older ideas about the virtues of monogamy and chastity and permanence and the special respect owed to the celibate."

83. But Douthat's conservative, religiously inflected vision is not a genuine alternative to Hanson's proposal to recognize a state-enforced right to sex. Monogamous marriage, the heteronormative family, and norms of chastity are—like Hanson's government subsidies for incels—parts of a patriarchal infrastructure designed to secure men's access to women's bodies and minds. From the feminist perspective, it does not matter if it is the state or society that is enforcing men's sexual entitlement—and in truth it is always both.

84. As for the special respect owed to the celibate, this is all well and good, so long as that respect is not a consolation prize for the gay man or woman taught to loathe their own desires.

85. Douthat is right to say, as radical feminists have long insisted, that the sexual revolution of the 1960s has left us wanting. But it did not create, as he claims, "new winners and losers" or a new hierarchy to displace the old.

86. Indeed, what is remarkable about the sexual revolution—this is why it was so formative for the politics of a generation of radical feminists—is how much was left unchanged. Women who say no still really mean yes, and women who say yes are still sluts. Black

and brown men are still rapists, and the rape of black and brown women still doesn't count. Girls are still asking for it. Boys still must learn to give it.

87. Whom exactly, then, did the sexual revolution set free?

88. We have never yet been free.

On Not Sleeping with Your Students

In 1992, Jane Gallop, Distinguished Professor of English and Comparative Literature at the University of Wisconsin at Milwaukee, was accused of sexual harassment by two of her women graduate students. After a long investigation, the university found Gallop guilty of violating, in the case of one of the students, a prohibition on "consensual amorous relations" between faculty and students. She was gently reprimanded. Five years later, Gallop published a book, *Feminist Accused of Sexual Harassment*, defending herself against the accusations. Yes, she said, she had made out with one of the women at a bar in front of other graduate students; she had announced at a conference that graduate students were her "sexual preference"; she had deliberately made her pedagogical relationships intense, flirtatious, and sexually charged; and she had slept with many students, graduates and undergraduates, at least before 1982, when she met the man who became her life partner. What's more, she said, there was nothing wrong with any of this:

At its most intense—and, I would argue, its most productive—
the pedagogical relation between teacher and student is, in fact,
"a consensual amorous relation." And if schools decide to prohibit not only sex but "amorous relations" between teacher and
student, the "consensual amorous relation" that will be banned
from our campuses might just be teaching itself.[1]

Teaching, Gallop suggests, is in its ideal form already an amorous,
erotic relation; so what harm could there be in allowing that relation
to manifest physically in sex? To rule out student-faculty sex is to
rule out erotically charged pedagogy—the best sort, Gallop thinks.

In the early 1980s, US universities began discouraging, and sometimes prohibiting, sex between professors and their students.
(Outside the US such prohibitions remain rare. The policy at Oxford,
where I teach, reads: "While the University does not wish to regulate
the private lives of its staff, it strongly advises staff not to enter into
a close personal or intimate relationship with a student for whom
they have any responsibility, and alerts them to the complications
that may result.") The introduction of these policies on US campuses was an outgrowth of the feminist campaign against sexual harassment in the 1970s and 1980s. While employment discrimination
"on the basis of sex" had been outlawed since the passage of the US
Civil Rights Acts in 1964, women in the 1960s and 1970s had strug-
gled to recruit the law in their fight against sexual harassment in the
workplace. Judges routinely decided that workplace sexual harassment was a "personal" matter, or that it was discrimination not "on
the basis of sex" but on the basis of something else, like being the
sort of woman who didn't want to have sex with her boss—a characteristic which, unlike sex, was not protected by anti-discrimination
legislation. (Using a similar logic, one court found in favor of an
employer who had fired a woman for not conforming to a dress
code that required women to wear skirts, reasoning that she wasn't

being discriminated against on the basis of sex, but on the basis of being a woman with an "affection for pantsuits."[2])

Feminists of this era fought to make the courts see what is to many of us now obvious: that far from being a merely personal matter, or a matter orthogonal to gender, sexual harassment expresses and reinforces women's political subordination. In 1974, Paulette Barnes, who had recently been fired from her job as an administrative assistant at the Environmental Protection Agency, brought a suit against her former employer for sex discrimination. Her boss, Douglas Costle, had fired Barnes after she refused his persistent sexual overtures. The case was dismissed, but was then taken to the District of Columbia Court of Appeals for review. Catharine MacKinnon, then a law student at Yale, slipped a working paper that would eventually become her groundbreaking book *The Sexual Harassment of Working Women* (1979) to one of the law clerks involved with the appeal. The court ruled that what had happened to Barnes constituted sex discrimination, and was therefore a violation of Title VII of the Civil Rights Act.[3]

A few years later, MacKinnon, by this time working as one of the leaders of the progressive New Haven Law Collective, helped a group of Yale undergraduates sue the university for the sexual harassment they and their peers had suffered as students, and the failure of the institution to do anything about it. The students lost the case, but *Alexander v. Yale* (1980) nonetheless established that sexual harassment constituted sex discrimination under Title IX of the Education Amendments Act of 1972. The ruling prompted universities across the country to draw up sexual harassment codes and grievance procedures.

Sexual harassment, by legal definition, involves "unwanted" sexual advances. That would seem not to include consensual relationships between professors and students—and indeed, early sexual harassment policies were silent on such relationships. But in 1986, the US Supreme Court decided that consent wasn't necessarily a bar to sexual harassment. The case that prompted this ruling, *Meritor*

Savings Bank v. Vinson, involved a young woman, Mechelle Vinson, who had been fired from her job at a bank for taking "excessive" leave. Vinson's supervisor, Sidney Taylor, had begun asking Vinson to have sex with him soon after she started at the bank four years earlier. At first she had refused, but eventually gave in out of fear of losing her job. Vinson estimated that she had agreed to have sex with Taylor as many as fifty times, and testified that she had been forcibly raped by him on several occasions. (Like Paulette Barnes before her, and the women in other key sexual harassment cases,[4] Mechelle Vinson was black; it is black women in the US who have borne the brunt of sexual harassment and the legal battle against it.) The court pointed out that Vinson's consent to her boss's sexual demands did not mean she welcomed them, since her consent was secured by a fear of the consequences of saying no.

Extending the logic of *Meritor* to the university campus, it was now possible to argue that professors were sexually harassing the students with whom they were having consensual sex. Students' consent to such relationships might, after all, be an expression not of genuine want, but fear. Universities, worried about their potential liability, began in the 1980s to expand their sexual harassment policies to cover consensual relationships between professors and students. In 1989, only an estimated 17 percent of American universities had consensual relationship policies; by 2004, the figure was 57 percent;[5] in 2014, a survey found that it had risen to 84 percent.[6] The policies are also getting increasingly strict. In 2010, Yale became the first US university to impose a blanket prohibition on relationships between faculty and undergraduate students. (Previously, Yale had prohibited faculty members from having relationships with students, undergraduate or graduate, with whom they had or were likely to have a supervisory relationship.[7] That policy had been devised in 1997, after an apparently consensual affair between a seventeen-year-old freshman and her mathematics professor left the student feeling, in her words, "betrayed" and "used."[8]) After Yale implemented its blanket ban, many other US universities quickly followed. In 2020, University College London was the third British university to adopt a prohibition on teacher–student relationships.[9] Universities invariably justify these prohibitions by citing the difference in power between teacher and student—a difference, they say, that casts doubt on the meaningfulness of the student's consent.[10]

The expansion of campus sexual harassment policies to cover consensual faculty–student relationships is part of the legacy of the women's liberation movement. Yet as soon as this expansion began, some feminists denounced it as a profound betrayal of their principles. To deny that women students could consent to sex with their professors, they argued, inverted the rapist's logic of "no means yes" into the moralizing logic "yes means no." Were women university students not adults? Were they not entitled to have sex with whom they pleased? Did such policies not play into the hands of the resurgent religious right, which was all too keen to control women's sex lives? (As Ann Snitow, Christine Stansell, and Sharon Thompson wrote in a gently critical letter to Adrienne Rich in 1981: "In the Reagan era, we can hardly afford to romanticize any old norm of a virtuous and moral sexuality."[11]) Some feminists in the 1980s and 1990s also objected to the way in which these policies reinforced a hierarchical, and thus anti-feminist, understanding of pedagogy: powerful professor versus vulnerable student. (Predictably, male opponents of the new prohibitions complained that they represented a prudish attack on personal freedom and—in one notorious case—that they ignored the benefits to young women of losing their virginity to their male professors.[12]) But in the last two decades these arguments have been less prominent, and comprehensive prohibitions on teacher–student relationships have had little pushback from feminists.[13] This is in keeping with a deepening feminist anxiety about the ethics of sexual relationships inflected by large differentials of power. When the relatively powerless consent to sex with the powerful, is it consent worth the name?

It is, no doubt, sometimes the case that women students consent to sex they don't really want because they are afraid of what will happen if they don't—a bad grade, a lackluster recommendation, being ignored by their supervisor. But there are also many women students who consent to sex with their professors out of genuine desire. And there are professors whose romantic and sexual overtures are very much wanted. To insist that the power differential between professor and student precludes consent is either to see women students, like children, as intrinsically incapable of consent to sex—or to see them as somehow incapacitated by the dazzling force of the professor. And which professor is really *that* good?

But this is not to say that genuinely wanted teacher–student sex is unproblematic. Imagine a professor who happily accepts the infatuated attentions of his student, takes her out on dates, has sex with her, makes her his girlfriend, perhaps as he has done with many students before. The student has consented, and not out of fear. Are we really prepared to say that there is nothing troubling here? But if there is something troubling, and the problem isn't a lack of consent, then what is it?

Is it too sterile, too boring to suggest that instead of sleeping with his student, this professor should have been—*teaching* her?

In her formal response to her students' sexual harassment complaints, Jane Gallop appealed to Freud's notion of transference, the patient's tendency to unconsciously project feelings associated with significant figures from childhood (usually a parent) onto the analyst. In many cases the result is what Freud called "transference-love," in which the object of the child's devotion, infatuation, and eagerness to please is displaced from parent onto analyst. Transference, Gallop says, "is also an inevitable part of any relationship we have to a teacher who really makes a difference."[14] Falling in love with our teachers, in other words, is a sign that pedagogy has gone well.

Perhaps. Certainly many of us ended up as professors because some teacher or teachers—at school, at university—prompted in us new desires and wants. And those of us who teach will likely recognize something akin to transference not only in the students in whom we prompt similar desires, but also in the students who experience the exercise of our pedagogical authority as if it were a mortal attack on their independence, prompting outsized hostility rather than (outsized) adoration.[15] Even so, Gallop overlooks Freud's insistence that analysts are "absolutely debarred" from engaging romantically or sexually with their analysands.[16] For Freud, as one reader puts it, "the analyst responds but does not respond *in kind*."[17] The analyst must not, that is, respond with either love or hostility to the analysand, and must not use the transference as a vehicle for their own emotional or physical gratification. (Freud helpfully reminds the analyst that the "patient's falling in love is induced by the analytic situation and is not to be ascribed to the charms of his person."[18]) Instead, Freud says, the analyst must use the transference-relation as a tool in the therapeutic process. The skilled analyst does this by drawing the analysand's attention to the transference at work, and, Freud says, "convinces" her—I shall return to the ambiguity of that formulation—that her transference-feeling is nothing more than a projection of repressed emotion. "In this way," Freud says, "the transference is changed from the strongest weapon of the resistance into the best instrument of the analytic treatment . . . the most difficult as well as the most important part of the technique of analysis."[19]

What might it be for the professor to respond to the student's transference-love, but not respond in kind—instead turning it to good use in the pedagogical process? It would involve, presumably, the professor "convincing" the student that her desire for him is a form of projection: that what she really desires isn't the professor at all, but what he represents. To switch from Freud's terms to Plato's, the teacher must redirect the student's erotic energies from himself toward their proper object: knowledge, truth, understanding. (Plato, like Freud, is often invoked in defenses of professor–student sex, but in fact Socrates did not sleep with his students—to the apparent frustration of some of them. Indeed, in the *Republic*, Socrates tells us that "sexual pleasure mustn't come into" relationships between philosopher-guardians and the young boys they are educating, "if they are to love and be loved in the right way."[20]) It is the bad teacher who absorbs the student's erotic energies into himself. As Freud puts it, "however highly he may prize love," the good teacher must "prize even more highly the opportunity to help" his student.[21]

What about that ambiguity in Freud's remark that the therapist must "convince" the analysand that her transference feelings aren't real feelings for the analyst, but mere projections? Does this mean the analyst must reveal a truth, or persuade the analysand of a lie? Freud's answer is something in between. The patient's transference really is a projection of repressed feelings: the therapist is loved as a symbol. But this doesn't make the patient's love any less genuine, for projection is, Freud says, "the essential character of every love."[22] Transference-love "has perhaps a degree less of freedom than the love which appears in ordinary life . . . it displays its dependence on the infantile pattern more clearly, is less adaptable and capable of modification; but that is all and that is nothing essential."[23] So too, perhaps, with the student's love for her professor. We can say that she is "really" in love with what he represents, rather than the man himself. But who falls in love any other way? (Proust: "We fall in love for a smile, a look, a shoulder. That is enough; then, in the long hours of hope or sorrow, we fabricate a person, we compose a character.")

The differences here, between the infatuation a student has for her professor, and the infatuation anyone has for anyone else, are a matter of degree, not kind. The problem with teacher–student relationships is not that they can't involve genuine romantic love. Many professors are married to former students (a fact that defenders of teacher–student relationships frequently trot out, as if we were in a Shakespearean comedy, where all that ends in marriage ends well). But the question, as Freud shows us, isn't whether "real" romantic love is possible in the pedagogical context, but whether real teaching is.

Or, to put it another way, the question is what sort of love teachers, as teachers, should show toward their students. In an essay from 1999, "Embracing Freedom: Spirituality and Liberation," bell hooks commands teachers to ask "How can I love these strangers, these others that I see in the classroom?"[24] The love hooks is referring to isn't the exclusive, jealous, dyadic love of lovers, but something more distanced, more controlled, more open to others and the world. It is no lesser a love for that.

When we speak of the power differential between teacher and student, it isn't simply that the teacher has more influence on how the student's life will go than the student has on the fate of her teacher. Indeed, to represent it that way is to invite the counter that, really, women students have all the power, since they can get their male professors fired. (That's the premise of David Mamet's *Oleanna*.) Instead, the teacher–student relationship is characterized, in its nature, by a profound epistemic asymmetry. Teachers understand and know how to do certain things; students want to understand and know how to do those same things. Implicit in their relationship is the promise that the asymmetry will be reduced: that the teacher will confer on the student some of his power; will help her become, at least in one respect, more like him. When the teacher takes the student's longing for epistemic power and transposes it into a sexual key, allowing himself to be—or worse, making himself—the object of her desire, he has failed her as a teacher.

Here is an account from a former student-girlfriend:

For a long time, I went around feeling naive, humiliated, and ashamed. Many of his colleagues knew the extent of the errands

I ran for him . . . Many of his colleagues were also my professors, and the humiliation I felt in their presence was great. I was
ridiculed by students who were aware of what was going on. My
emotional attachment to him earned me the title "Professor X's
pitbull," as though I could not think for myself, only defend my
master on command.[25]

The relationship between teacher and student is upended. It was
supposed to serve her needs; now, in the eyes of her professor-
boyfriend, she serves his (doing his errands, feeding his ego). She
is also—or so she imagines, but do we think she is wrong?—
transformed in the eyes of her academic community as a whole. She
is unable to relate any longer to her other professors as her teachers; they are now her boyfriend's (judgmental) colleagues. She may
still be enrolled, but is she really a student any longer? If she were
to leave, would we be surprised?

In a discussion in *Critical Inquiry* following the publication of
Feminist Accused of Sexual Harassment, James Kincaid, a professor of
English at the University of Southern California, defended Gallop
from the charge of sexual harassment—a charge that, in his view,
lacks a sense of "fun."[26] Kincaid opens his case by transcribing a letter he received from a student the previous semester:

Dear Professor Kinkade:
    I never do this kind of thing, but my roommate keeps telling
me I should, she says, go ahead and tell him if you feel like it, so
I am. I really like your class and the way you have of explaining
things. I mean I read these poems and they don't mean a thing
to me until you start talking and then they do. It's the way you
talk that is different from the other teachers I have had in the
English Department, who may know more than you but can't
get it across if you know what I mean. But when you were saying
that the Romantic poets wrote about feelings, unlike the 17th-
century poets like Pope, who didn't, I knew right away what you

meant. I have a lot of feelings myself, though I am not exactly a poet ha ha. But anyhow, I just wanted to say thanks and hope you keep it up because I really like it.

Kincaid reads the note as flirtatious, an initiation, a come-on:

That note, unsigned and heartfelt, expresses true desire . . . My admirer hopes that I will keep it up because he or she likes it, and he or she writes me this note hoping that I will like it. I will like it and he or she will like it and we will, together, keep it up because it is fun for both of us to like and be liked and to keep being liked without end. Nobody reaches the finish line; nobody is empowered, and nobody is victimized, either. If my perceptive student and I go beyond writing notes and make all this material, it will not be because I have something to give and he or she to take, or vice versa, but because we like it and want to keep it up. A physical relationship will not be progress, just difference.

Kincaid, whose profession it is to interpret and to teach others to interpret, is here engaged in what would be a satire of a certain sort of "perverse" psychoanalytic interpretation, if the occasion for it weren't, as Kincaid says, a "heartfelt" letter from a young woman. (Kincaid insists on the ambiguity of the student's gender—"he or she"—but we know that this is a young woman, if not from the tone of the letter, then from the gender of the writer's dorm roommate. What investment does Kincaid have in acting as if this letter and his response have nothing to do with gender?)

As it is, Kincaid's reading of the letter is a kind of abuse, a pornification of a sweet, earnest declaration of feeling. The student, for the first time, gets the meaning of poetry, and she is awestruck by this professor who has, alone among all the professors she has had, been able to show her what poetry means. Kincaid ignores all this, and focuses instead on the final line, "I hope you keep it up because I really like it," turning it into a crude sexual pun. He is hard for his student, and she's enjoying it, and wants it to continue, ad infinitum, just because it's fun.

But that isn't what his student said. She wants him to "keep it up"—that is, keep on *teaching*—not just because it's enjoyable, though it is that too, but because it helps her understand what poetry means: "I mean I read these poems and they don't mean a thing to me until you start talking and then they do." She wants for herself the capacity to understand poetry, not just the pleasure of watching him exercise that capacity. It is Kincaid's insistence on the masturbatory aspect of his student's desire that allows him to say, of an imagined future in which he and his student "go beyond writing notes and make all this material," that "nobody is empowered, and nobody is victimized, either."

Is there no difference in power between Kincaid, author of *Child-Loving: The Erotic Child and Victorian Culture*, and his student? I want to leave aside the (un-fun) matter of institutional power: who grades whom, who writes recommendations for whom, and so on. There are other differences in power here. First, epistemic power. Kincaid knows how to read in a way that makes reading meaningful; the student lacks, but wants to have, this power. Part of what is particularly disturbing about Kincaid's reading of the letter is that the student is not intellectually sophisticated. Kincaid's calling her "perceptive" feels manipulative and cruel, giving her a simulacrum of what she wants—the teacher's own mastery. Indeed, Kincaid only reproduces the letter, presumably without her permission, because he is confident that she isn't the type to read *Critical Inquiry*. But what if she did read it? How might she be expected to feel, seeing her youthful earnestness exhibited as a sexual trophy?

Second, there is Kincaid's power to interpret not only poetry, but the student herself. This is a sort of metaphysical power: that is, a power not only to reveal the truth, but to make it. He tells us that her letter is latently sexual, that its natural fulfillment would be sex—that sex would do no more than "make all this material." What would happen if Kincaid offered this reading to the student herself, who trusts him to reveal the truth in things written? Did Kincaid have the power to *make* it true that her letter was, in a sense, sexual all along?

Kincaid would perhaps protest that her letter *is* sexual, albeit latently. It isn't as if there aren't any expressions of desire to be found there. It opens as if it were a confession of love: "I never do this kind of thing . . ." The student declares that she has "a lot of feelings," and then immediately makes fun of herself for it ("ha ha"). Kincaid is special, "different from the other teachers." He is perhaps correct in implying that he could sleep with this student if he wanted to—without any need for coercion, threats, or offers of a quid pro quo. Maybe he wouldn't have to do much more than read her some Wordsworth, call her "perceptive," and lead her to the bedroom. So what? Are we really to believe that Kincaid isn't deliberately sexualizing this interaction, that he is merely passive and obedient in the face of his student's will?

Of course, it is hard to read someone's mind on the basis of one letter. Perhaps the student simply admires and wants to be like Kincaid. Or maybe she doesn't know what she wants: to be like Kincaid, or to have Kincaid. Or she wants both, and takes having Kincaid as a means to, or a sign of, being like him. Or she believes that she can't ever be like Kincaid, and so longs, as a second best, to have him instead. Perhaps, even, she just wants to have sex with Kincaid, and all the talk of poetry is just an attempt at seduction. Still, whichever of these possibilities is right, it may well be possible for Kincaid to get his student consensually to have sex with him. Where a student's desire is inchoate—*Do I want to be like him, or to have him?*—it is all too easy for the teacher to steer it in the second direction. Likewise when the student (wrongly) thinks that sleeping with her teacher is a means to becoming like her teacher, or a sign that she is like him already (*He wants me so I must be brilliant*). Even where it is clear that the student's desire is to be like the teacher, it's not hard for a teacher to convince the student that her desire is really for him, or that sleeping with him is a way to become like him. (What better way to understand the "feelings" of the Romantic poets than to experience those feelings yourself?)

Whatever may be in the student's mind, it is surely the case that Kincaid's focus, as a teacher, should be on directing his student's desire away from himself, and toward its proper object: her epistemic empowerment. If this is what the student wants already, then all Kincaid has to do is exercise some restraint, and not sexualize what is a sincere expression of her desire to learn. If the student is ambivalent or confused in her desires, Kincaid must go a step further and draw boundaries, redirecting the student's desires in the proper direction. Freud thinks that in psychoanalysis this should be done explicitly, by telling the patient that she is experiencing transference. In the pedagogical context, taking that approach would be deeply awkward. (For all the intimacy of the teacher–student relationship, teachers aren't supposed to be reading their students' hearts, even if we can.) But there are subtler ways to redirect a student's energies, quiet ways of stepping back, drawing attention away from oneself and toward an idea, a text, a way of seeing. By failing even to try to do this, Kincaid fails to be what his student is praising him for being: a good teacher.

Teachers must resist the temptation to allow themselves to be, or to make themselves, the receptacle of their students' desires. I am not saying that teaching can or should be entirely free of narcissistic satisfactions. But there is a difference between enjoying the desires you ignite in your students even as you deflect them away from yourself, and making yourself their object. This sort of narcissism is the enemy of good teaching. Sexualization is its most obvious manifestation, but it can take other forms. Part of what is striking about the case of Avital Ronell, the NYU professor of German and Comparative Literature who in 2018 was suspended from teaching for sexually harassing a graduate student, is how little of the abuse she allegedly perpetrated was sexual in nature. She demanded that he spend countless hours in her presence or talking with her on the phone, that he "schedule his life around her wants and needs," that he "distance himself from friends and family," that he not travel out of New York. Had Ronnell not also touched him and sent him sexually explicit messages, presumably NYU would not have found that she had violated Title IX. But she would still have failed in her duties as a teacher, insofar as she used her student to gratify her own narcissistic needs. Here we see one limit of sexual harassment policies in the classroom. At best, such policies prohibit certain egregious failures of good teaching. But they do not teach us how to teach well.

Earlier I asked what investment Kincaid might have in talking about his student as if she could be of any gender. What is it that he doesn't want to face? Most obviously, that the situation he is in fact describing—older, male professor; younger, female student— is the most common form of teacher–student relationship. Kincaid doesn't want us to see him as a cliché. He also presumably doesn't want us thinking about—or isn't himself aware of—the gender dynamics that underpin this cliché. By this I don't only mean the way that boys and men are socialized to find domination sexy, and girls and women to find subordination sexy; or the way that some male professors blend sexual entitlement with intellectual narcissism, seeing sex with women students as the delayed reward for suffering through an adolescence in which brawn or cool were prized more highly than brains. What I mean, most importantly, is the way that women are socialized to interpret their feelings about men they admire.

Adrienne Rich described the institution of "compulsory heterosexuality" as a political structure that compels all women, straight and gay alike, to regulate their relations to other women in a way that is congenial to patriarchy.[27] One of its mechanisms is the tacit instruction of women in how they should feel, or interpret their feelings, about women they admire. The appropriate response is envy, not desire. You must want to be *like* that woman; it could never be that you simply *want* her. But when it comes to the men they find compelling, the opposite applies: it must be that you *want* him, it can't be that you want to be *like* him.

Regina Barreca, speaking of and to women who ended up as professors, asks: "At what point . . . did the moment come for each of us when we realized that we wanted to be the teacher, and not sleep with the teacher?"[28] The default for most women, Barreca suggests, is to interpret the desire sparked in her by a (male) teacher as a desire *for* the teacher: an interpretation she must overcome if she is ever going to become the teacher herself. Male students, meanwhile, relate to their male professors as they are socialized to do: by wanting to be *like* them (and, at the limit, wanting to destroy and replace them: its own source of psychic drama). This difference between women and men in how likely they are to see their teachers as objects of emulation rather than attraction isn't the effect of some natural, primordial difference in disposition. It is the result of gendered socialization.

To be clear: it is no less a pedagogical failure for a woman professor to sleep with her male student, or for her to sleep with a woman student, or for a male professor to sleep with a male student.[29] But an ethical appraisal of the phenomenon of consensual teacher–student sex misses something crucial if it doesn't register that it typically involves male professors sleeping with women students. The professor's failure in such cases—that is, most actual cases of consensual teacher–student sex—isn't just a failure to redirect the student's erotic energies toward its proper object. It is a failure to resist taking advantage of the fact that women are socialized in a particular way under patriarchy—that is, socialized in a way that conduces *to* patriarchy. And, what is just as important, it reproduces the very dynamics on which it feeds, by making sure that the benefits of education will not accrue equally to men and women.

Adrienne Rich, in a lecture she gave in 1978 to the teachers of women students, spoke of what she called the "misleading concept" of "coeducation": "that because women and men are sitting in the same classrooms, hearing the same lectures, reading the same books, performing the same laboratory experiments, they are receiving an equal education."[30] For women do not enter or exist in the classroom on equal terms with men. They are assumed to be less intellectually capable, encouraged to take fewer risks and be less ambitious, given less mentoring, socialized to be less confident and to take themselves less seriously, told that evidence of a mind is a sexual liability and that their self-worth depends on their capacity to attract men's sexual attention. They are groomed to be caretakers and mothers and doting wives rather than scholars or intellectuals. "If it is dangerous for me to walk home late of an evening from the library, *because I am a woman and can be raped*," asked Rich, "how self-possessed, how exuberant can I feel as I sit working in that library?"[31] Equally, we might ask: if I know that my professor sees me not (only) as a student to be taught, but (also) as a body to be fucked, how self-possessed, how exuberant can I feel sitting in his classroom?

Early feminist theorists of workplace sexual harassment argued that the harm it did to women's lives wasn't a mere contingency—was not, that is, just a matter of women's negative psychological response to certain patterns of male behavior. Rather, it was the *function* of sexual harassment to harm women in these ways: to police and enforce their subordinate roles both as women and as workers.[32] Is it such a stretch to think that the function, however unconscious, of the widespread practice of male professors making sexual advances on their female students is to impress on women their proper place in the university? That women are allowed into the university to play the role not of student or would-be professor, but of sexual conquest, fawning girlfriend, emotional caretaker, wife, secretary? Is it a stretch to think that this practice represents not just a failure of pedagogy, but a reinforcement of patriarchal gender norms?

A friend of mine, an exceptionally brilliant woman academic, once explained to a male colleague that, had any of her male mentors, in college or grad school, ever so much as put a hand on her knee, it would have "destroyed" her. The colleague was taken aback. He recognized that such an action would have been creepy, wrong, an instance of sexual harassment—but how could such a small gesture destroy anyone? What he didn't know, she explained to him, was what it is like to have one's sense of intellectual worth rest so precariously on the approbation of men.

In "Eros, Eroticism and the Pedagogical Process" bell hooks writes of her experience as a new professor: "No one talked about the body in relation to teaching. What did one do with the body in the classroom?"[33] What you are supposed to do or not do with your body, and with your students' bodies, is something university teachers do not, as a rule, talk about. Or, when they do talk about it, the discussion has almost always been set up by anxious administrators, in the form of mandatory sexual harassment training—training that has little to do with what is special or particular about the pedagogical relationship. Lessons from the workplace are transferred to the classroom, with no thought given to the way teaching might be characterized by peculiar risks and peculiar responsibilities.

Sometimes these conversations happen informally. A friend of mine, a young professor of law, recently described to me the awkwardness of sharing a gym with his undergraduates. They are free to look at his body, he said, while he "of course pretends they don't have bodies at all." I like that he said "of course": it is self-evident to him that he cannot be a good teacher while also contemplating his students to any degree as potential sexual partners.[34]

But this is not self-evident to many, sometimes with poignant consequences. Another friend, when he was a graduate student, was mortified to learn that some of his women students were complaining that he stared at their legs when they wore shorts or skirts to class. No one had told this graduate student what it might mean for him, as a man, to teach under patriarchy: that if he just let his gaze go where it "naturally" went, let his conversations and interactions with his students proceed as they "naturally" might, he would likely fail to treat his women students on equal terms with his male students. No one told him that, unless he stopped himself doing what came "naturally" to him, he would likely end up treating the women in his class not fully as students, but also as bodies to be consumed, prizes to be won, emotional reservoirs from which to draw. What's more, no one had told him that his women students, raised as they had been on unequal terms from the start, might well go along with it. As a result, the young women he taught had been let down. But so, too, had this graduate student, whose own teachers had failed to teach him how to teach.

In 2019, Danielle Bradford sued the University of Cambridge, from which she had recently graduated, under the UK's Equality Act for its gross mishandling of her complaints of persistent sexual harassment by a graduate student instructor. The university had upheld Bradford's claim, but the only action it took was to insist, first, that the instructor write Bradford a letter of apology, and second that he have no further contact with her—a condition the university ensured would be met partly by restricting Bradford (not her harasser) from entering certain campus buildings. The instructor, meanwhile, continued to teach undergraduates. On Twitter, Bradford complained that the university did not make her harasser undergo any training in how to teach. The firm handling Bradford's case is run by Ann Olivarius, one of the women who, as an undergraduate at Yale in 1977, sued the university for its failure to deal with complaints of sexual harassment. That suit ushered in a new era for the regulation of sexual harassment on US campuses. But the conversation about the sexual ethics of teaching in that era was at best incomplete. Will Bradford's suit make a difference?

The contrast is striking, on this score, between university teaching and the profession of psychotherapy. Learning to anticipate and negotiate the dynamics of transference is central to the training of therapists, and involves an emphasis on the importance of not responding to the patient's desires in kind. The training of university professors involves none of this; in the US, at least, graduate students and junior professors are given little pedagogical training of any sort. But this difference in training does not, it seems to

141

me, track a fundamental difference in kind between therapy and teaching. In both cases, there is an asymmetrical relation of need and trust; in both cases, intense emotions can be expected to arise; in both cases, sex undermines the aims of the practice. There is nothing obviously distinctive about university teaching that makes teacher–student sex permissible, but not therapist–patient sex. Is the difference a function of the contingencies of history? Freud wrote thoughtfully but unequivocally about the sexual ethics of psychoanalysis at the start of the twentieth century, setting out principles and norms for nearly all schools of psychotherapy thereafter. Pedagogy has not, in this respect, had its Freud. Plato, who perhaps came closest, is all too easily misread.

Perhaps it isn't too late. The trend toward increased regulation of sex on campus creates an opportunity for professors, as a group, to think about the aims of pedagogical practice, and the norms of conduct appropriate to achieving them. Professors have a strong incentive to take these things seriously: if they don't regulate themselves, they will—there have already been instances—be regulated from above, with all the attendant consequences. Top-down regulation is unlikely to take into account the ethical and psychic complexities of teaching; instead, it will reflect administrators' desires to cover their backs, and the law's tendency to see the classroom on the model of the workplace. It is striking that when the law does regulate therapist–patient relationships, it almost always does so in the terms accepted by therapists themselves: the terms, that is, of what therapists as therapists owe to their patients as patients. What might it be for professors to lead administrators and the law in thinking not merely in the familiar terms of consent, coercion, and conflict of interest—but in terms of what university teachers, as teachers, owe their students, as students? What might it be for us to set out a sexual ethics of pedagogy?

I magine a student who, infatuated with her professor, pursues him and, thrilled when he returns her attentions, has sex with him, dates him, only eventually to realize that she was just the latest in a string of students, and that their affair is less a sign of her special-ness than it is of his vanity. What happens next? Feeling betrayed and embarrassed, she can no longer take his classes, or spend time in his department (her department); she worries about which of his colleagues (her teachers) know about the relationship, and whether they might hold it against her; she suspects (rightly) that her aca-demic successes will be chalked up to her relationship with him. Now recognize that this is an experience that happens to many women, and almost no men; and, further, that this isn't because of some natural division of sexual labor, but because of the psycho-sexual order into which men and women are inducted, from which men disproportionately benefit and by which women are dispro-portionately harmed. I think it is clear that our imaginary young woman was not sexually harassed by her professor. But was she not denied the benefits of education "on the basis of sex"?

While consensual professor–student relationships do not fit the definition of sexual harassment, they might still count as sex discrimination. For such relationships often—predictably, and seriously—harm women's educations.[35] And they do so *on the ba-sis of sex*. On the conventional legal understanding of sex discrimina-tion, discriminating "on the basis of sex" involves treating women and men differently. Clearly, the male professor who only has sexual relationships with women students treats his female and male stu-dents differently. So does the male professor who only has sexual relationships with male students, or the female professor who only has sexual relationships with male students. Bisexuality poses a problem for this understanding of sex discrimination. (Is it not sex discrimination if a boss hits on both his female and male subordi-nates?) This is one reason to favor an alternative understanding of what it means to discriminate "on the basis of sex." For Catharine MacKinnon, Lin Farley, and other feminist pioneers of sexual ha-rassment theory, the essence of sex discrimination lies not in differ-ential treatment but treatment that reproduces inequality. Take the boss who hits on his secretary, a woman. The problem isn't that the boss doesn't also hit on his male underlings, but that his unwanted sexual advances, as MacKinnon puts it, "express and reinforce the social inequality of women to men."[36]

Can the same be said of consensual professor–student relationships? Perhaps there are some male professors who sleep with their students but are entirely unaroused by their status *as* students. Perhaps. Even so, are we really to believe that the more typical situation isn't one in which everyday heterosexual desire is erotically underscored by the professor–student dynamic? I know of a woman who, as an undergraduate, began a relationship with her professor that lasted several years beyond college. When she finally broke up with him, she explained that "there's just something about an adult man who wants to date his freshman." That "something," I take it, was an erotic investment in gendered domination.

Leaving aside the question of what teacher–student relationships express, it is easy enough to say what they produce. They often, if not universally, harm women in ways that derail their education. This is obviously true in the case of women who stop going to class, who become convinced they are not cut out for academic life, who drop out of college or grad school. But it is also true in the case of women who stay on with a diminished sense of their intellectual capacities, newly suspicious when other male professors show an interest in their work and anxious that, should they succeed, their successes will be attributed to someone or something else. These relationships are sometimes, often, wanted. Are they any less discriminatory for that?

A m I moralizing? There is something prurient in the cultural fascination with professor–student sex that should make us suspicious of the impulse to regulate it.[37] Transgression is not grounds for regulation, especially where sex is concerned. But discrimination does potentially provide those grounds. What matters is the effect that teacher–student relationships have on the lives of the students—usually women—who participate in them, and on the lives and fortunes of women as a class. Yet the truth is that under patriarchy, as a system, women are subjected to discrimination "on the basis of sex" wherever they go, including the university. How could it be otherwise? The question for feminists is which forms of inequality we will use the law to address, and which forms are susceptible only to the forces of social change.

Title IX and the sexual harassment policies it yielded are regulatory instruments intended, at least officially, to make university campuses more equal, fair, and just for women. But they have done so, in part, by making campuses less fair and just in other respects—a fact that many feminists are loath to acknowledge. Sometimes the victims of this injustice are women. In 1984, the year after the first consensual relationship policies appeared on US campuses, the courts upheld the sanctioning of a graduate student, Kristine Naragon, at Louisiana State University, for conducting a romantic relationship with a woman freshman student she wasn't teaching.[38] At the time, LSU did not officially prohibit such relationships, but Naragon was sanctioned after persistent complaints from the student's parents about the lesbian relationship. No sanction had been handed out to a male professor in the same department who had conducted an affair with a woman student whose work he had the responsibility of grading.

The Office for Civil Rights, which administers Title IX, does not track racial statistics for allegations of Title IX violations. Campus Title IX officers are charged with protecting students from discrimination on the basis of sex, but not from discrimination on the basis of race, sexuality, immigration status, or class. Thus, as a matter of Title IX law, it is of no concern that the small minority of black students at Colgate University have been disproportionately targeted for sexual violation complaints; and, as a matter of law, no notes are kept on where else this might be happening.[39] Janet Halley, a professor of law at Harvard, has spent years documenting the unseen wages of campus sexual harassment policies, including accusations that unfairly target men of color, undocumented immigrants, and trans students. "How can the left care about these people when the frame is mass incarceration, immigration or trans-positivity," she asks, "and actively reject fairness protections for them under Title IX?"[40]

So, we must ask: would legally recognizing faculty–student relationships as sex-discriminatory—and thus a violation of Title IX—make campuses fairer for all women, for queer people, for immigrants, for the precariously employed, for people of color? Or would it lead to further failures of due process, unfair in themselves but doubly so in that they disproportionately target people who are already marginalized? Would it inadvertently strengthen the hand of cultural conservatives who are all too keen to control women under the guise of protecting them? Would it be used as a means to suppress academic freedom? Would it be seen, however falsely, as the ultimate *reductio ad absurdum* of campus sexual harassment policies, a clear sign, if one were needed, that the feminists had well and truly lost their minds?

The history of sexual harassment law is a story of the mobilization of the law in service of gender justice. But it's a history that also points to the limits of the law. Where precisely those limits are—the point beyond which the law must cease trying to guide culture, but instead wait impatiently for it—is a question not of principle, but of politics.

I began writing a version of this essay in 2012, five years after I had finished my undergraduate degree at Yale, and two years after Yale implemented its blanket prohibition on faculty–student sex. I was then a graduate student in philosophy, a discipline with its unfair share of both sexual harassment and consensual faculty–student relationships. I was struck then, as I am today, by how limited philosophers' thinking was on the question of whether professors should have sex with or date their students. How could the same people who were used to wrestling with the ethics of eugenics and torture (issues you might have imagined were more clear-cut) think that all there was to say about professor–student sex was that it was fine if consensual?

Many philosophers prefer to see complexity only where it suits them. Philosophy is a discipline dominated by men, including many men who feel—or historically have felt—powerless in the face of women, and who trade on their professional status for sex as a way of getting their just deserts. I remember once reading on an anonymous philosophy blog a comment by a philosopher—I can't imagine it was a woman—who asked why there should be any difference between a professor asking to have sex with a student and asking to play tennis with her. Why, indeed? "When you are a woman and a philosopher," wrote the French philosopher Michèle Le Dœuff, "it is useful to be a feminist in order to understand what is happening to you."[41]

As a graduate student I wanted to explain to the men in my discipline, as I have tried to explain here, that the absence of consent isn't the only indicator of problematic sex; that a practice which is consensual can also be systemically damaging; that the pedagogical relationship might come with certain responsibilities beyond the ones we owe each other as persons. I wanted to explain to them that it was precisely because pedagogy was or could be an erotically charged experience that it could be harmful to sexualize it. I wanted to explain that refraining from having sex with their students wasn't the same as treating students as children.

Now that I am a professor, I confess that some of these arguments don't grip me in the way they once did. Not because I think they are wrong—I still think they are right—but because I no longer feel them to be, in a sense, necessary. As a teacher, I see that my undergraduate students, and in some cases my graduate students, for all their maturity, intelligence and self-directedness, are, in an important sense, still children. I don't mean this as a claim about their legal or cognitive or moral status. They are perfectly capable of consent, and have the right to determine the course of their lives just as I have the right to determine the course of mine. I simply mean that my students are so very young. I didn't know, when I was in their place, how young I was, and how young I must have seemed even to those professors who were kind enough to treat me like the fully fledged intellectual I mistakenly thought I was. There are plenty of people my students' age, most of them not in university and will never be, who are adults in ways that my students simply aren't. My students' youthfulness has much to do with the sort of institutions at which I have taught, filled with the sort of young people who have been allowed, by virtue of their class and race, to remain young, even as many of their peers have been required to grow up too quickly.

The youthfulness of my students, undergrad and grad, has a lot to do, too, with the peculiar liminal space in which they, as students, exist. Their lives are intense, chaotic, thrilling: open and largely as yet unformed. It is hard sometimes not to envy them. Some professors find it difficult to resist the temptation to try and assimilate themselves to their students. But it seems obvious to me—not as a general moral precept, but in the specific sense of what is called for in the moments of confrontation with our own past selves which are part of what it is to teach—that one must stand back, step away and leave them to get on with it. Jane Tompkins, in *A Life in School* (1996), writes: "Life is right in front of me in the classroom, in the faces and bodies of the students. *They* are life, and I want us to share our lives, make something together, for as long as the course lasts, and let that be enough."[42]

In my very first week as a new professor, I attended a dinner with faculty members and graduate students in my department. I was closer in age to the grad students than I was to most of the faculty members, and I remember feeling relaxed and happy in their company. After dinner, the wine not yet finished, everyone buzzing, the head of the department told me he was calling it a night. Eyeing two graduate students horsing around across the table, he laughed: "When they start sitting on each other, I think it's time to head home." He was right, and I followed him out, leaving my students to get on with it.[43]

Sex, Carceralism, Capitalism

A black professor I know likes to tell his students they should have a plan for what to do if they win. What should feminists do if they win? The question will strike many as extravagantly hypothetical. Feminists do not have power, they will say; instead, they "speak truth to power," from a place of relative powerlessness. Except that some feminists, like it or not, have quite a lot of power. This is true, for example, of the feminists who have been instrumental in the shaping of university and workplace sexual harassment policies, the priorities of global NGOs, and the treatment of women in domestic and international law. It is true of the self-styled feminists who have slotted into existing systems of power as political leaders and CEOs. It is true of the feminists whose aims converge, however unintentionally, with those of the political right: for example, the anti-porn and anti-prostitution feminists of the 1970s and 1980s, and the trans-exclusionary feminists of today. And it is increasingly true of the feminists who, through social media, have been able to direct public attention toward the behavior of sexually abusive men. To be sure, these feminists with power are almost all wealthy, and usually white and from western countries. In that sense, feminism has reproduced the world's inequalities within its own ranks. But the fact that most women—working-class and immigrant women of the global north, the poor brown and black women of the global south—remain relatively disempowered is no reason to deny that some feminists wield considerable power. What should they do with it?

I n September 2019, the *Guardian* reported on the emergence of government-sponsored "drive-thru brothels" in Cologne, Germany:

> Located on the edge of town, the result is a kind of sex drive-through. Customers drive down a one-way street, into a roughly two-acre open-air space where sex workers can offer their services. Once hired, the sex worker accompanies the customer into a semi-private parking stall. For safety, each stall allows sex workers to easily flee if necessary—the stall is designed so that the driver's door can't be opened, but the passenger one can—and there's an emergency button to call for help. Social workers are present on site and offer a space to rest, stay warm and access services.[1]

Karen Ingala Smith, the CEO of nia, a London-based charity set up "to end violence against women and children," tweeted the article with the comment: "For me, images of these drive-in brothels, looking so much like live-stock sheds, or garages, exemplify the dehumanisation of prostituted women."[2] Making Herstory, another British charity that works to end violence against women, tweeted: "Anything to safeguard easy access to abused, impoverished and trafficked-in victims, right?"[3] The image accompanying the article—a large wooden shed, divided into car-sized lots by colored metal dividers—is a provocation to feminist sensibilities. The semiotics of the building make its function explicit: the anonymous and routinized sexual ser-vicing of men by women. Its panic buttons and escape routes are a frank acknowledgment that a proportion of the clients will be vio-lent. The building is expressive of everything feminists loathe about the state of relations between men and women: a built testament to men's physical, sexual, and economic dominance.

Yet if we read the image differently—not as a symbol of the state of relations between men and women, but as a pragmatic response to it—we can perceive an impulse to make the world more livable for a particular group of women. Once we take it as given that under current economic conditions many women will be compelled to sell sex, and that under current ideological conditions many men will buy it, the most important question remaining is: what can we do to strengthen the hand of women in this bargain? Nicole Schulze, a sex worker in Cologne, told the *Guardian*: "I think every city should have a secure space for sex workers to work, to rest. Every city should have that because there's prostitution in every city."

The feminist debate about sex work very often involves a tension between these two levels of analysis: between the symbolic force of sex work and its reality. At the level of the symbol, prostitution is seen as a distillation of women's condition under patriarchy. The prostitute is the perfected figure of women's subordinate status, just as the john is the perfected figure of male domination. Their sexual transaction, defined by inequality and often accompanied by vio-lence, stands in for the state of sexual relations between women and men more generally. Seen this way, the prostitute calls out to be saved, the john to be punished, and their transactional sex to be stopped—for the good of all women.

Anti-prostitution feminists propose to answer this call through the criminalization of sex work: making the buying, and sometimes also the selling, of sex illegal. But the criminalization of sex work does not, on the whole, help sex workers, much less "save" them. Indeed we know, because sex workers have long been telling us, that

legal restrictions on sex work make their lives harder, more dangerous, more violent, and more precarious.[4] When prostitution is criminalized, as in most of the US, sex workers are raped by johns, and
by the police, with impunity. When prostitution is partly legalized,
as in the UK, women who work together for safety are arrested for
"brothel-keeping," and—if they are immigrants—deported. When
prostitution is legalized but heavily state-regulated, as in Germany
and the Netherlands, male managers and brothel-keepers grow
rich, while women who are unable to meet licensing requirements
join a shadowy criminal class, susceptible to trafficking and forced
prostitution. When buying but not selling sex is illegal, as in the
"Nordic model," johns demand increased privacy for their trans-
actions with sex workers, forcing women to take greater risks to
make the same money.[5] Under none of these criminalizing regimes
are sex workers, as a class, better off.

I am not suggesting that anti-prostitution feminists—Catharine
MacKinnon, Andrea Dworkin, Susan Brownmiller, Kathleen Barry,
Julie Bindel, Sheila Jeffreys—think of themselves as engaging in a symbolic politics. Far from it: most anti-prostitution feminists are clearly
conscious of, and exercised by, the grim reality of much sex work. (I
say "most" anti-prostitution feminists because some are by their own
admission indifferent to the welfare of sex workers; Julie Burchill, for
example, has said that when "the sex war is won prostitutes should be
shot as collaborators for their terrible betrayal of all women."[6]) At the
same time, sex workers insist that anti-prostitution efforts make their
lives worse, not better. What are we to make of this?

What affective investment do anti-prostitution feminists have in
the criminalization of sex work, such that their genuine concern for
sex workers ends, paradoxically, in a refusal to hear what they have
to say? When Molly Smith and Juno Mac began writing *Revolting
Prostitutes* (2018), a formidable defense of sex workers' rights, they
formed a reading group with other sex workers on the history of
anti-prostitution writing, much of it by feminists. "For feminist
women," they write,

the figure of the prostitute often comes to represent the trauma that is inflicted on all women within patriarchy—the ultimate symbol of women's pain, of the violence that women suffer. The client thus becomes the symbol of all violent men: he is the avatar of unadulterated violence against women, the archetypal predator. We deeply sympathise with this perspective. Our lives too have been shaped by gendered violence, and we understand the political impulse to punish the man who has come to symbolise this trauma ... And, of course, proponents of the Nordic model are right in identifying prostitution as a deeply unequal transaction—one scarred by patriarchy as well as by white supremacy, poverty, and colonialism. It seems intuitively right to criminalise the men who *are*, in many ways, the living embodiments of these huge power differentials.[7]

For Smith and Mac, it is the desire to punish the men who buy sex—as individuals, but also as stand-ins for all violent men—which explains the contradictions of a feminism that makes life worse for sex workers. Smith and Mac understand that desire. They don't deny that johns are "in many ways" apt symbols of patriarchy. But they do insist that a choice must be made between satisfying the desire to punish men and empowering the women who sell sex in order to live. Put another way, the psychic, and perhaps moral, satisfactions of punishing men can be had only at the cost of women—and often the women whose lives are most precarious. Anti-prostitution feminists, who are as a rule not themselves sex workers, maintain the fantasy that there is no choice to be made here: that there is a satisfying convergence between the punishment of men who indulge their patriarchal entitlement and the welfare of the worst-off women. In so doing, they forget Max Weber's warning that to do politics is to enter "into relations with the satanic powers that lurk in every act of violence."[8] For sex workers themselves, the choice between men's punishment and their own survival is all too clear.

Symbolism, of course, matters: patriarchy establishes itself at the level of words and signs, not just bodies. But the demands of the symbolic can stand in tension with those of the real women who must pay their bills, feed their children, and sometimes are assaulted by the men to whom they sell sex. When these women are assaulted, will they have any recourse—or will they be trapped in a closed space with a violent man, a quiet sacrifice in a war of symbols?

Perhaps I am oversimplifying. It is undeniable, I think, that anti-prostitution feminists are symbolically invested in the punishment of sexually entitled men, and that this prevents them from acknowledging the choice between punishing the men who buy sex and improving conditions for women who sell it. But these feminists might counter that they are responding to another, equally real choice, which proponents of sex workers' rights ignore: the choice between making life better for the women who sell sex now, and bringing into existence a world in which sex is no longer bought and sold. A few years ago, French anti-prostitution activists successfully campaigned to implement a law that punishes the purchase of sex. Asked whether the criminalization of clients makes prostitutes more vulnerable, one of the campaigners said: "Of course it will! I am not scared to say it. But think of the abolition of slavery, it also made life bad for some former slaves. We need to think about the future!"[9]

In calling themselves "abolitionists," anti-prostitution feminists deliberately invoke the historical campaign against slavery. Sex workers object not only to the assimilation of sex work to the condition of chattel slavery, but also to the idea that outlawing sex work, like outlawing slavery, is genuinely a step toward its eradication. The criminalization—in part or in full—of sex work has never, in practice, got rid of prostitution. Sex work has thrived under every legal regime; what has varied are the conditions under which sex is bought and sold, and in particular whether clients and workers are subject to the coercive power of the state. So long as women need money to pay their bills and feed their children, so long as sex work is better than the available alternatives, and so long as women's subordination is eroticized, there will be prostitution. The criminalization of sex work is in this sense a symbolic abolition: a striking out of prostitution in the law, but not in reality. In 2018, a Spanish court voided the by-laws of a sex workers' labor union, under intense pressure from anti-prostitution feminists, on the grounds that sex work is not work. The ruling does not apply to those women who work in "gentlemen's clubs"—brothels, that is, almost always operated by men. Spanish sex workers who want to work for themselves, and not for men, enjoy no labor protections, cannot receive state pensions or social security, and are routinely fined by the police under vague public safety laws. Now they cannot unionize. The motto of the Spanish anti-prostitution feminists who led the campaign is #*SoyAbolicionista*. But what exactly have they abolished?

There is a striking parallel to this dialectic, between those who are invested in a symbolic abolition of sex work and those who work to improve the immediate lives of sex workers, in the debate about an issue on which sex workers and most anti-prostitution feminists adamantly agree: abortion. Feminists have long tried to explain to opponents of abortion that criminalizing it doesn't reduce the number of abortions carried out, but does increase the number of women who die from them.[10] A real movement to abolish abortion would presumably involve massive investment in (non-abstinence-based) sex education; effective, safe, and freely available contraception; state-guaranteed parental leave; and universal childcare and maternal health care. Of course, some opponents of abortion actually do want women who seek abortions to die; the former *Atlantic* writer Kevin Williamson commented that he "would totally go with treating it like any other crime, up to and including hanging."[11] But if most opponents of abortion are to be taken at their word, they are concerned not with the punishment of women, but the protection of the unborn. Whatever one thinks of the idea that the "unborn" represent a class in need of protection, it is fairly clear that the criminalization of abortion does not serve this end. If so, then we can say that anti-abortionists too are engaged in a symbolic politics whose aim, however unconscious, isn't so much to end abortion as to have it denounced in the law.

Would the decriminalization of sex work fare any better? Not in improving the conditions for current sex workers—there the case for decriminalization is clear—but in achieving the outright abolition of sex work? After all, in countries where prostitution has been decriminalized, the size of the sex work industry has not substantially decreased, even as conditions for workers in the industry have improved.[12]

Smith and Mac argue that the title of "abolitionist" properly belongs to the proponents of decriminalization because, they say, it is only through the political recognition of sex workers as workers—in need of legal protection rather than censure or salvation—that they will be empowered to refuse the sex they don't want to have.[13] Here Smith and Mac invoke the Marxist feminist Silvia Federici, who claimed in the context of the Wages for Housework campaign, begun in the early 1970s by Selma James and Mariarosa Dalla Costa, that calling something "work" was the first step toward refusing to do it.[14] By forcing the recognition that women's unwaged reproductive labor is a necessary precondition of capitalist production, Federici argued, wages for housework would allow women to *refuse that work as the expression of our nature*, and therefore . . . refuse precisely the female role that capital has invented for us."[15] The demand for wages disrupts the illusion that domestic labor is the natural task of women—an expression of their innate femininity—and, in so doing, "forces capital to restructure social relations in terms more favorable to us and consequently more favorable to the unity of the [working] class."[16] In *Women, Race & Class* (1981) Angela Davis countered Federici and other Wages for Housework feminists by arguing that a housework wage might marginally improve the lot of working-class women, but only at the cost of further entrenching their role as domestic laborers.[17] "Cleaning women, domestic workers, maids," Davis wrote, "these are the women who know better than anyone else what it means to receive wages for housework."[18] Wages for housework would not improve working-class women's social standing, Davis said, nor offer them "psychological liberation."[19] It would instead "further legitimize this domestic slavery."[20] Could wages for housework, Davis asked, really be "a concrete strategy for women's liberation?"[21]

The debate between Federici and Davis, viewed through a wider political lens, is over which demands are truly revolutionary and which merely reformist—that is, which demands set the groundwork for the undoing of a system of domination, and which only secure the grip of that system by relieving its most egregious symptoms. Federici sees wages for housework as a revolutionary demand because, she says, it would strengthen the hand of women in their struggle against both capitalism and sexism, in turn giving them more collective control over the processes of social production and reproduction. It is a demand, she says, not just for a "thing" (money) but moreover for the power to remake social relations. Here Federici alludes to André Gorz, who wrote in his essay "Reform and Revolution" (1967) that for the reformist

> at stake in the reforming action is merely "things"—wages, public amenities, pensions, etc.—which the state is to dispense from on high to individuals maintained in their dispersion and impotent with respect to the process of production.

By contrast, for revolutionary socialists, "each partial improvement, each reform demanded should be articulated into a general project aiming at producing global change."[22] Davis, in Gorz's terms, thinks the Wages for Housework campaign is essentially, and merely, reformist: by making the oppressive life of the housewife slightly more bearable, she says, paying her a wage would buttress both sexism and capitalism. The truly revolutionary demand, in Davis's view, would be for the "*abolition* of housework as the private responsibility of individual women": that is, the socialization of childcare, cooking, and cleaning.[23]

There is an analogous dialectic in the debate over sex work. Both anti-prostitution and pro-decriminalization feminists claim that their aim is to overthrow the system that produces sex work: hence the wrangling over which side is entitled to call itself "abolitionist." Proponents of decriminalization like Smith and Mac argue that strengthening the labor power of sex workers wouldn't just make their lives more livable; it would give them more power to demand a restructuring of economic and social relations such that they will no longer have to sell sex to live. Seen this way, theirs is a revolutionary politics. As anti-prostitution feminists might see it, though, decriminalization is at best a reformist measure, which marginally improves the lives of sex workers while shoring up both patriarchy and the neoliberal commodification of sex.

Who is right? To be honest, it's hard to know. As Gorz writes, "any reform whatsoever . . . may be emptied of its revolutionary significance and re-absorbed by capitalism."[24] Perhaps the decriminalization of sex work would in the long run, despite the intentions of its radical proponents, stabilize the place of sex work within capitalist societies. And perhaps, by turning sex workers into workers like any other, decriminalization would vitiate rather than strengthen their insurrectionary potential.[25] Perhaps. Meanwhile, there isn't much reason to think that throwing sex workers and their clients in jail will eventually lead to the end of sex work. (It certainly hasn't done so yet.) There is, though, every reason to think that decriminalization makes life better for the women who sell sex. From this perspective, to choose criminalization is to choose the certain immiseration of actual women as a putative means to the notional liberation of all women. It is a choice that again reveals, deep in the logic of anti-prostitution feminism, an investment in symbolic politics.

But let's suppose, just for the sake of argument, that we knew for a fact a tragic choice had to be made between improving the conditions of the women who sell sex today, and accelerating a future in which there will be no prostitution. If we really did know this, as feminists, how should we proceed? The Combahee River Collective, a black lesbian feminist group, explained its political methodology in its April 1977 manifesto as follows:

> In the practice of our politics, we do not believe that the end always justifies the means. Many reactionary and destructive acts have been done in the name of achieving "correct" political goals. As feminists we do not want to mess over people in the name of politics. [26]

This basic principle—of not "messing over" people as a means to a political end—implies that any choice between improving the lives of existing people and holding the line for a better future must be settled in favor of the former. Many, perhaps most, anti-prostitution feminists simply deny that they face such a choice—insisting, fantastically, that criminalization can secure abolition and help sex workers at the same time. But some anti-prostitution feminists no doubt think there is a choice to be made, and are prepared to live with the immiseration of sex workers if it means gaining the psychic satisfaction of punishing men, the symbolic erasure of prostitution in the law, and the hastening, or so they imagine, of a world without patriarchy. These feminists might not wish to shoot prostitutes as patriarchal collaborators. But they are happy, one way or another, to mess them over.

In 2007, the sociologist Elizabeth Bernstein coined the term "carceral feminism" to describe a politics that looks to the coercive power of the state—police, criminal courts, prisons—to achieve gender justice. [27] Over the last fifty years, a carceral response to prostitution, domestic violence, and rape has become increasingly accepted as common sense in most countries. The problem, as the particular case of sex work shows, is that carceral "solutions" tend to make things worse for the women who are already worst off. This is because carceral feminism invites the wielding of the state's coercive power against the women who suffer most from gendered violence—poor women, immigrant women, women of color, low-caste women—as well as the men with whom their lives are fatefully entwined. At the same time, the carceral approach fails to address those social realities—poverty, racism, caste—that lie at the root of most crime, and which make certain groups of women particularly susceptible to gendered violence.

In 2006, Brazil passed the Maria da Penha Law, named after a woman who had survived repeated beatings and two murder attempts by her husband, one of which left her paralyzed from the waist down; it took twenty years for da Penha to get her husband tried and convicted by a Brazilian court. The new law, passed in large part because of the campaigning efforts of feminist organizations, introduced mandatory prison sentences for perpetrators of domestic violence, and special courts for the adjudication of domestic violence cases. Some Brazilian academics have pointed out that the Maria da Penha Law has resulted in a drop in the reporting of domestic violence. This is not because the new law has decreased the incidence of domestic violence. It is because the poor Brazilian women who disproportionately suffer from domestic violence no longer feel that they can turn to the police for help: they fear their partners will be imprisoned under terrible conditions, and worry about their ability to run a household alone, in the absence of state economic support.[28]

Starting in the 1980s, some US feminists successfully campaigned for states to adopt "mandatory arrest" policies, which require the police to make an arrest whenever they are called out on a domestic violence complaint. As many black and Latina feminists predicted, these policies increased the incidence of domestic violence against women of color.[29] Numerous studies have shown that retaliatory violence after arrest is linked with poverty, unemployment, and drug and alcohol use—factors that disproportionately afflict black and Latino communities.[30] One 1992 study in Milwaukee found that

the mandatory arrest policy reduced the amount of violence perpetrated by employed white men while increasing the amount of
violence perpetrated by unemployed black men: "If three times as
many blacks as whites are arrested in a city like Milwaukee, which
is a fair approximation, then an across-the-board policy of mandatory arrests prevents 2,504 acts of violence against primarily white
women at the price of 5,409 acts of violence against primarily
black women."[31] Indeed, the world over, male joblessness is linked
with domestic violence against women.[32] But poor abused women
cannot, as a rule, turn to the state to employ their husbands, or
for the money they would need in order to be able to leave them.
Instead, they can only ask that their husbands be locked up, which
many are understandably reluctant to do. When these women do
call on the carceral state for help, they are sometimes directly punished themselves. Under mandatory and "dual-arrest" policies in
the US, women of color—instead of or as well as their abusers—
frequently end up arrested.[33]

In 1984, bell hooks wrote about the tendency of the women's liberation movement to focus solely on what women could be said
to have in common:

> Although the impulse towards unity and empathy that informed
> the notion of common oppression was directed at building soli-
> darity, slogans like "organize around your own oppression" pro-
> vided the excuse many privileged women needed to ignore the
> differences between their social status and the status of masses
> of women. It was a mark of race and class privilege . . . that
> middle-class white women were able to make their interests the
> primary focus of the feminist movement and employ a rheto-
> ric of commonality that made their condition synonymous with
> "oppression."[34]

On its face, the notion of "common oppression" contains a promise of universal women's solidarity. The rich woman and the poor woman, the citizen and the refugee, the white woman and the black and brown woman, the high-caste woman and the Dalit woman: all women are oppressed on the basis of their sex, and this will be the foundation of their empathetic and strategic alliance. But it is precisely those forms of harm that are not common to all women— those from which some women, by virtue of their wealth, race, citizenship status or caste, are insulated—that are the most grievous to the women who suffer them. A feminism that addresses only sexual oppression will pursue strategies that are of little use to women whose sex is just one cause of their political predicament. To make common oppression your rallying cry, bell hooks points out, isn't just to ignore, but to guarantee, the oppression of the worst-off women.

Carceral approaches to gender justice tend to presuppose a subject who is a "pure" case of women's "common oppression," uncomplicated by such factors as class and race. The belief that a sex worker will be helped by the criminalization of her trade rests on the assumption that she has other choices available to her—that it is prostitution, rather than, say, poverty or immigration law, that is her fundamental problem. Likewise, the belief that incarceration is the way to deal with domestic violence does not take into account the women whose fates are bound up with the men who perpetrate it: the women who are financially dependent on the men who beat them, and who have a large stake in how the men in their community are treated by the police, courts, or prisons.

The carceral approach also neglects the more than half a million women worldwide who are themselves incarcerated—and subject, in prison, to sexual abuse, violence, humiliation, forced sterilization, and the loss of their children. In the US, which holds 30 percent of the world's incarcerated women (by comparison, China has 15 percent and Russia 7.5 percent), the women's incarceration rate has grown at twice the rate of men's in recent decades.[35] The disproportionate poverty of women means they are less able to bail themselves out of pre-trial custody, thus increasing the number of children who are separated from their primary caregivers: 80 percent of women in jail in the US are mothers.[36] In Thailand, the only country whose rate of women's incarceration rivals the rate in the US, 80 percent of women are imprisoned for nonviolent, drug-related offenses.[37] In the UK, detainees on hunger strike at Yarl's Wood, an immigration detention center where women can be held indefinitely, were warned by the Home Office that their protest might accelerate their deportation.[38] The vast majority of incarcerated women the world over are poor, undereducated, and have backgrounds involving violence. That many mainstream feminists have little to say to these women comes as no surprise, implicated as they themselves are in the carceral system.

When feminists embrace carceral solutions—cops on the street, men sent to prison—it gives cover to the governing class in its refusal to tackle the deepest causes of most crime: poverty, racial domination, borders, caste.[39] These are also the deepest causes of women's inequality, in the sense that it is these forces and their corollaries—lack of housing, health care, education, childcare, decent jobs—that are responsible for the greater part of women's misery. Globally, most women are poor, and most poor people are women. This is why feminism understood as the fight against "common oppression" comes apart from a feminism that fights for the equality and dignity of all women. A feminism focused on women's common oppression leaves untouched the forces that most immiserate most women, instead seeking gender-equal admission to existing structures of inequality.

The turn toward carceralism is part of a broader shift in emphasis within feminism since the 1970s, away from the transformation of socio-economic life toward securing women's equality in the pre-existing structures of capitalism. As Susan Watkins pointed out in

New Left Review in 2018, the radical women's liberationists of the late 1960s and 1970s in the anglophone world, like their contemporaries in social democratic Europe and the decolonizing Third World, were interested in transforming the social order that produced not only gender inequality but also racialized and class-based inequalities.[40] They demanded universal childcare, health care, and education; the right to reproductive self-determination and the demise of the heteronormative nuclear family; wealth redistribution, union rights, wages for unwaged domestic work, and democratic ownership of the means of production. In 1974 the New York Radical Feminists published *Rape: The First Sourcebook for Women*. In it they wrote: "It must be made clear that rape is not a law-and-order issue. Women are not demanding castration nor are women demanding capital punishment ... We do not want to make rape laws more punitive."[41] Rape could only be eliminated, they said, through "a transformation of the family, of the economic system and the psychology of men and women so that sexual exploitation" becomes "unimaginable." Rape, they said, "is not a reformist but a revolutionary issue."[42]

But such transformative demands soon gave way, in the US, to what Watkins calls the "anti-discrimination" paradigm, according to which the real problem for women was that they did not exist on equal terms with men in the workforce—"to bring women," as Betty Friedan's National Organization for Women put it, "into full participation in the mainstream of American society."[43] This sort of feminism was, and remains, congenial to the women who were already beneficiaries of US capitalism: the rich, largely white women who were now freed from the tedium of domesticity to become doctors, lawyers, bankers, and academics. It was also congenial, as Watkins observes, to the American right, who saw in the anti-discrimination paradigm a solution to the so-called "Negro problem"—the public spectacle of an immiserated people clamoring for racial and economic equality. The "problem," from the right's perspective, was not how to achieve this equality, but how to avoid international embarrassment during its fight against communism and anti-colonial insurrection.[44] By securing access for some black men and women to the professional middle class, the Nixon administration set about bifurcating the black population. There would be one class, in Nixon's words, of "black capitalists," and a second vast black underclass, to be disciplined in the decades ahead by means of a series of "wars"—on drugs, on crime, on "welfare queens." (These wars—like the "war on terrorism" to come—were also waged on immigrants, who were made to bear the blame for white poverty.) The strategy was explicitly carceral, and has helped the US achieve the largest prison population in the world.[45] At the same time, the pursuit of "anti-discrimination" feminism from the mid-1970s onward laid bare the division between a newly empowered class of largely white professional women, and the class of poor, largely non-white and immigrant women who took over the tasks of caring for their children and cleaning their houses.[46]

The feminists of the early US women's liberation movement, like European and Third World feminists, had not, on the whole, looked to the state's coercive apparatus for a solution to gendered violence. Skeptical of state power, they created and ran their own grassroots rape crisis centers, domestic violence shelters, and abortion networks.[47] But by the 1980s, mainstream feminists had fully embraced "law and order" as the way to deal with domestic violence, prostitution, pornography, and rape. Why the shift? In part it reflected broader changes in the US in this period: increasing anxiety about violent crime,[48] together with the taking hold of an individualist ideology which implied that crime was a personal failing rather than a social pathology. In 1984, Ronald Reagan complained that liberals had sold Americans the lie that "individual wrongdoing . . . was always caused by a lack of material goods, and underprivileged background, or poor socio-economic conditions." "Is it any wonder," he said, "that a new privileged class emerged . . . of repeat offenders and career criminals who thought they had the right to victimize their fellow citizens with impunity."[49] In 1989, Donald Trump, then a New York City playboy and real-estate mogul, took out full-size ads in four of the city's newspapers, including the *New York Times*, calling for the execution of the five teenage boys, four black and one Latino, falsely accused of raping a woman in Central Park. (These ads, while distinctively Trumpian in their bombast and orgiastic celebration of state violence, also serve as a reminder that Trump's politics were formed in the context of a broader history of US carceralism.)

The carceral turn of feminism was in keeping, then, with the shifting material and ideological conditions of the postwar US.[50] But US feminists in this period also actively facilitated the growth of the carceral state, whether or not this was their intention.[51] Seeking mainstream legitimacy and access to funding, some feminists became professional "anti-violence" experts—counselors, victim advocates, project administrators—who, as Beth Richie puts it, began to function as apologists for the system rather than agents of its transformation.[52] At the same time, feminist lawyers led the way in redefining gendered violence as a problem of law and law enforcement.[53] In 1976, it was argued in a class action lawsuit, *Bruno v. Codd*, that battered women had a right to police intervention. Two years later, feminists participated in the federal Commission on Civil Rights hearings on "wife abuse," which laid the ground for government anti-battering initiatives, including mandatory arrest requirements. In the 1980s, feminists co-operated with Republicans to introduce civil legislation against pornographers;[54] participated in a child sex abuse moral panic that sent innocent day-care workers to prison;[55] supported the creation of sex offender registries that include juveniles;[56] and launched a campaign to "abolish" prostitution and sex trafficking through intensified criminalization.[57] In 1994, Bill Clinton signed into law the Violence Against Women Act (the bill had been co-sponsored by Senator Joe Biden), which provided $1.6 billion for the investigation and prosecution of violent crimes against women. US feminists, who had played a crucial role in the creation and passage of VAWA, rejoiced. It was part of the bipartisan Violent Crime Control and Law Enforcement Act, which also created sixty new death-penalty offenses and got rid of federal funding for prison education programs. Two years later, Clinton made good on his campaign promise to "end welfare as we know it," leaving poor women and their children more susceptible to violence. "Pro-arrest" laws for domestic violence increased the numbers of poor men and women in prison.

All this took place against a background in which the end of the Cold War and the spiraling of Third World debt had ushered in an era of US hegemony. "Global" feminism took on a distinctively American character.[58] The ambitions of socialist and anti-colonial feminists to create a new world order, in which women's emancipation would go hand in hand with economic justice, gave way to a new priority: to bring the world's women into the global capitalist economy, with the US at its helm. Western governments, NGOs, and private foundations invested in women's education and health care, but the most important tool in this assimilationist project was microfinance: the extension of credit to the poor women of the world. It didn't register that what poor women said they needed was more public provision—water, electricity, and sanitation. (In 1984 the Indian feminist Devaki Jain warned that "Economic development, that magic formula . . . has become women's worst enemy.") Instead, it was decided that women's empowerment would be achieved through the issuing of small loans at 20 percent interest rates by foreign private-sector lenders. Together with access to credit, poor women were also given the "protection" of the carceral state. The 1995 Beijing Platform, adopted by 189 countries at the Fourth United Nations World Conference on Women, listed violence against women as one of its twelve critical areas of concern. It called on states to enact "penal, civil, labour and administrative sanctions . . . to punish and redress the wrongs done to women and girls who are subjected to any form of violence" and to legislate for "the prevention of violence and the prosecution of offenders."[59]

While the Beijing Platform also encouraged states to take steps to eliminate sexist practices and equip women with the means of subsistence, global women's rights activists went on to focus largely on carceral solutions to gendered violence.[60] By framing gendered violence as an issue of international human rights, these activists also provided cover for western military intervention.[61] In a radio address in November 2001, soon after her husband inaugurated the "war on terror" by invading Afghanistan, Laura Bush explained that "the fight against terrorism is also a fight for the rights and dignity of women."[62] She did not mention the historical role of the US in making Afghanistan one of the world's worst places to be a woman[63]— a distinction it retains to this day.[64] After decades of foreign military intervention, including the US's longest ever war, economic devastation has left Afghans more hopeless about their lives than the people of any other country on record.[65] Women pay a disproportionate price: 90 percent of Afghan women have experienced domestic abuse, and 80 percent of suicides are by women.[66]

It is an embarrassment to feminism that decades of improving conditions for some of the world's women in some respects— greater legal rights; better representation in tertiary education, elite professions, electoral politics, and the media; improved access to reproductive health care; widespread agreement in polite society that women are men's equals; an increased willingness among men to question the strictures of gender; the growing acceptance of non-hegemonic sexualities—have coincided with an increase across the board in other forms of inequality, especially economic inequality. I am not suggesting that the improvements in women's lives are not real or hard-won, or that they are a benefit only to rich women. They are not. A poor woman in India also needs her husband to know he is not entitled to beat her; she must be able to have her day in court. She should be able to send her daughter, if she can scrape together the fees, to university; and her daughter must be free to love whom she wants. But this woman must also have the means to ensure her own and her family's survival: land, water, food, but also safety, solidarity, community. The history of US feminism, which for some time has been the most globally powerful form of feminism, is a history of women—some women—wielding, to great effect, state power, and ultimately supranational power. But it is also a history of the capitalist state channeling the power of women in ways that are conducive to its own sustenance—ways, ultimately, that do little to threaten the ruling class.

The most recent inflection point of American feminism, the #MeToo campaign of 2017, gained its motive force from the simple fact that all working women, or near enough, have experienced sexual harassment: lewd remarks, humiliation, groping, sexual threats, sabotage. On social media platforms, first in the US and then beyond, women recognized their own stories in the testimonies of other women. "Women come into the movement from the unspecified frustration of their own private lives," as Juliet Mitchell put it in 1971, then "find that what they thought was an individual dilemma is a social predicament and hence a political problem."[67] Many men looked on and were surprised by what they saw. But almost immediately, the limits of "Me Too" as a universal rallying cry began to show. The slogan had been pioneered by Tarana Burke, a black anti-violence campaigner, more than ten years earlier. Black women resented being asked to stand in solidarity with white women when their own protests against sexual harassment had been ignored for so long. When the actress Rose McGowan had her Twitter account suspended for posting about her treatment by Harvey Weinstein, Alyssa Milano and other white women called for a women's boycott of the platform with the hashtag #WomenBoycottTwitter. Many high-profile black women, including Ava DuVernay and Roxane Gay, accused white women of being selective in their concern.[68] April Reign, a media consultant and the woman behind the #OscarsSoWhite hashtag, told the *New York Times*: "If there is support for Rose McGowan—which is great—you need to be consistent across the board. All women stand with all women."[69]

But the problem with Me Too as a mass women's movement isn't just a lack of "consistent" application of concern and outrage across racial lines. Its fundamental problem is the presupposition that any such movement must be grounded in what women have universally in common. Sexual harassment is a reality for working women. But for many women, being sexually harassed is not the worst thing about their jobs. There is a profound difference between the situation of a wealthy white woman like Rose McGowan, or well-off black women like Roxane Gay and Ava DuVernay, and the poor immigrant women who clean Hollywood's bathrooms. When these woman are sexually harassed, it only underscores the misery of their low-wage, precarious work. Thanks to the Hollywood actresses of Me Too, these women can now appeal to the Time's Up Legal Defense Fund to sue if they are sexually harassed. But to whom should they turn when they need money to escape an abusive partner, or health care for a sick child, or when immigration comes to ask for their papers?[70] Few if any feminists believe that harassment should be tolerated, that employers shouldn't be sued, or that laws against sexual harassment haven't done much to help working women, poor women included.[71] But a feminist politics which sees the punishment of bad men as its primary purpose will never be a feminism that liberates all women, for it obscures what makes most women unfree.

The feminists of Me Too appear, on the whole, to have a great deal of faith in the coercive powers of the state. They protested Brock Turner's comparatively light sentence for sexual assault, celebrated when the judge in Larry Nassar's trial seemed to express the hope that he might be raped in prison, and crowed when the verdict on Harvey Weinstein came in. They champion the move to stricter notions of sexual consent both in the law and on university campuses, and have denounced critics of these developments as rape apologists. It is hard to blame them. For centuries men haven't only assaulted and degraded women, but have used the state's coercive apparatus to enforce their right to do so. Is it not time women got to wield some of that same power—to express their outrage and to take revenge?

Except that once you have started up the carceral machine, you cannot pick and choose whom it will mow down. Feminism's embrace of carceralism, like it or not, gives progressive cover to a system whose function is to prevent a political reckoning with material inequality.[72] This is not to say that there are no difficult choices to be made. There are poor women who want to see their abusive partners in prison, just as there are sex workers who long for violent johns to be arrested. Some opponents of carceralism think that no one deserves to be punished, that violence must never be met with more violence. But feminists need not be saints. They must only, I am suggesting, be realists. Perhaps some men deserve to be punished. But feminists must ask what it is they set in motion, and against whom, when they demand more policing and more prisons.[73]

The renewed media attention given to the Black Lives Matter movement, in the wake of George Floyd's murder by a Minneapolis police officer in May 2020, introduced to many people for the first time the idea that the police, and the broader carceral complex of which it forms a part, might be radically shrunk or abolished. Calls to "defund the police" have met with bafflement from those, including feminists, who cannot imagine a society that isn't regulated by the violent power of the state. Who would enforce law and order, if not the police? The assumption here is that, broadly speaking, the police and prisons do serve law and order: that such things as extrajudicial executions, false imprisonment, forced hysterectomies, and sexual violence are the exception and not, in the treatment of some people, the rule. And there are some, of course, who believe in any case that law and order properly consists in the unjust treatment of poor people, people of color, and immigrants—that these people either deserve no better, or that their mistreatment is a reasonable price to pay for an orderly society.

The question—"If not the police, then who?"—also betrays a misunderstanding of the abolitionist tradition. For most abolitionist thinkers—most notably, among the feminists in this tradition, Angela Davis and Ruth Wilson Gilmore—the proposal is not, needless to say, that the angry energies of those who are made to exist on society's margins should be simply let loose. Abolitionists see that carceral practices substitute control for provision: that "criminalisation and cages" serve as "catchall solutions to social problems."[74] As Davis wrote in June 1971, sitting in a Marin County jail awaiting trial on charges of helping to arm black activists, "the necessity to resort to such repression is reflective of profound social crisis, of systemic disintegration."[75] What if, rather than relying on police and prisons to manage the symptoms of social crisis, that crisis were met head-on? As the legal academic James Forman Jr. puts it, abolitionism asks us to "imagine a world without prisons, and then . . . work to try to build that world."[76] What would that take? It would involve the decriminalization of activity, like drug use and sex work, whose criminalization is known to exacerbate rather than reduce violence.[77] It would involve a restructuring of economic relations such that crimes of survival—food theft, border-crossing, homelessness—were unnecessary. (George Floyd was killed after using a counterfeit bill to buy cigarettes. He had recently lost his job.) It would involve putting in place the social and political arrangements to meet the needs that, when they go unfulfilled, produce interpersonal violence: public housing, health care, education, and childcare; decent jobs in democratically organized workplaces; guaranteed basic income; local democratic control of community spending and priorities; spaces for leisure, play, and social gathering; clean air and water. And it would involve creating a justice system that, wherever possible, sought repair and reconciliation. Abolition, Gilmore explains, "isn't just absence . . . abolition is a fleshly and material presence of social life lived differently."[78]

The abolitionist tradition sees that carceralism works as a cover for the deprivations of racial capitalism, and that a transformation in our social and economic relations would at least partly undermine the rationale and need for the carceral state. Implicit in the call to "defund the police," then, is the demand for a massive redistribution of wealth and power from the rich to the poor. Like the radical feminists of the early women's liberation movement, the activists and organizers of the Movement for Black Lives have little interest in finding a place in a system built on someone else's terms. (Though it is true that the same cannot be said of many of their "allies.") The movement's 2016 manifesto, "A Vision for Black Lives," lists six demands, including divestment from carceral institutions and investment in education and health, together with "economic justice for all and a reconstruction of the economy to ensure our communities have collective ownership, not merely access." Here the manifesto echoes Fred Hampton, the Black Panther assassinated by the police and FBI in 1969: "We don't think you fight fire with fire best, we think you fight fire with water best . . . We say we're not going to fight capitalism with black capitalism, but we are going to fight it with socialism."[79]

So the Movement for Black Lives is not, as some critics on the left—most notably the Marxist political theorist Adolph Reed—have claimed, a movement that simply seeks black people's inclusion in the reigning capitalist order, with its few lucky winners and outsized population of losers.[80] Reed rightly objects to an anti-discrimination approach to racism, which doesn't seek genuine equality but, as he and Walter Benn Michaels put it, "proportional *inequality*":[81] that is, the proportional representation of people of color at every level of an unequal economic system. Reed isn't wrong that anti-racism, like feminism, can and often does come in a form that is congenial to capitalism. Capitalism, historically, has depended, in different ways, on the creation of hierarchies based on race, caste, and gender—allowing, to take just one example, the exploited white male worker to be subdued with reassurances of his superiority to his wife and to his black fellow workers. But capitalism is also well served by the logic of anti-discrimination. Sexist, racist, and anti-immigrant discrimination disrupt the smooth functioning of meritocracy, potentially depriving capital of the most talented workers. Anti-discrimination measures increase the efficiency of the labor market, leaving its underlying logic—that some people must sell their labor to survive—untouched. Following the murder of George Floyd, the CEOs of Google, Amazon, Twitter, and Nike all called on their employees to honor "Juneteenth": the commemoration on June 19 of the end of US slavery. Jeff Bezos, the CEO of Amazon, encouraged his employees to cancel all their meetings for the day—which didn't do much for the Amazon warehouse workers who go without bathroom breaks and incur repetitive strain injuries as they labor under the constant threat of algorithmic censure.

Reed and other left critics of "identity politics" tend to think that proportional inequality is the best that anti-racist politics can aspire to.[82] If that's right, the US—and other racially stratified societies too—may be doomed. For the historical absence of a mass working-class movement in the US has plausibly much to do with white racism and nativism, themselves a historical product of class antagonism.[83] As W.E.B. Du Bois put it in *Black Reconstruction in America* (1935), white racial supremacy has served as a "compensation" for the immiseration that capitalism brings on white workers, precluding the possibility of working-class solidarity across the color line.[84] It is no doubt true that a working-class movement in the US cannot succeed by alienating poor white people, still less by treating them as objects of contempt. But it is truer still that such a movement cannot succeed without speaking to—indeed, unless it emerges from—the increasing proportion of the working class that is not white or native-born—the growing number of people, that is, whose lives are directly devastated by the entanglement of capitalism, racism, and xenophobia.[85] This is not just because these people increasingly *are* the working class, and that for them the force of "class" is experientially inseparable from the workings of "race."[86] It is because their lives, in their greater devastation, contain within them the demand for the most revolutionary change.

Theorists like Reed think this dilemma can be resolved, not by creating a multiracial and pro-immigrant working-class politics, but by focusing on the "common oppression" of all poor Americans—namely, their exploitation under capitalism, narrowly understood. But, as bell hooks said of white feminism, this approach threatens not just to cover up but to perpetuate the oppression of the worst-off. What's more, to the extent that a psychic investment in whiteness and "native" status plays a role in the antipathy of poor whites toward immigrant workers and workers of color—as recent events in the US and UK suggest it does—the delayed confrontation with racism and xenophobia guarantees misery for poor whites as well.[87] In a letter to Angela Davis as she sat in jail in 1970, James Baldwin lamented that

> only a handful of the millions of people in this vast place are aware that the fate intended for you . . . is a fate which is about to engulf them, too. White lives, for the forces which rule in this country, are no more sacred than Black ones . . . the American delusion is not only that their brothers all are white but that the whites are all their brothers.[88]

The question, therefore, is not: Can the anti-racist movement ever be sufficiently anti-capitalist? Instead, we should ask: Can a working-class movement afford not to be anti-racist?

So too with the relationship between feminism and anti-capitalism. Marxist feminists of the 1970s pointed out that capitalism rested on the unwaged labor of women in the household. Working-class women, they observed, not only birthed, clothed, and fed male workers, but also soothed their egos, absorbed their frustrations, and created homes that offered them some respite from alienated labor.[89] Increasingly, in advanced capitalist countries, women's work, the work of social care (cleaning, nursing, feeding, child-rearing, teaching the young, tending to the old), is now bought and sold. Low-wage women are becoming the face of the new working class, and they are at the heart of its most hopeful protests.[90] The COVID-19 pandemic has given a stark demonstration of how the patriarchal ideology of the self-sufficient nuclear family entraps not only women but men in lives that are deemed, in that contradiction of contemporary capitalism, at once "essential" and disposable.[91] It has made clear to many what certain feminists have long insisted: that the work of social reproduction must be the work of society. The question isn't whether feminism can be a working-class movement, but whether a working-class movement can afford to be anything but feminist.

To say that a working-class movement must be feminist and anti-racist is not to deny that capital is able to co-opt, and indeed has co-opted, feminist and anti-racist energies. It would be a mistake to underestimate the genius of capital: its ability to repurpose and reconstitute itself in accordance with cultural shifts. The same is true, after all, of even "purely" anti-capitalist demands, like universal basic income: a proposal that has been advanced by many socialists but also appeals to Silicon Valley billionaires who see it as a means of quieting resistance to the tech-abetted erosion of decently paid, middle-skilled jobs.[92] In 1973, the Notting Hill Women's Liberation Workshop Group explained that a statement of demands delivered by Selma James the year before—including wages for housework, equal pay, and community-controlled nurseries—was "not a statement of what we want, finally, to have." These demands, they said, did not constitute "a plan for an ideal society," and a society that satisfied them would not thereby "cease to be oppressive." Rather, the demands were simply meant to act as "a force against what capital wants and for what we want." For "ultimately the only demand which is not co-optable is the armed population demanding the end of capitalism."[93] There is no settling in advance on a political program that is immune to co-option, or that is guaranteed to be revolutionary rather than reformist. You can only see what happens, then plot your next move. This requires being prepared—strategically and emotionally—to abandon ways of thinking and acting to which you may have become deeply attached. In that sense, nostalgia is a barrier to any truly emancipatory politics. This is as true in feminism as anything else.

B ut what about the rapists?
This is the objection on which the critique of carceralism is supposed to crucially founder. Surely the example of the rapist shows us, if nothing else does, that abolitionism is unworkably

utopian. How can a feminist criticize patriarchal practices of punishment while demanding that the rapist be tried, convicted, and
locked up?

Some opponents of carceralism answer this challenge by insisting that sexual assault is a product of social problems that can be
solved through the application of non-carceral forms of state power,
most obviously the radical democratization of the economy and
political decision-making. But this makes the mistake of reducing
patriarchal oppression to economic and political oppression. Sexual
violence is indeed partly a function of those things: racial domination, economic inequality, and deficits in democracy are all predictors
for high rates of sexual assault.[94] In particular, crises of masculinity, precipitated by de-industrialization and wage depression, make
women particularly susceptible to sexual violence. But the reasons
underemployed and hopeless men turn their aggression on women
are not exhausted by economic forces: there are dimensions of gender relations that pre-exist our current economic arrangements. So
long as the critique of capital is made in terms of economic relations alone, it will never fully account for, or remedy, sexual violence. A full critique of capital must see gendered subordination
as an essential aspect of the broader capitalist system—economic,
yes, but also social, ecological, psychic, and so on—that is its proper
object.[95] Otherwise, an anti-capitalist politics threatens to abandon
women to civil society, which has for them, as Catharine MacKinnon
aptly put it, "more closely resembled a state of nature."[96]

But what about the rapists? The question is sometimes played as a
trump card. But in fact it's a question about which abolitionist feminists have plenty to say. They begin by asking: which rapists? In the
US, after excessive force, sexual misconduct is the most common
complaint brought against cops. Between 2005 and 2013, 405 police
officers were arrested for forcible rape, and 219 for forcible sodomy.[97] In England and Wales, there were 1,500 accusations of sexual
misconduct against police officers between 2012 and 2018.[98] When,
in March 2021, a police officer was charged with the kidnapping and

murder of a young British woman, the UK government responded by announcing that plainclothes police officers would begin patrolling bars and clubs at closing time, as part of an initiative called "Project Vigilance." In India in 2014, a woman was gang-raped by four police officers; she had gone to the police station to seek her husband's release.[99] Theorists and practitioners of feminist abolitionism—often poor women of color—are building, in various places, democratic, community-based institutions to manage interpersonal violence, including sexual violence, without turning to the coercive apparatus of the state. They seek new ways of holding men accountable, insisting at the same time that men not use their treatment at the hands of the state as an excuse for their own violence.[100] These projects, for their various successes, have proved grueling, calling on precisely the women most susceptible to gendered violence to create the institutions that will be needed to end it. If they were supported by a different form of state power—not carceral, but socialist—such projects would no doubt be far easier. Guaranteed income, housing, and childcare would free the world's poor women to think about how to make their communities safer and more just—how to teach their sons and brothers and partners what it means to live on equal terms with women and girls. But it would be grueling work nonetheless, asking women to do what the law has not and, in my view, cannot: transform the most basic terms of engagement between women and men.

There is a paradox in powerlessness. Collectivized, articulated and represented, powerlessness can become powerful. This is not in itself a bad thing. But with new power come new difficulties and new responsibilities. This is especially true for those whose acquisition of power rests on their ethical authority: on their promise to bring into being something new and better. Feminists need not abjure power—it is, in any case, too late for that—but they must make plans for what to do when they have it. Too often, feminists with power have denied their own entanglement with violence, acting as if there were no hard choices to be made: between helping some and harming others, between symbolism and efficacy, between punishment and liberation.

It is often the case that those with power are the ones least capable of seeing how it should be wielded. But this needn't be, for feminists at least, a cause for despair. Feminism is a movement. In it there have always been, always are, those for whom power remains elusive—those who have still not won, those for whom winning so far means surviving. It is these women, at the sharp end of power, to whom the rest of us must turn, and then, turning, follow.

Acknowledgments

First, my profound thanks to Karolina Sutton, for knowing before I did that this was the book I wanted to write; and to my editors, Alexis Kirschbaum and Mitzi Angel, for breathing life into it.

My endless gratitude to Mary-Kay Wilmers, who gave my writing its first home, and who especially gave a home to "The Right to Sex" ("never too much sex for an LRB piece"); to Katherine Rundell, bold and wise and kind friend, who told me, two days after my twenty-sixth birthday, that I should try to write; to Katie Geminder, in whose home I wrote some of these essays; and to Robin Bierstedt and Peter Mayer, in whose home I wrote others; to Ted Fertik, for comradeship and criticism; to Dennis Zhou, for meticulous fact-checking and more; to my students Simple Rajrah and Robert Cheah for helping to prepare the manuscript; to Susan Brison, who at the eleventh hour read the manuscript with great generosity and care; and to the many students I have taught at Oxford and UCL, some of whose stories I have told here.

ACKNOWLEDGMENTS

I owe an unpayable debt to my colleagues in Politics and Philosophy at Oxford; and to the Warden, fellows, and staff of All Souls, which has been more than a second home.

My love and thanks to my parents, Chitra and Anand, for letting me surprise them and surprising me in turn; to my sister, Sveta, for usually taking my side, and to Saana, Simran, and Joe; to my grandmothers, Ammama and Patuma, for wanting more; to my aunt and uncle, Radhi and Ramesh, for refuge; to my cousin Madhu, for solidarity; to Cindy, for unyielding kindness; to Monique, for laughter; to Dick and Mandy Russell, for wild generosity over many years; to my goddaughter Clio, for almost always being in excellent cheer; and to Goose, you are my whole heart.

Friendship is a bewildering miracle. For conversations about this book, and support while writing it, my love and thanks to Alex Cole, Alice Spawls, Ambrogio Cesare-Bianchi, Amrou Al-Kadhi, Camilla Dubini, Cat Normile, Cécile Fabre, Chas Tyler, Christian Nakarado, Clare Birchall, Cressie St. Aubyn, Daniel Rothschild, Danny Grossman, Danny Rubens, Ed Hollingsworth, Eli Schachar, Emma Hogan, Fabienne Hess, Fazeelat Aslam, Fred Wilmot-Smith, Henrik Isackson, Hermione Hoby, Jane Friedman, Joanna Biggs, Jonathan Gingerich, Jonny Yarker, Justin Zaremby, Kate Saunders-Hastings, Liz Chatterjee, Marcel Przymusinski, Mary Wellesley, Matthew Campbell, Matt Knott, Merve Emre, Mirra Vane, Nick Mayer, Osh Jones, Paul Lodge, Philippa Hetherington, Polly Russell, Rob Simpson, Sanja Bogojevic, Steve Rose, Tabitha Goldstaub, Tom Adams, Vikrom Mathur, and Zeynep Pamuk.

Finally, I reserve special love and gratitude—the kind that brings my heart up short—for three people, all of whom were also close readers of the manuscript:

To Paul Myerscough, who hates the cult of the editor, but deserves a cult, and not just for editing this book. Thank you for putting up with how much I love you.

To my fellow traveler on the road to freedom, my brilliant friend, my best friend, Daniela Dover.

ACKNOWLEDGMENTS

To Sophie Smith, who is as much in this book as I am. *I knew that this experience, this writing-on-the-wall before me . . . could not be shared with anyone except the girl who stood so bravely there beside me. This girl said without hesitation, "Go on." It was she really who had the detachment and the integrity of the Pythoness of Delphi. But it was I . . . who was seeing the pictures, who was reading the writing or who was granted the inner vision. Or perhaps in some sense, we were "seeing" it together, for without her, admittedly, I could not have gone on* (H.D.).

Notes

Preface

1. See Judith Butler, *Gender Trouble: Feminism and the Subversion of Identity* (Routledge, 2010 [1990]), p. 10.
2. Simone de Beauvoir, *The Second Sex*, trans. Constance Borde and Sheila Malovany-Chevallier (Vintage, 2011 [1949]), pp. 765–6.
3. For a discussion of some of these recent developments, see Verónica Gago, *Feminist International: How to Change Everything*, trans. Liz Mason-Deese (Verso, 2020).
4. David R. Roediger, *The Wages of Whiteness: Race and the Making of the American Working Class* (Verso, 2007 [1991]), p. x.
5. Bernice Johnson Reagon, "Coalition Politics: Turning the Century" [1981], in *Home Girls: A Black Feminist Anthology*, ed. Barbara Smith (Kitchen Table: Women of Color Press, 1983): 356–68, p. 359.

The Conspiracy Against Men

1. Liz Kelly, Jo Lovett, and Linda Regan, "A gap or a chasm?: Attrition in reported rape cases," Home Office Research Study 293 (2005): http://webarchive.nationalarchives.gov.uk/20100418065544 /homeoffice.gov.uk/rds/pdfs05/hors293.pdf, p. 50. The study, as

well as the National Registry of Exonerations that I go on to discuss, was brought to my attention by Sandra Newman's article "What kind of person makes false rape accusations?," *Quartz* (May 11, 2017): https://qz.com/980766/the-truth-about-false-rape-accusations/. My thanks to Newman for advice on using the Registry.

2. Kelly et al., "A gap or a chasm?," p. 47. The study notes that even the higher 8 percent figure "is considerably lower than the extent of false reporting estimated by police officers interviewed in this study" (ibid., p. xi).

3. Federal Bureau of Investigation, *Crime in the United States 1996, Section II: Crime Index Offenses Reported* (1997): https://ucr.fbi.gov/crime-in-the-u.s/1996/96sec2.pdf, p. 24.

4. Bruce Gross, "False Rape Allegations: An Assault on Justice," *The Forensic Examiner*, vol. 18, no. 1 (2009): 66–70, p. 66; and Kelly et al., "A gap or a chasm?." The Home Office report concluded that a "greater degree of acquaintance between victim and perpetrator decreased the likelihood of cases being designated false" (p. 48). At the same time, several police officers who were interviewed confessed to being personally prone to disbelieving women who knew the alleged perpetrators.

5. Joanna Jolly, "Does India have a problem with false rape claims?," *BBC News* (February 8, 2017): https://www.bbc.co.uk/news/magazine-38796457

6. Indian Ministry of Health and Family Welfare, "National Family Health Survey (NFHS-4)" (2015–2016): https://dhsprogram.com/pubs/pdf/FR339/FR339.pdf, p. 568.

7. Newman, "What kind of person makes false rape, accusations?"

8. In the UK, an estimated 12,000 men between the ages of sixteen and fifty-nine experience rape, attempted rape, or sexual assault by penetration in England and Wales alone every year (Home Office and the Office for National Statistics, "An Overview of Sexual Offending in England and Wales" [2013]: https://www.gov.uk/government/statistics/an-overview-of-sexual-offending-in-england-and-wales). Mass incarceration makes the US the only country in which the rape rate of men may rival that of women (Christopher Glazek, "Raise the Crime Rate," *n+1* [Winter 2012]: https://nplusonemag.com/issue-13/politics/raise-the-crime-rate/; and Jill Filipovic, "Is the US the only country where more men are raped than women?," *Guardian*

[February 21, 2012]: https://www.theguardian.com/commentisfree/cifamerica/2012/feb/21/us-more-men-raped-than-women).

9. "The National Registry of Exonerations," *The National Registry of Exonerations*: https://www.law.umich.edu/special/exoneration/Pages/about.aspx. Reliable estimates of wrongful conviction are hard to come by, as they are typically based on exoneration rates—at best a very loose proxy for wrongful conviction. On the complications of estimating wrongful conviction rates from exoneration data, see Jon B. Gould and Richard A. Leo, "One Hundred Years Later: Wrongful Convictions After a Century of Research," *Journal of Criminal Law and Criminology*, vol. 100, no. 3 (2010): 825–68. For a recent study that estimates the wrongful conviction rate for cases involving sexual assault in the state of Virginia to be as high as 11.6 percent, see Kelly Walsh, Jeanette Hussemann, Abigail Flynn, Jennifer Yahner, and Laura Golian, "Estimating the Prevalence of Wrongful Convictions," *Office of Justice Programs' National Criminal Justice Reference Service* (2017): https://www.ncjrs.gov/pdffiles1/nij/grants/251115.pdf

10. "The National Registry of Exonerations."

11. "Perpetrators of Sexual Violence: Statistics," *RAINN*: https://www.rainn.org/statistics/perpetrators-sexual-violence

12. Samuel R. Gross, Maurice Possley, and Klara Stephens, "Race and Wrongful Convictions in the United States," *National Registry of Exonerations* (2017): http://www.law.umich.edu/special/exoneration/Documents/Race_and_Wrongful_Convictions.pdf, p. iii.

13. Bernadette Rabuy and Daniel Kopf, "Prisons of Poverty: Uncovering the pre-incarceration incomes of the imprisoned," *Prison Policy Initiative* (July 9, 2015): https://www.prisonpolicy.org/reports/income.html

14. Quoted in Mia Bay, "Introduction," in Ida B. Wells, *The Light of Truth*, ed. Mia Bay (Penguin Classics, 2014): xix–xxxi, p. xxv.

15. Ida B. Wells, "A Red Record. Tabulated Statistics and Alleged Causes of Lynchings in the United States, 1892-1893-1894" [1895], in Wells, *The Light of Truth*: 220–312.

16. Sheila Weller, "How Author Timothy Tyson Found the Woman at the Center of the Emmett Till Case," *Vanity Fair* (January 26, 2017): https://www.vanityfair.com/news/2017/01/how-author-timothy-tyson-found-the-woman-at-the-center-of-the-emmett-till-case

17. For discussions of false rape accusations in colonial contexts, see Amirah Inglis, *The White Women's Protection Ordinance: Sexual Anxiety and Politics in Papua* (Chatto and Windus, 1975); Norman Etherington, "Natal's Black Rape Scare of the 1870s," *Journal of Southern African Studies*, vol. 15, no. 1 (1988): 36–53; John Pape, "Black and White: The 'Perils of Sex' in Colonial Zimbabwe," *Journal of Southern African Studies*, vol. 16, no. 4 (1990): 699–720; Vron Ware, *Beyond the Pale: White Women, Racism and History* (Verso, 1992); Jenny Sharpe, *Allegories of Empire: The Figure of Woman in the Colonial Text* (University of Minnesota Press, 1993); Alison Blunt, "Embodying war: British women and domestic defilement in the Indian 'Mutiny,' 1857–8," *Journal of Historical Geography*, vol. 26, no. 3 (2000): 403–28; David M. Anderson, "Sexual Threat and Settler Society: 'Black Perils' in Kenya, *c*. 1907–30," *The Journal of Imperial and Commonwealth History*, vol. 38, no. 1 (2010): 47–74; and David Sheen, "Israel weaponizes rape culture against Palestinians," *The Electronic Intifada* (January 31, 2017): https://electronicintifada.net/content/israel-weaponizes-rape-culture-against-palestinians/19386

18. Black men in the US are seven times more likely to be falsely convicted of murder than white men (Gross et al., "Race and Wrongful Convictions," p. 4). On average, black men are given 20 percent longer sentences than white men for the same crimes (Joe Palazzolo, "Racial Gap in Men's Sentencing," *The Wall Street Journal* (February 14, 2013): https://www.wsj.com/articles/SB10001424127887324432004578304463789858002). Black girls receive more severe sentences when they enter the juvenile justice system than girls of any other race (Kimberlé Williams Crenshaw, Priscilla Ocen, and Jyoti Nanda, "Black Girls Matter: Pushed Out, Overpoliced and Underprotected," *African American Policy Forum* [2015]: https://www.atlanticphilanthropies.org/wp-content/uploads/2015/09/BlackGirlsMatter_Report.pdf, p. 6). Black boys are suspended from school three times more often than white boys, while black girls are suspended six times more often than white girls (ibid., p. 16). In New York City, where black people make up 27 percent of the population, 53.4 percent of all women stopped by the police are black, and 55.7 percent of all men stopped are black (Kimberlé Williams Crenshaw, Andrea J. Ritchie, Rachel Anspach, Rachel Gilmer, and Luke Harris, "Say Her Name: Resisting Police Brutality Against Black Women," *African American Policy Forum* [2015]: https://

www.aapf.org/sayhername, p. 5). Black men are 2.5 times more likely to be killed by police over the course of their lives than are white men, while black women are 1.4 times more likely to be killed by police over the course of their lives than white women (Frank Edwards, Hedwig Lee, and Michael Esposito, "Risk of being killed by police use of force in the United States by age, race–ethnicity, and sex," *Proceedings of the National Academy of Sciences of the United States of America*, vol. 116, no. 34 [2019]: 16,793–8).

19. For a discussion of the phenomenon of black men sympathizing with Brett Kavanaugh, see Jemele Hill, "What the Black Men Who Identify With Brett Kavanaugh Are Missing," *The Atlantic* (October 12, 2018): https://www.theatlantic.com/ideas/archive/2018/10/why-black-men-relate-brett-kavanaugh/572776/

20. Dan A. Turner, "Letter from Brock Turner's Father" (2016), available at: https://www.stanforddaily.com/2016/06/08/the-full-letter-read-by-brock-turners-father-at-his-sentencing-hearing/

21. "Brett Kavanaugh's Opening Statement: Full Transcript," *New York Times* (September 26, 2018): https://www.nytimes.com/2018/09/26/us/politics/read-brett-kavanaughs-complete-opening-statement.html

22. Kate Kelly and David Enrich, "Kavanaugh's Yearbook Page Is 'Horrible, Hurtful' to a Woman It Named," *New York Times* (September 24, 2018): https://www.nytimes.com/2018/09/24/business/brett-kavanaugh-yearbook-renate.html

23. Mollie Hemingway and Carrie Severino, "Christine Blasey Ford's Father Supported Brett Kavanaugh's Confirmation," *The Federalist* (September 12, 2019): https://thefederalist.com/2019/09/12/christine-blasey-fords-father-supported-brett-kavanaughs-confirmation/

24. See for example JoAnn Wypijewski, "What We Don't Talk About When We Talk About #MeToo," *The Nation* (February 22, 2018): https://www.thenation.com/article/archive/what-we-dont-talk-about-when-we-talk-about-metoo/

25. Emily Yoffe, "The Uncomfortable Truth about Campus Rape Policy," *The Atlantic* (September 6, 2017): https://www.theatlantic.com/education/archive/2017/09/the-uncomfortable-truth-about-campus-rape-policy/538974/

26. Shulamith Firestone, *The Dialectic of Sex* (Verso, 2015 [1970]).

27. Angela Y. Davis, *Women, Race & Class* (Penguin Modern Classics, 2019 [1981]), p. 163.

28. Libby Purves, "Indian women need a cultural earthquake," *The Times* (December 31, 2012): https://www.thetimes.co.uk/article/indian-women-need-a-cultural-earthquake-mtgbgxd3mvd

29. On the myth of "unrapeability" as it applies to Native American and First Nations women, see Andrea Smith, *Conquest: Sexual Violence and American Indian Genocide* (South End Press, 2005); Jacki Thompson Rand, *Kiowa Humanity and the Invasion of the State* (University of Nebraska Press, 2008); and Maya Seshia, "Naming Systemic Violence in Winnipeg's Street Sex Trade," *Canadian Journal of Urban Research*, vol. 19, no. 1 (2010): 1–17. For the same phenomenon in South Africa, see Pumla Dineo Gqola, *Rape: A South African Nightmare* (MF Books Joburg, 2015); and Rebecca Helman, "Mapping the unrapeability of white and black womxn," *Agenda: Empowering women for gender equality*, vol. 32, no. 4 (2018): 10–21. For Australia, see Ann McGrath, "'Black Velvet': Aboriginal women and their relations with white men in the Northern Territory 1910–40," in *So Much Hard Work: Women and Prostitution in Australian History*, ed. Kay Daniels (Fontana Books, 1984): 233–97; Greta Bird and Pat O'Malley, "Kooris, Internal Colonialism, and Social Justice," *Social Justice*, vol. 16, no. 3 (1989): 35–50; Larissa Behrendt, "Consent in a (Neo)Colonial Society: Aboriginal Women as Sexual and Legal 'Other,'" *Australian Feminist Studies*, vol. 15, no. 33 (2000): 353–67; and Corrinne Tayce Sullivan, "Indigenous Australian women's colonial sexual intimacies: positioning indigenous women's agency," *Culture, Health & Sexuality*, vol. 20, no. 4 (2018): 397–410. The historian Pamela Scully notes a "curious feature of the historiography: that authors have in general been more concerned with the elusive myths concerning white women as victims of black rapists, than with the ways in which colonialism created conditions that authorised the pervasive rape of black women by white men" (Pamela Scully, "Rape, Race, and Colonial Culture: The Sexual Politics of Identity in the Nineteenth-Century Cape Colony, South Africa," *The American Historical Review*, vol. 100, no. 2 [1995]: 335–59, p. 337).

30. Scully, "Rape, Race, and Colonial Culture," pp. 335ff.

31. Carolyn M. West and Kalimah Johnson, "Sexual Violence in the Lives of African American Women," *National Online Resource Center on Violence Against Women* (2013): https://vawnet.org/sites/default/files/materials/files/2016-09/AR_SVAAWomenRevised.pdf, p. 2.

32. Joanna Bourke, *Rape: A History from 1860 to the Present Day* (Virago, 2007), p. 77.

33. Rebecca Epstein, Jamilia J. Blake, and Thalia González, "Girlhood Interrupted: The Erasure of Black Girls' Childhood," *Georgetown Center on Poverty and Inequality* (2017): https://ssrn.com/abstract=3000695

34. Kimberlé Williams Crenshaw, "I Believe I Can Lie," *The Baffler* (January 17, 2019): https://thebaffler.com/latest/i-believe-i-can-lie-crenshaw

35. In the US, an estimated 41.2 percent of non-Hispanic black women will experience physical violence from an intimate partner during their lifetimes, as compared with 30.5 percent of non-Hispanic white women. The number is 51.7 percent for Native American women and 29.7 percent for Hispanic women (Matthew J. Breiding, Sharon G. Smith, Kathleen C. Basile, Mikel L. Walters, Jieru Chen, and Melissa T. Merrick, "Prevalence and Characteristics of Sexual Violence, Stalking, and Intimate Partner Violence Victimization— National Intimate Partner and Sexual Violence Survey, United States, 2011," *Center for Disease Control and Prevention: Morbidity and Mortality Weekly Report*, vol. 63, no. 8 [2014]: https://www.cdc.gov/mmwr/preview/mmwrhtml/ss6308a1.htm, table 7). Black women in the US are murdered at three times the rate of white women (Emiko Petrosky, Janet M. Blair, Carter J. Betz, Katherine A. Fowler, Shane P.D. Jack, and Bridget H. Lyons, "Racial and Ethnic Differences in Homicides of Adult Women and the Role of Intimate Partner Violence—United States, 2003–2014," *Morbidity and Mortality Weekly Report*, vol. 66, no. 28 [2017]: 741–6, p. 742).

36. Beth E. Richie, *Arrested Justice: Black Women, Violence, and America's Prison Nation* (NYU Press, 2012).

37. Shatema Threadcraft, "North American Necropolitics and Gender: On #BlackLivesMatter and Black Femicide," *South Atlantic Quarterly*, vol. 116, no. 3 (2017): 553–79, p. 574.

38. Ibid., p. 566.

39. Joe Coscarelli, "R. Kelly Faces a #MeToo Reckoning as Time's Up Backs a Protest," *New York Times* (May 1, 2018): https://www.nytimes.com/2018/05/01/arts/music/r-kelly-timesup-metoo-muterkelly.html

40. In *Surviving R. Kelly*, Chance the Rapper, one of Kelly's musical collaborators, admitted that he hadn't credited the accusers' stories "because they were black women." ("Chance the Rapper

Apologizes for Working With R. Kelly," *NBC Chicago* (January 8, 2019): https://www.nbcchicago.com/news/local/Chance-the-Rapper -Apologizes-for-Working-With-R-Kelly-504063131.html)

41. Alan Blinder, "Was That Ralph Northam in Blackface? An Inquiry Ends Without Answers," *New York Times* (May 22, 2019): https:// www.nytimes.com/2019/05/22/us/ralph-northam-blackface -photo.html

42. "Virginia's Justin Fairfax Compared Himself To Lynching Victims In An Impromptu Address," *YouTube* (February 25, 2019): https://www .youtube.com/watch?v=ZTaTssa2d8E

43. Anubha Bhonsle, "Indian Army, Rape Us," *Outlook* (February 10, 2016): https://www.outlookindia.com/website/story/indian -army-rape-us/296634. My thanks to Durba Mitra for drawing this case, and its extraordinary aftermath, to my attention.

44. On the role of the low-caste, "sexually deviant" women in the social formation of colonial and post-colonial India, see Durba Mitra, *Indian Sex Life: Sexuality and the Colonial Origins of Modern Social Thought* (Princeton University Press, 2020).

45. "Hathras case: A woman repeatedly reported rape. Why are police denying it?," *BBC News* (October 10, 2020): https://www.bbc.co.uk /news/world-asia-india-54444939

46. Adrija Bose, "'Why Should I be Punished?': Punita Devi, Wife of Nirbhaya Convict, Fears Future of 'Shame,'" *News 18* (March 19, 2020): https://www.news18.com/news/buzz/why-should-i-be -punished-punita-devi-wife-of-nirbhaya-convict-fears-future-of -shame-delhi-gangrape-2543091.html

47. Ibid. On the Indian feminist (largely carceral) response to Singh's gang rape, and the criticism it has received from Marxist femi- nists, see Prabha Kotiswaran, "Governance Feminism in the Postcolony: Reforming India's Rape Laws," in Janet Halley, Prabha Kotiswaran, Rachel Rebouché, and Hila Shamir, *Governance Feminism: An Introduction* (University of Minnesota Press, 2018): 75– 148. For a critique of carceral responses to sexual violence, see "Sex, Carceralism, Capitalism" (this volume).

48. Claudia Jones, "An End to the Neglect of the Problems of the Negro Woman!" [1949], in *Claudia Jones: Beyond Containment*, ed. Carole Boyce Davies (Ayebia Clarke Publishing, 2011): 74–86; Frances M. Beal, "Double Jeopardy: To Be Black and Female" [1969], *Meridians: feminism, race, transnationalism*, vol. 8, no. 2 (2008): 166–76;

NOTES TO PAGES 18-19

Enriqueta Longeaux y Vásquez, "The Mexican-American Woman," in *Sisterhood is Powerful: An Anthology of Writings from the Women's Liberation Movement*, ed. Robin Morgan (Vintage, 1970): 379–84; Selma James, *Sex, Race and Class* (Falling Wall Press, 1975); The Combahee River Collective, "A Black Feminist Statement" [1977], in *Home Girls: A Black Feminist Anthology*, ed. Barbara Smith (Kitchen Table: Women of Color Press, 1983): 272–92; Lorraine Bethel and Barbara Smith, eds., *Conditions: Five: The Black Women's Issue* (1979); Davis, *Women, Race & Class*; Cherríe Moraga and Gloria E. Anzaldúa, eds., *This Bridge Called My Back: Writings by Radical Women of Color* (Persephone Press, 1981); bell hooks, *Ain't I a Woman? Black women and feminism* (South End Press, 1981); bell hooks, *Feminist Theory: From Margin to Center* (Routledge, 1984); and Kimberlé Crenshaw, "Demarginalizing the Intersection of Race and Sex: A Black Feminist Critique of Antidiscrimination Doctrine, Feminist Theory and Antiracist Politics," *University of Chicago Legal Forum*, vol. 1989, no. 1 (1989): 139–67.

49. For an elaboration of this phenomenon see "Sex, Carceralism, Capitalism" (this volume).

50. Ida B. Wells, "Southern Horrors: Lynch Law in All Its Phases" [1892], in *Southern Horrors and Other Writings: The Anti-Lynching Campaign of Ida B. Wells, 1892–1900*, ed. Jacqueline Jones Royster (Bedford Books, 1997): 49–72, p. 59.

51. Jia Tolentino, "Jian Ghomeshi, John Hockenberry, and the Laws of Patriarchal Physics," *New Yorker* (September 17, 2018): https://www.newyorker.com/culture/cultural-comment/jian-ghomeshi-john-hockenberry-and-the-laws-of-patriarchal-physics

52. Patrick Smith and Amber Jamieson, "Louis C.K. Mocks Parkland Shooting Survivors, Asian Men, And Nonbinary Teens In Leaked Audio," *BuzzFeed News* (December 31, 2018): https://www.buzzfeednews.com/article/patricksmith/louis-ck-mocks-parkland-shooting-survivors-asian-men-and

53. Meanwhile, the only TV show to take direct action in response to C.K.'s behavior, Tig Notaro and Diablo Cody's brilliant and moving *One Mississippi*, on which C.K. had worked as an executive producer, was canceled by Amazon after two seasons.

54. Glenn Whipp, "A year after #MeToo upended the status quo, the accused are attempting comebacks—but not offering apologies," *Los Angeles Times* (October 5, 2018): https://www.latimes.com

/entertainment/la-ca-mn-me-too-men-apology-20181005-story
.html

55. John Hockenberry, "Exile," *Harper's* (October 2018): https://harpers
.org/archive/2018/10/exile-4/

56. Kevin Spacey (@KevinSpacey), *Twitter* (October 30, 2017): https://
twitter.com/KevinSpacey/status/924848412842971136

57. Kevin Spacey, "Let Me Be Frank," *YouTube* (December 24, 2018):
www.youtube.com/watch?v=JZveA-NAIDI

58. Michelle Goldberg, "The Shame of the MeToo Men," *New York Times*
(14 September 2018): https://www.nytimes.com/2018/09/14/opinion
/columnists/metoo-movement-franken-hockenberry-macdonald
.html

59. Catharine A. MacKinnon, *Toward a Feminist Theory of the State* (Harvard
University Press, 1991 [1989]), p. 180.

60. *R v. Cogan and Leak* (1976) QB 217.

61. Leak was convicted of aiding and abetting rape, though, from the
perspective of the law, no rape had been attempted or occurred. He
wasn't charged with raping his wife: the "marital rape exception" was
overturned by the House of Lords only in 1991.

62. Melena Ryzik, Cara Buckley, and Jodi Kantor, "Louis C.K. Is Accused
by 5 Women of Sexual Misconduct," *New York Times* (November 9,
2017): https://www.nytimes.com/2017/11/09/arts/television/louis
-ck-sexual-misconduct.html

63. "The Reckoning: Women and Power in the Workplace," *New York Times
Magazine* (December 13, 2017): https://www.nytimes.com/interac
tive/2017/12/13/magazine/the-reckoning-women-and-power-in
-the-workplace.html

64. In 2018, Ian Buruma, who had recently been appointed editor of the
New York Review of Books, published a personal essay by Jian Ghomeshi
("Reflections from a Hashtag," *New York Review of Books* [October
11, 2018]: https://www.nybooks.com/articles/2018/10/11/reflec
tions-hashtag/), who had been fired from CBC Radio in 2014 after
being accused of sexual assault by several women. The piece was
a garbled self-exoneration, which neglected to mention that the
charges brought by one of the women were dropped only after
Ghomeshi agreed to apologize to her. Feminists, including me,
tweeted their distaste for Buruma's decision to publish Ghomeshi.
Soon after, Buruma was forced out of his job. The *New York Times*

story on the firing included a screen-grab of my tweet. I felt uneasy. On one hand, I thought that Buruma had exercised poor editorial judgment, and from what I heard and was later reported, had imposed his will over the dissent of his staff, some of whom were senior women who had worked at the magazine for a long time. I hope this is why he was forced out: by his own staff, for being a bad editor and a dictatorial boss. But what if he had been made to resign, as Buruma himself claims, merely because a "social media mob" (of which I was a part) had forced the hand of the *NYRB*'s board? That an editor provokes the fury of people on Twitter isn't a good reason to fire him, even if that fury is justified. Not pissing people off on social media isn't part of what it is to be a good editor, any more than it's part of being a good academic. Feminists, who piss off a great deal of people, should be the first to insist that institutions dedicated to truth-seeking—literary magazines, universities—shouldn't depend for their existence on public approbation.

65. Complaint, *Bonsu v. University of Massachusetts—Amherst*, Civil Action No. 3:15-cv-30172-MGM (District of Massachusetts, September 25, 2015), p. 9.

66. Yoffe, "The Uncomfortable Truth."

67. Complaint, *Bonsu v. Univ. of Mass.*, p. 10.

68. Ibid.

69. Massachusetts is one of the US states that continues to define rape in terms of force and threat, rather than in terms of consent ("affirmative" or not); rape is thus "sexual intercourse or unnatural sexual intercourse with a person" where the perpetrator "compels such person to submit by force and against his will, or compels such person to submit by threat of bodily injury." See Mass. Gen. Law 265, §22.

70. Yoffe, "The Uncomfortable Truth."

71. Jacob Gersen and Jeannie Suk, "The Sex Bureaucracy," *California Law Review*, vol. 104, no. 4 (2016): 881–948. See also Janet Halley, "Trading the Megaphone for the Gavel in Title IX Enforcement," *Harvard Law Review Forum*, vol. 128 (2015): 103–17; Janet Halley, "The Move to Affirmative Consent," *Signs*, vol. 42, no. 1 (2016): 257–79; Laura Kipnis, *Unwanted Advances: Sexual Paranoia Comes to Campus* (HarperCollins, 2017); Elizabeth Bartholet, Nancy Gertner, Janet Halley, and Jeannie Suk Gersen, "Fairness For All Students Under Title IX," *Digital Access to Scholarship at Harvard* (August 21, 2017): http://

nrs.harvard.edu/urn-3:HUL.InstRepos:33789434; and Wesley
Yang, "The Revolt of the Feminist Law Profs: Jeannie Suk Gersen
and the fight to save Title IX from itself," *The Chronicle of Higher
Education* (August 7, 2019): https://www.chronicle.com/article
/the-revolt-of-the-feminist-law-profs/

72. Gersen and Suk, "The Sex Bureaucracy," p. 946, emphasis mine.

73. Ruth Bader Ginsburg said that the "criticism of some college
codes of conduct for not giving the accused person a fair opportunity to be heard" was correct, and that "everyone deserves a fair
hearing" (Jeffrey Rosen, "Ruth Bader Ginsburg Opens Up About
#MeToo, Voting Rights, and Millennials," *The Atlantic* (15 February
2018): https://www.theatlantic.com/politics/archive/2018/02
/ruth-bader-ginsburg-opens-up-about-metoo-voting-rights-and-mil
lenials/553409/).

74. Gersen and Suk, "The Sex Bureaucracy," p. 946.

75. In "Rape Redefined," MacKinnon writes that "gender belongs on the
list of inequalities that, when drawn upon as a form of power and
used as a form of coercion in sexual interactions, make sex rape"
(Catharine A. MacKinnon, "Rape Redefined," *Harvard Law & Policy
Review*, vol. 10, no. 2 (2016): 431–77, p. 469).

76. Cal. Educ. Code §67386. On the role that Jerry Brown played in
the growth of mass incarceration in California, see Ruth Wilson
Gilmore, *Golden Gulag: Prisons, Surplus, Crisis, and Opposition in
Globalizing California* (University of California Press, 2007).

77. Ezra Klein, "'Yes Means Yes' is a terrible law, and I completely support it," *Vox* (13 October 2014): https://www.vox.com/2014/10
/13/6966847/yes-means-yes-is-a-terrible-bill-and-i-completely
-support-it

78. MacKinnon, "Rape Redefined," p. 454. For related discussion of the
limits of the consent paradigm, see Linda Martín Alcoff, *Rape and
Resistance* (Polity, 2018); and Joseph J. Fischel, *Screw Consent: A Better
Politics of Sexual Justice* (University of California Press, 2019).

79. New Jersey: "In order to establish effective consent by the putative
victim of a sexual assault, a defendant must demonstrate the presence
of 'affirmative and freely-given permission . . .'" (*State v. Cuni*, 733
A.2d 414, 159 N.J. 584 [1999], p. 424). Oklahoma: "The term 'consent' means the affirmative, unambiguous and voluntary agreement to
engage in a specific sexual activity during a sexual encounter which can
be revoked at any time." (Okla. Stat. 21 §113). Wisconsin: "'Consent'

NOTES TO PAGES 30–35

means words or overt actions by a person who is competent to give informed consent indicating a freely given agreement to have sexual intercourse or sexual contact" (Wis. Stat. § 940.225[4]).

80. Complaint, *Bonsu v. Univ. of Mass.*, p. 10.
81. Tolentino, "Jian Ghomeshi, John Hockenberry, and the Laws of Patriarchal Physics."
82. Jian Ghomeshi, "Reflections from a Hashtag."
83. Goldberg, "The Shame of the MeToo Men."

Talking to My Students About Porn

1. Its actual, rather less racy, title was "The Scholar and the Feminist IX: Towards a Politics of Sexuality."
2. *Diary of a Conference on Sexuality* (1982), available at: http://www .darkmatterarchives.net/wp-content/uploads/2011/12/Diary-of-a -Conference-on-Sexuality.pdf, p. 38.
3. Lorna Norman Bracewell, "Beyond Barnard: Liberalism, Antipornography Feminism, and the Sex Wars," *Signs*, vol. 42, no. 1 (2016): 23–48, p. 23.
4. *Diary of a Conference on Sexuality*, p. 72.
5. Alice Echols, "Retrospective: Tangled Up in Pleasure and Danger," *Signs*, vol. 42, no. 1 (2016): 11–22, p. 12.
6. Rachel Corbman, "The Scholars and the Feminists: The Barnard Sex Conference and the History of the Institutionalization of Feminism," *Feminist Formations*, vol. 27, no. 3 (2015): 49–80, p. 59.
7. Coalition for a Feminist Sexuality and against Sadomasochism, [The Barnard Leaflet], reproduced in *Feminist Studies*, vol. 9, no. 1 (1983): 180–2.
8. *Diary of a Conference on Sexuality*, p. 72.
9. Gayle Rubin, "Blood Under the Bridge: Reflections on 'Thinking Sex,'" *GLQ: A Journal of Lesbian and Gay Studies*, vol. 17, no. 1 (2011): 15–48, pp. 26–7.
10. Elizabeth Wilson, "The Context of 'Between Pleasure and Danger': The Barnard Conference on Sexuality," *Feminist Review*, vol. 13, no. 1 (1983): 35–41, p. 40.
11. Ibid., p. 35.
12. Rubin, "Blood Under the Bridge," p. 34.
13. See for example Sheila Jeffreys, "Let us be free to debate transgenderism without being accused of 'hate speech,'" *Guardian* (May 29,

2012): https://www.theguardian.com/commentisfree/2012/may /29/transgenderism-hate-speech

14. Rubin, "Blood Under the Bridge," p. 16.

15. Ubiquitous and instantaneous, that is, for about half of the world's population. The other half do not have internet access. China and India, in absolute terms, have the world's highest number of internet users, but only 54 percent and 30 percent of their populations, respectively, are online. In Afghanistan, that number is 10 percent. In the Democratic Republic of Congo, it is 6 percent (Max Roser, Hannah Ritchie, and Esteban Ortiz-Ospina, "Internet," *Our World in Data* (2017): https://ourworldindata.org/internet).

16. Alice Echols, *Daring to Be Bad: Radical Feminism in America 1967–1975* (University of Minnesota Press, 2011 [1989]), p. 361 fn. 7; Bracewell, "Beyond Barnard," pp. 29–30 fn. 19; and Robin Morgan, "Goodbye to All That" [1970], in *The Sixties Papers: Documents of a Rebellious Decade*, ed. Judith Clavir Albert and Stewart Edward Albert (Praeger, 1984): 509–16.

17. Andrea Dworkin, "Suffering and Speech," in *In Harm's Way: The Pornography Civil Rights Hearings*, ed. Catharine A. MacKinnon and Andrea Dworkin (Harvard University Press, 1997): 25–36, p. 28; and Bracewell, "Beyond Barnard," pp. 28–30.

18. Robin Morgan, "Theory and Practice: Pornography and Rape" [1974], in *Take Back the Night: Women on Pornography*, ed. Laura Lederer (William Morrow and Company, 1980): 134–47, p. 139.

19. Rubin, "Blood Under the Bridge," pp. 29–30.

20. Georgia Dullea, "In Feminists' Antipornography Drive, 42d Street Is the Target," *New York Times* (July 6, 1979): https://www.nytimes .com/1979/07/06/archives/in-feminists-antipornography-drive -42d-street-is-the-target.html

21. Ibid.

22. Morgan, "Theory and Practice," p. 139.

23. Catharine A. MacKinnon, *Only Words* (Harvard University Press, 1996 [1993]), pp. 21–2.

24. As quoted in Patricia Hill Collins, *Black Feminist Thought* (Routledge, 1991 [1990]), p. 168.

25. Ibid., pp. 167–8.

26. Ann Snitow, Christine Stansell, and Sharon Thompson, eds., *Powers of Desire: The Politics of Sexuality* (Monthly Review Press, 1983), p. 460.

This quotation comes from a prefatory note by the editors at the start of Ellen Willis's essay "Feminism, Moralism, and Pornography."

27. MacKinnon, *Only Words,* pp. 19–20.

28. Michael Castleman, "Surprising New Data from the World's Most Popular Porn Site," *Psychology Today* (March 15, 2018): https://www .psychologytoday.com/us/blog/all-about-sex/201803/surprising -new-data-the-world-s-most-popular-porn-site

29. Gert Martin Hald, Neil M. Malamuth, and Carlin Yuen, "Pornography and Attitudes Supporting Violence Against Women: Revisiting the Relationship in Nonexperimental Studies," *Aggressive Behavior,* vol. 36, no. 1 (2010): 14–20, p. 18.

30. Ibid.

31. Paul J. Wright and Michelle Funk, "Pornography Consumption and Opposition to Affirmative Action for Women: A Prospective Study," *Psychology of Women Quarterly,* vol. 38, no. 2 (2014): 208–21.

32. Elizabeth Oddone-Paolucci, Mark Genius, and Claudio Violato, "A Meta-Analysis of the Published Research on the Effects of Pornography," in *The Changing Family and Child Development* (Ashgate, 2000): 48–59.

33. Neil M. Malamuth, Tamara Addison, and Mary Koss, "Pornography and Sexual Aggression: Are There Reliable Effects and Can We Understand Them?," *Annual Review of Sex Research,* vol. 11, no. 1 (2000): 26–91.

34. Joetta L. Carr and Karen M. VanDeusen, "Risk Factors for Male Sexual Aggression on College Campuses," *Journal of Family Violence,* vol. 19, no. 5 (2004): 279–89.

35. Matthew W. Brosi, John D. Foubert, R. Sean Bannon, and Gabriel Yandell, "Effects of Sorority Members' Pornography Use on Bystander Intervention in a Sexual Assault Situation and Rape Myth Acceptance," *Oracle: The Research Journal of the Association of Fraternity /Sorority Advisors,* vol. 6, no. 2 (2011): 26–35.

36. "Study exposes secret world of porn addiction," *University of Sydney* (May 10, 2012): http://sydney.edu.au/news/84.html?newscategory id=1&newsstoryid=9176

37. Gustavo S. Mesch, "Social Bonds and Internet Pornographic Exposure Among Adolescents," *Journal of Adolescence,* vol. 32, no. 3 (2009): 601–18.

38. Jon Ronson, "The Butterfly Effect," *Audible* (2017): www.jonronson .com/butterfly.html, episode 4: "Children."

39. Maddy Coy, Liz Kelly, Fiona Elvines, Maria Garner, and Ava Kanyeredzi, "'Sex without consent, I suppose that is rape': How Young People in England Understand Sexual Consent," *Office of the Children's Commissioner* (2013): https://www.childrenscommissioner .gov.uk/report/sex-without-consent-i-suppose-that-is-rape/. Rae Langton discusses this study and its implications for the feminist porn debate in "Is Pornography Like The Law?," in *Beyond Speech: Pornography and Analytic Feminist Philosophy*, ed. Mari Mikkola (Oxford University Press, 2017): 23–38.

40. Rae Langton, "Speech Acts and Unspeakable Acts," *Philosophy and Public Affairs*, vol. 22, no. 4 (1993): 293–330, p. 311.

41. Stoya, "Feminism and Me," *Vice* (August 15, 2013): https://www.vice .com/en/article/bn5gmz/stoya-feminism-and-me

42. Stoya, "Can There Be Good Porn?," *New York Times* (March 4, 2018): https://www.nytimes.com/2018/03/04/opinion/stoya-good -porn.html

43. Peggy Orenstein, *Girls & Sex: Navigating the Complicated New Landscape* (One World, 2016), pp. 7–8.

44. In a large study of straight US undergraduates conducted between 2005 and 2008, researchers found that in first-time hookups involving oral sex, men alone received in 55 percent of cases; women, meanwhile, received oral sex alone in just 19 percent of such cases. The researchers also found that in first-time hookups, three times as many men as women reached orgasm; that gap narrows but does not close in relationships, where women undergraduates experience orgasm 79 percent as often as their male partners (Elizabeth A. Armstrong, Paula England, and Alison C. K. Fogarty, "Orgasm in College Hookups and Relationships," in *Families as They Really Are*, 2nd edition, ed. Barbara J. Risman and Virginia E. Rutter (W. W. Norton, 2015), pp. 280–96).

45. Nancy Bauer, "Pornutopia," *n+1* (Winter 2007): https://nplusone mag.com/issue-5/essays/pornutopia/

46. Part of that interview appears in Polly Russell's "Unfinished Business" podcast series (*British Library* [2020]: https://www.bl.uk/podcasts, series 2, episode 2: "The Politics of Pleasure").

47. Zoë Heller, "'Hot' Sex & Young Girls," *New York Review of Books* (August 18, 2016): https://www.nybooks.com/articles/2016/08/18/hot-sex -young-girls/

48. Vincent Canby, "What Are We To Think of 'Deep Throat'?," *New York Times* (January 21, 1973): https://www.nytimes.com/1973/01/21/archives/what-are-we-to-think-of-deep-throat-what-to-think-of-deep-throat.html

49. Stuart Taylor Jr., "Pornography Foes Lose New Weapon in Supreme Court," *New York Times* (February 25, 1986): https://www.nytimes.com/1986/02/25/us/pornography-foes-lose-new-weapon-in-supreme-court.html, emphasis mine.

50. *R.A.V. v. City of St. Paul, Minnesota*, 505 U.S. 377 (1992).

51. St. Paul Bias-Motivated Crime Ordinance, St. Paul, Minn. Legis. Code § 292.02 (1990).

52. MacKinnon, *Only Words*, p. 12.

53. *R. v. Butler* (1992) 1 S.C.R. 452.

54. MacKinnon, *Only Words*, p. 103.

55. *R v. Scythes* (1993) OJ 537. See Becki L. Ross, "'It's Merely Designed for Sexual Arousal': Interrogating the Indefensibility of Lesbian Smut" [1997], in *Feminism and Pornography*, ed. Drucilla Cornell (Oxford University Press, 2007 [2000]): 264–317, pp. 264ff. For a qualified defense of *Butler*, see Ann Scales, "Avoiding Constitutional Depression: Bad Attitudes and the Fate of *Butler*" [1994], in *Feminism and Pornography*, ed. Drucilla Cornell (Oxford University Press, 2007 [2000]): 318–44.

56. Jeffrey Toobin, "X-Rated," *New Yorker* (October 3, 1994): pp. 70–8.

57. Ellen Willis, "Feminism, Moralism, and Pornography" [1979], in *Powers of Desire: The Politics of Sexuality*, ed. Ann Snitow, Christine Stansell, and Sharon Thompson (Monthly Review Press, 1983): 460–7, p. 464.

58. Bracewell, "Beyond Barnard," p. 35 fn. 29.

59. "Attorney General's Commission on Pornography: Final Report," *U.S. Department of Justice* (1986), vol. 1, p. 78.

60. Morgan, "Theory and Practice," p. 137.

61. Christopher Hooton, "A long list of sex acts just got banned in UK porn," *Independent* (December 2, 2014): https://www.independent.co.uk/news/uk/a-long-list-of-sex-acts-just-got-banned-in-uk-porn-9897174.html

62. Frankie Miren, "British BDSM Enthusiasts Say Goodbye to Their Favorite Homegrown Porn," *Vice* (December 1, 2014): https://www.vice.com/en_uk/article/nnqybz/the-end-of-uk-bdsm-282

63. Tracy McVeigh, "Can Iceland lead the way towards a ban on violent online pornography?," *Observer* (February 16, 2013): https://www.theguardian.com/world/2013/feb/16/iceland-online-pornography

64. Katrien Jacobs, "Internationalizing Porn Studies," *Porn Studies*, vol. 1, no. 1–2 (2014): 114–19, p. 117.

65. "UK's controversial 'porn blocker' plan dropped," *BBC News* (October 16, 2019): https://www.bbc.co.uk/news/technology-50073102

66. Tom Crewe, "The p-p-porn ban," *London Review of Books* (April 4, 2019): https://www.lrb.co.uk/the-paper/v41/n07/tom-crewe/short-cuts

67. Ryan Thorneycroft, "If not a fist, then what about a stump? Ableism and heteronormativity within Australia's porn regulations," *Porn Studies*, vol. 7, no. 2 (2020): 152–67.

68. Anirban K. Baishya and Darshana S. Mini, "Translating Porn Studies: Lessons from the Vernacular," *Porn Studies*, vol. 7, no. 1 (2020): 2–12, p. 3.

69. Pornhub Insights, "The 2019 Year in Review," *Pornhub* (December 11, 2019): www.pornhub.com/insights/2019-year-in-review

70. Joe Pinsker, "The Hidden Economics of Porn," *The Atlantic* (April 4, 2016): https://www.theatlantic.com/business/archive/2016/04/pornography-industry-economics-tarrant/476580/

71. Jon Millward, "Deep Inside: A Study of 10,000 Porn Stars and Their Careers," *Jon Millward: Data Journalist* (February 14, 2013): https://jonmillward.com/blog/studies/deep-inside-a-study-of-10000-porn-stars/; and Shira Tarrant, *The Pornography Industry: What Everyone Needs to Know* (Oxford University Press, 2016), p. 51.

72. Gabrielle Drolet, "The Year Sex Work Came Home," *New York Times* (April 10, 2020): https://www.nytimes.com/2020/04/10/style/camsoda-onlyfans-streaming-sex-coronavirus.html

73. Blake Montgomery (@blakersdozen), *Twitter* (March 31, 2020): https://twitter.com/blakersdozen/status/1245072167689060353

74. Nana Baah, "This Adult Site Is Offering Ex-McDonald's Employees Camming Work," *Vice* (March 24, 2020): https://www.vice.com/en_uk/article/dygjvm/mcdonalds-workers-coronavirus-employment

75. "SRE—the evidence," *Sex Education Forum* (January 1, 2015): http://www.sexeducationforum.org.uk/resources/evidence/sre-evidence

76. "Statutory RSE: Are teachers in England prepared?," *Sex Education Forum* (2018): https://www.sexeducationforum.org.uk/resources /evidence/statutory-rse-are-teachers-england-prepared

77. "Give parents the right to opt their child out of Relationship and Sex Education," *Petitions: UK Government and Parliament* (2019): https:// petition.parliament.uk/petitions/235053

78. "Sex and HIV Education," *Guttmacher Institute* (January 1, 2021): https:// www.guttmacher.org/state-policy/explore/sex-and-hiv-education

79. "Abstinence Education Programs: Definition, Funding, and Impact on Teen Sexual Behavior," *Kaiser Family Foundation* (June 1, 2018): https:// www.kff.org/womens-health-policy/fact-sheet/abstinence-education -programs-definition-funding-and-impact-on-teen-sexual-behavior/

80. "SRE—the evidence," *Sex Education Forum* (January 1, 2015): http:// www.sexeducationforum.org.uk/resources/evidence/sre-evidence

81. "International technical guidance on sexuality education," *United National Educational, Scientific and Cultural Organization (UNESCO)*, rev. ed. (2018): https://www.unaids.org/sites/default/files/media _asset/ITGSE_en.pdf, p. 23.

82. Laura Mulvey, "Visual Pleasure and Narrative Cinema," *Screen*, vol. 16, no. 3 (1975): 6–18, p. 12.

83. Quoted in Linda Williams, *Hard Core: Power, Pleasure, and the "Frenzy of the Visible"* (University of California Press, 1999 [1989]), p. 93.

84. Quoted in ibid., p. 291.

85. Willis, "Feminism, Moralism, and Pornography," p. 464.

86. See Parveen Adams, "Per Os(cillation)," *Camera Obscura*, vol. 6, no. 2 (1988): 7–29.

87. Jennifer C. Nash, "Strange Bedfellows: Black Feminism and Antipornography Feminism," *Social Text*, vol. 26, no. 4 (2008): 51– 76, p. 67. See also Jennifer C. Nash, *The Black Body in Ecstasy: Reading Race, Reading Pornography* (Duke University Press, 2014).

88. Leslie Green, "Pornographies," *Journal of Political Philosophy*, vol. 8, no. 1 (2000): 27–52, p. 47.

89. Pornhub Insights, "2017 Year in Review," *Pornhub* (January 9, 2018): https://www.pornhub.com/insights/2017-year-in-review

90. Pinsker, "The Hidden Economics of Porn."

91. Candida Royalle, "Porn in the USA" [1993], in *Feminism and Pornography*, ed. Drucilla Cornell (Oxford University Press, 2007 [2000]): 540– 50, p. 547.

92. Marianna Manson and Erika Lust, "Feminist Porn Pioneer Erika Lust on the Cultural Cornerstones of Her Career," *Phoenix* (May 31, 2018): https://www.phoenixmag.co.uk/article/feminist-porn-pio neer-erika-lust-on-the-cultural-cornerstones-of-her-career/

93. Japanese law requires that all genitalia be pixelated in porn, one of the unintended effects of which has been the proliferation of hardcore and aggressive forms of pornography; rape porn and animated child porn are legal.

94. Alexandra Hambleton, "When Women Watch: The Subversive Potential of Female-Friendly Pornography in Japan," *Porn Studies*, vol. 3, no. 4 (2016): 427–42.

95. Andrea Dworkin, *Intercourse* (Basic Books, 2007 [1987]), pp. 60–1.

The Right to Sex

1. Catharine A. MacKinnon, "Sexuality, Pornography, and Method: 'Pleasure under Patriarchy,'" *Ethics*, vol. 99, no. 2 (1989): 314–46, pp. 319–320.

2. Ibid., p. 324.

3. Quoted in Alice Echols, *Daring to Be Bad: Radical Feminism in America 1967–1975* (University of Minnesota Press, 2011 [1989]), p. 171. Emphasis mine.

4. Valerie Solanas, *SCUM Manifesto* (Verso, 2015 [1967]), p. 61.

5. Quoted in Echols, *Daring to be Bad*, p. 164.

6. Ibid., chapter 4.

7. "Redstockings Manifesto" [1969], in *Sisterhood is Powerful: An Anthology of Writings from the Women's Liberation Movement*, ed. Robin Morgan (Vintage, 1970): 533–6, p. 534.

8. Echols, *Daring to be Bad*, p. 146.

9. Ibid.

10. Ibid., p. 213. The woman was the important lesbian feminist and organizer Rita Mae Brown.

11. Ibid., p. 232.

12. Sheila Jeffreys, "The Need for Revolutionary Feminism," *Scarlet Woman*, issue 5 (1977): 10–12.

13. Ibid., p. 11.

14. Jeska Rees, "A Look Back at Anger: the Women's Liberation Movement in 1978," *Women's History Review*, vol. 19, no. 3 (2010): 337–56, p. 347.

15. For discussions of the history of the BritishWLM, see Beverley Bryan, Stella Dadzie, and Suzanne Scafe, *The Heart of the Race: Black Women's Lives in Britain* (Virago, 1985); Anna Coote and Beatrix Campbell, *Sweet Freedom: The Struggle for Women's Liberation* (Picador, 1982); Michelene Wandor, *Once a Feminist: Stories of a Generation* (Virago, 1990); Jeska Rees, "A Look Back at Anger"; Martin Pugh, *Women and the Women's Movement in Britain since 1914* (Palgrave, 2015 [1992]); Margaretta Jolly, *Sisterhood and After: An Oral History of the UK Women's Liberation Movement, 1968–present* (Oxford University Press, 2019).

16. Ellen Willis, "Lust Horizons: Is the Women's Movement Pro-Sex?" [1981], in *No More Nice Girls: Countercultural Essays* (University of Minnesota Press, 2012 [1992]): 3–14, pp. 6–7.

17. On sexual racism among gay and bisexual men, see Denton Callander, Martin Holt, and Christy E. Newman, "Just a Preference: Racialised Language in the Sex-Seeking Profiles of Gay and Bisexual men," *Culture, Health & Sexuality*, vol. 14, no. 9 (2012): 1,049–63; and Denton Callander, Christy E. Newman, and Martin Holt, "Is Sexual Racism *Really* Racism? Distinguishing Attitudes Towards Sexual Racism and Generic Racism Among Gay and Bisexual Men," *Archives of Sexual Behavior*, vol. 14, no.7 (2015): 1,991–2,000. On sexual racism among gay men, and how it compares with the (much rarer) phenomenon of sexual racism among gay women, see Russell K. Robinson and David M. Frost, "LGBT Equality and Sexual Racism," *Fordham Law Review*, vol. 86, issue 6 (2018): 2,739–54. Robinson and Frost point to ways in which sexual racism extends beyond mere partner preference: "A man of color may be deemed desirable only insofar as he adheres to sexualized racial stereotypes . . . gay men of various races use race as a proxy to label a man as a 'top' or a 'bottom.' Black men are expected to embody the insertive or 'top' role (which is associated with masculinity) while Asian men are expected to assume the receptive or 'bottom' role (which is regarded as relatively feminine). White men, by contrast, are permitted to assume the role of their choice—top, bottom, or versatile—without being constrained by racial stereotypes" ("LGBT Equality and Sexual Racism," p. 2,745).

18. A trans philosopher I know objected to me that, for them, using Grindr and other dating apps has been a sexually and romantically liberating experience, opening up possibilities for new attractions and attachments.

19. Judith N. Shklar, "The Liberalism of Fear," in *Liberalism and the Moral Life*, ed. Nancy L. Rosenblum (Harvard University Press, 1989): 21–38.

20. Rebecca Solnit, "Men Explain *Lolita* to Me," *Literary Hub* (December 17, 2015): https://lithub.com/men-explain-lolita-to-me/

21. Quoted in Jonathan Beecher, "Parody and Liberation in *The New Amorous World* of Charles Fourier," *History Workshop Journal*, vol. 20, no. 1 (1985): 125–33, p. 127. See also Jonathan Beecher, *Charles Fourier: The Visionary and His World* (University of California Press, 1986), chapter 15.

22. Andrea Long Chu, "On Liking Women," *n+1* (Winter 2018): https://nplusonemag.com/issue-30/essays/on-liking-women/

23. Ibid.

24. Lindy West, *Shrill: Notes from a Loud Woman* (Quercus, 2016), pp. 76–7.

25. For related discussion, see Ann J. Cahill, "Sexual Desire, Inequality, and the Possibility of Transformation," in *Body Aesthetics*, ed. Sherri Irvin (Oxford University Press, 2016): 281–91; Sonu Bedi, "Sexual Racism: Intimacy as a Matter of Justice," *The Journal of Politics*, vol. 77, no. 4 (2015): 998–1,011; Robin Zheng, "Why Yellow Fever Isn't Flattering: A Case Against Racial Fetishes," *Journal of the American Philosophical Association*, vol. 2, no. 3 (2016): 400–19; and Uku Tooming, "Active Desire," *Philosophical Psychology*, vol. 32, no. 6 (2019): 945–68.

26. A version of this essay was originally published in the *London Review of Books*, vol. 40, no. 6 (March 22, 2018). My thanks to the editors of the *LRB* for permission to reprint the essay here in revised form.

Coda: The Politics of Desire

1. Kate Manne (@kate_manne), *Twitter* (August 25, 2018): https://twitter.com/kate_manne/status/1033420304830349314

2. Adrienne Rich, "Compulsory Heterosexuality and Lesbian Existence" [1980], in *Journal of Women's History*, vol. 15, no. 3 (2003): 11–48.

3. Ibid., pp. 26–7.

4. William S. Wilkerson, *Ambiguity and Sexuality: A Theory of Sexual Identity* (Palgrave Macmillan, 2007), p. 49.

5. Silvia Federici, "Wages Against Housework" [1975], in *Revolution at Point Zero: Housework, Reproduction, and Feminist Struggle* (PM Press, 2012): 15–22, p. 22.

6. Andrea Long Chu and Anastasia Berg, "Wanting Bad Things: Andrea Long Chu Responds to Amia Srinivasan," *The Point* (July 18, 2018): https://thepointmag.com/2018/dialogue/wanting-bad-things-andrea-long-chu-responds-amia-srinivasan

7. Audre Lorde, "Uses of the Erotic: The Erotic as Power" [1978], in *Sister Outsider* (Crossing Press, 1984): 53–9, pp. 57–8.

8. Sandra Lee Bartky, *Femininity and Domination: Studies in the Phenomenology of Oppression* (Routledge, 1990), p. 50. See also Ann J. Cahill, "Sexual Desire, Inequality, and the Possibility of Transformation," in *Body Aesthetics*, ed. Sherri Irvin (Oxford University Press, 2016): 281–91, p. 286.

9. For a contemporary feminist text that asks us to rethink, once again, these and many related issues, see Sophie Lewis, *Full Surrogacy Now: Feminism Against Family* (Verso, 2019). On the importance of feminist and queer challenges to the nuclear family as a strategy for upending neoliberalism, see Melinda Cooper, *Family Values: Between Neoliberalism and the New Social Conservatism* (Zone Books, 2017).

10. For the notion of "experiments of living," see John Stuart Mill, "On Liberty," in *On Liberty, Utilitarianism, and Other Essays*, ed. Mark Philp and Frederick Rosen (Oxford World Classics, 2015 [1859]): 1–112, pp. 56ff. See also Sara Ahmed, *Living a Feminist Life* (Duke University Press, 2017).

11. Sekai Farai (@SekaiFarai), *Twitter* (March 17, 2018): https://twitter.com/SekaiFarai/status/975026817550770177

12. Katherine Cross (@Quinnae_Moon), *Twitter* (May 3, 2018): https://twitter.com/Quinnae_Moon/status/992216016708165632

13. Yowei Shaw (u/believetheunit), "NPR reporter looking to speak with asian women about internalized racism in dating," *Reddit* (June 6, 2018): https://www.reddit.com/r/asiantwoX/comments/8p3p7t/npr_reporter_looking_to_speak_with_asian_women/

14. Heather J. Chin (@HeatherJChin), *Twitter* (June 8, 2018): https://twitter.com/HeatherJChin/status/1005103359114784769. Chin later softened her position, writing: "I am no longer wary of [Yowei Shaw's] . . . story . . . Her source call notes desire for care, nuance + after [speaking with] hapa [women] I didn't expect to be affected by this, I realize 1st step is needed & who better to tackle than folks [with] yowei & NPR's record?" (Heather J. Chin (@HeatherJChin), *Twitter* (June 9, 2018): https://twitter.com/HeatherJChin/status/1005403920037015552).

15. Celeste Ng, "When Asian Women Are Harassed for Marrying Non-Asian Men," *The Cut* (October 12, 2018): https://www.thecut.com/2018/10/when-asian-women-are-harassed-for-marrying-non-asian-men.html

16. Anon. (u/aznidentity), "Sub's Take on AF," *Reddit* (April 15, 2016): https://www.reddit.com/r/aznidentity/comments/4eu80f/the_subs_take_on_af/

17. Wesley Yang, "The Face of Seung-Hui Cho," *n+1* (Winter 2008): https://nplusonemag.com/issue-6/essays/face-seung-hui-cho/

18. Wesley Yang, "The Passion of Jordan Peterson," *Esquire* (May 1, 2018): https://www.esquire.com/news-politics/a19834137/jordan-peterson-interview/

19. Yowei Shaw and Kia Miakka Natisse, "A Very Offensive Rom-Com" (2019), NPR's *Invisibilia*: https://www.npr.org/programs/invisibilia/710046991/a-very-offensive-rom-com

20. Celeste Ng (@pronounced_ing), *Twitter* (June 2, 2015): https://twitter.com/pronounced_ing/status/605922260298264576

21. Celeste Ng (@pronounced_ing), *Twitter* (March 17, 2018): https://twitter.com/pronounced_ing/status/975043293242421254

22. Audrea Lim, "The Alt-Right's Asian Fetish," *New York Times* (January 6, 2018): https://www.nytimes.com/2018/01/06/opinion/sunday/alt-right-asian-fetish.html

23. Cristan Williams and Catharine A. MacKinnon, "Sex, Gender, and Sexuality: The TransAdvocate Interviews Catharine A. MacKinnon," *The TransAdvocate* (April 7, 2015): https://www.transadvocate.com/sex-gender-and-sexuality-the-transadvocate-interviews-catharine-a-mackinnon_n_15037.htm

24. Jordan Peterson, "Biblical Series IV: Adam and Eve: Self-Consciousness, Evil, and Death," *The Jordan B. Peterson Podcast* (2017): https://www.jordanbpeterson.com/transcripts/biblical-series-iv/

25. "Technology And Female Hypergamy, And The Inegalitarian Consequences," *Château Heartiste* (January 4, 2018): https://heartiste.org/2018/01/04/technology-and-female-hypergamy-and-the-inegalitarian-consequences/

26. For a characteristically astute discussion of these issues, see Mike Davis, "Trench Warfare: Notes on the 2020 Election," *New Left Review*, no. 126 (Nov/Dec 2020): https://newleftreview.org/issues/ii126/articles/mike-davis-trench-warfare

27. Katherine Cross (@Quinnae_Moon), *Twitter* (May 3, 2018): https://twitter.com/Quinnae_Moon/status/992216016708165632?s=20

28. Kate Julian, "Why Are Young People Having So Little Sex?," *The Atlantic* (December 2018): https://www.theatlantic.com/magazine/archive/2018/12/the-sex-recession/573949/

29. Simon Dedeo, "Hypergamy, Incels, and Reality," *Axiom of Chance* (November 15, 2018): http://simondedeo.com/?p=221

30. On the relationship between misogyny and the far right, see Michael Kimmel, *Angry White Men: American Masculinity at the End of an Era* (Nation Books, 2013); Kyle Wagner, "The Future Of The Culture Wars Is Here, And It's Gamergate," *Deadspin* (October 14, 2014): https://deadspin.com/the-future-of-the-culture-wars-is-here-and-its-gamerga-1646145844; Cara Daggett, "Petro-masculinity: Fossil Fuels and Authoritarian Desire," *Millennium*, vol. 47, no. 1 (2018): 25–44; Bonnie Honig, "The Trump Doctrine and the Gender Politics of Power," *Boston Review* (July 17, 2018): http://bostonreview.net/politics/bonnie-honig-trump-doctrine-and-gender-politics-power; Matthew N. Lyons, *Insurgent Supremacists: The U.S. Far Right's Challenge to State and Empire* (PM Press and Kersplebedeb, 2018); Aja Romano, "How the alt-right's sexism lures men into white supremacy," *Vox* (April 26, 2018): https://www.vox.com/culture/2016/12/14/13576192/alt-right-sexism-recruitment; Ashley Mattheis, "Understanding Digital Hate Culture," *CARR: Centre for the Analysis of the Radical Right* (August 19, 2019): https://www.radicalrightanalysis.com/2019/08/19/understanding-digital-hate-culture/; Alexandra Minna Stern, *Proud Boys and the White Ethnostate: How the Alt-Right Is Warping the American Imagination* (Beacon Press, 2019); the essays in Agniezska Graff, Ratna Kapur, and Suzanna Danuta Walters, eds., *Signs*, vol. 44, no. 3, "Gender and the Rise of the Global Right" (2019); Kristin Kobes Du Mez, *Jesus and John Wayne: How White Evangelicals Corrupted a Faith and Fractured a Nation* (Liveright, 2020); and Talia Lavin, *Culture Warlords: My Journey Into the Dark Web of White Supremacy* (Hachette, 2020).

31. Patrick Stedman (@Pat_Stedman), *Twitter* (October 30, 2020): https://twitter.com/Pat_Stedman/status/1322359911871819778).

32. Ross Douthat, "The Redistribution of Sex," *New York Times* (May 2, 2018): https://www.nytimes.com/2018/05/02/opinion/incels-sex-robots-redistribution.html

33. Meghan Murphy, "Ross Douthat revealed the hypocrisy in liberal feminist ideology, and they're pissed," *Feminist Currents* (May 4,

2018): https://www.feministcurrent.com/2018/05/04/ross-douthat
-revealed-hypocrisy-liberal-feminist-ideology-theyre-pissed/

34. Rebecca Solnit, "A broken idea of sex is flourishing. Blame capitalism," *Guardian* (May 12, 2018): www.theguardian.com/comment
isfree/2018/may/12/sex-capitalism-incel-movement-misogyny
-feminism. In 1911 Alexandra Kollontai warned that "In a society based
on competition, in a society where the battle for existence is fierce
and everyone is involved in a race for profit, for a career, or for just a
crust of bread, there is no room left for the cult of the demanding and
fragile Eros" (Alexandra Kollontai, "Love and the New Morality," in
Sexual Relations and the Class Struggle / Love and the New Morality, trans.
Alix Holt [Falling Wall Press, 1972], p. 20).

35. Mariarosa Dalla Costa and Selma James, "Women and the Subversion
of the Community" [1971], in *The Power of Women and the Subversion of
the Community* (Falling Wall Press, 1975 [1972]): 21–56; Mariarosa
Dalla Costa, "A General Strike" [1974], in *All Work and No Pay: Women,
Housework, and the Wages Due*, ed. Wendy Edmond and Suzie Fleming
(Power of Women Collective and the Falling Wall Press, 1975): 125–7;
Federici, "Wages Against Housework"; Nancy Fraser, "Behind
Marx's Hidden Abode," *New Left Review*, issue 86 (March–April
2014): 55–72; and Nancy Fraser, "Contradictions of Capital and Care,"
New Left Review, issue 100 (July–August 2016): 99–117. On the rela-
tionship between neoliberal capitalism and the nuclear family, see
Melinda Cooper, *Family Values*.

On Not Sleeping with Your Students

1. Jane Gallop, *Feminist Accused of Sexual Harassment* (Duke University
Press, 1997), p. 57.

2. *Lanigan v. Bartlett & Co. Grain*, 466 F. Supp. 1388 (W.D. Mo. 1979),
p. 1,391.

3. One of the three judges on the case was George MacKinnon, a conservative Republican and Catharine MacKinnon's father. In his opinion he wrote that "Sexual advances may not be intrinsically offensive,
and no policy can be derived from the equal employment opportunity laws to discourage them. We are not here concerned with
racial epithets or confusing union authorization cards, which serve
no one's interest, but with social patterns that to some extent are
normal and expectable. It is the abuse of the practice, rather than

the practice itself, that arouses alarm." One can only convince one's father of so much.

4. See e.g., *Miller v. Bank of America*, 418 F. Supp. 233 (N.D. Cal. 1976), in which a black woman clerk sued her white male supervisor, and *Munford v. James T. Barnes & Co.*, 441 F. Supp. 459 (E.D. Mich. 1977), in which a black woman assistant manager sued her white male employer. The central plaintiff in *Alexander v. Yale*, 459 F. Supp. 1 (D.Conn. 1979), 631 F.2d 178 (2nd Cir. 1980), Pamela Price, was also black.

5. Eileen Sullivan, "Perceptions of Consensual Amorous Relationship Polices (CARPs)," *Journal of College and Character*, vol. 5, no. 8 (2004).

6. Tara N. Richards, Courtney Crittenden, Tammy S. Garland, and Karen McGuffee, "An Exploration of Policies Governing Faculty-to-Student Consensual Sexual Relationships on University Campuses: Current Strategies and Future Directions," *Journal of College Student Development*, vol. 55, no. 4 (2014): 337–52, p. 342.

7. Margaret H. Mack, "Regulating Sexual Relationships Between Faculty and Students," *Michigan Journal of Gender & Law*, vol. 6, no. 1 (1999): 79–112, p. 91.

8. Jeffrey Toobin, "The Trouble with Sex," *New Yorker* (February 9, 1998): 48–55, p. 54. Toobin laments that the mathematics professor, Jay Jorgenson, and others like him, "can expect . . . to have their careers destroyed." Jorgenson is currently a tenured professor at the City College of New York.

9. David Batty and Rachel Hall, "UCL to ban intimate relationships between staff and their students," *Guardian* (February 20, 2020): https://www.theguardian.com/education/2020/feb/20/ucl-to-ban-intimate-relationships-between-staff-and-students-univesities. I had given a version of this essay as the Harriet and Helen Memorial Lecture at the UCL Philosophy Department just a few weeks before the policy change.

10. For appeals to this rationale in defense of regulations on professor–student relationships, see Phyllis Coleman, "Sex in Power Dependency Relationships: Taking Unfair Advantage of the 'Fair' Sex," *Albany Law Review*, vol. 53, no. 1 (1988): 95–142, pp. 95–6; Peter DeChiara, "The need for universities to have rules on consensual sexual relationships between faculty members and students," *Columbia Journal of Law and Social Problems*, vol. 21, no. 2 (1988): 137–62, p. 142; and Billie Wright Dziech and Linda Weiner, *The Lecherous Professor: Sexual Harassment On Campus* (University of Illinois Press, 1990 [1984]).

11. Adrienne Rich, "Compulsory Heterosexuality and Lesbian Existence" [1980], in *Journal of Women's History*, vol. 15, no. 3 (2003): 11–48, p. 38.

12. Jack Hitt, Joan Blythe, John Boswell, Leon Botstein, and William Kerrigan, "New Rules About Sex on Campus," *Harper's* (September 1993): 33–42, pp. 35–6.

13. A notable exception here is Laura Kipnis, *Unwanted Advances: Sexual Paranoia Comes to Campus* (HarperCollins, 2017).

14. Gallop, *Feminist Accused of Sexual Harassment*, p. 56.

15. As Corey Robin points out in an eviscerating essay in the *Chronicle of Higher Education*, those who wax lyrical about the erotics of pedagogy are, like me, almost always humanities professors at elite universities—that is, the sort of people (humanities professors) who are invested in a romanticized self-conception, working in the sort of institutions (elite universities) that allow for that conception's sustenance: offering the space and time for intense pedagogic relationships, with the sort of students who know how to share in "the easy rapport of people with money." Thus, Robin says, "the real shadow talk of the erotic professor is not sex but class" (Corey Robin, "The Erotic Professor," *The Chronicle of Higher Education* [May 13, 2018]: https:// www.chronicle.com/article/the-erotic-professor/). I feel the sting of Robin's critique. The picture of pedagogy I presuppose here *is* an elitist one: it is a picture that assumes that professors are not entirely consumed with bureaucratic hoop-jumping or huge teaching loads, and that students are not entirely consumed by financial or immigration worries. Like Robin, my political commitments mean that I think that such an education need not be elitist, that the "aim should not be to tear down Harvard but to lift up Brooklyn College" (ibid). But he is right to point out that this is an all-too-easy thing to say, and "the material conditions and teacher–student ratios that are necessary for a democratized intensity" would require a drastic redistribution of economic and social resources, at all levels of education.

16. Sigmund Freud, "Further Recommendations in the Technique of Psycho-Analysis: Observations on Transference-Love [1915]," in *Freud's Technique Papers*, trans. Joan Riviere and ed. Stephen Ellman (Other Press, 2002): 65–80, p. 79.

17. Chris Higgins, "Transference Love from the Couch to the Classroom: A Psychoanalytic Perspective on the Ethics of Teacher-Student Romance," in *Philosophy of Education* (Philosophy of Education Society, 1998): 357–65, p. 363.

18. Freud, "Further Recommendations in the Technique of Psycho-Analysis," p. 67.

19. Sigmund Freud, *An Autobiographical Study*, trans. James Strachey (Hogarth Press and The Institute of Psycho-Analysis, 1950 [1925]), p. 77.

20. Plato, *Republic,* trans. G. M. A. Grube and ed. C. D. C. Reeve (Hackett, 1991), 403b.

21. Freud, "Further Recommendations in the Technique of Psycho-Analysis," p. 79.

22. Ibid., p. 76.

23. Ibid., pp. 76–7.

24. bell hooks, "Embracing Freedom: Spirituality and Liberation," in *The Heart of Learning: Spirituality in Education*, ed. Steven Glazer (Tarcher/Putnam, 1999), p. 125.

25. Leslie Irvine, "A 'Consensual' Relationship" [1997], quoted in Carol Sanger, "The Erotics of Torts," *Michigan Law Review*, vol. 96, no. 6 (1998): 1,852–83, p. 1,875.

26. James R. Kincaid, "*Pouvoir, Félicité, Jane, et Moi* (Power, Bliss, Jane, and Me)," *Critical Inquiry*, vol. 25, no. 3 (1999): 610–16, p. 613.

27. Rich, "Compulsory Heterosexuality and Lesbian Existence."

28. Regina Barreca, "Contraband Appetites: Wit, Rage, and Romance in the Classroom," in *The Erotics of Instruction*, ed. Regina Barreca and Deborah Denenholz Morse (University Press of New England, 1997), p. 2. Quoted in Sanger, "The Erotics of Torts," p. 1,874.

29. On the particular challenges of managing transference between gay teachers and their students, see Michèle Aina Barale, "The Romance of Class and Queers: Academic Erotic Zones," in *Tilting the Tower*, ed. Linda Garber (Routledge, 1994): 16–24. See also bell hooks, "Eros, Eroticism and the Pedagogical Process," *Cultural Studies*, vol. 7, no. 1 (1993): 58–64.

30. Adrienne Rich, "Taking Women Students Seriously" [1978], in *On Lies, Secrets, and Silence: Selected Prose, 1966–1978* (Virago, 1984 [1980]): 237–45, p. 241.

31. Ibid., p. 242.

32. Lin Farley, *Sexual Shakedown: The Sexual Harassment Of Women On The Job* (McGraw-Hill, 1978); and Reva B. Siegel, "Introduction: A Short History of Sexual Harassment," in *Directions in Sexual Harassment Law*, ed. Catharine A. MacKinnon and Reva B. Siegel (Yale University Press, 2004): 1–39.

33. bell hooks, "Eros, Eroticism and the Pedagogical Process," p. 58.

34. In saying this, my friend didn't mean—just as I don't mean—that we should ignore the fact that students have bodies that are differently abled, that are differently racialized, that have different roles in the reproductive cycle, and so on. His point (and mine) is about treating our students as having bodies that might be sexually available to us.

35. For a discussion of such harms, see Caroline Forell, "What's Wrong with Faculty-Student Sex? The Law School Context," *Journal of Legal Education*, vol. 47, no. 1 (1997): 47–72; Sanger, "The Erotics of Torts"; and Mack, "Regulating Sexual Relationships Between Faculty and Students," section II.

36. Catharine A. MacKinnon, *Sexual Harassment of Working Women: A Case of Sex Discrimination* (Yale University Press, 1979), p. 174. See also Farley, *Sexual Shakedown*.

37. For a survey of recent cultural representations of professor–student relationships, see William Deresiewicz, "Love on Campus," *The American Scholar* (June 1, 2007): https://theamericanscholar.org/love-on-campus/

38. *Naragon v. Wharton*, 737 F.2d 1403 (5th Cir. 1984).

39. Lara Bazelon, "I'm a Democrat and a Feminist. And I Support Betsy DeVos's Title IX Reforms," *New York Times* (December 4, 2018): https://www.nytimes.com/2018/12/04/opinion/-title-ix-devos-democrat-feminist.html

40. Ibid. See also Janet Halley, "Trading the Megaphone for the Gavel in Title IX Enforcement," *Harvard Law Review Forum*, vol. 128 (2015): 103–17.

41. Michèle Le Dœuff, *Hipparchia's Choice: An Essay Concerning Women, Philosophy, etc.*, trans. Trista Selous (Columbia University Press, 2007 [1989]), p. 28.

42. Jane Tompkins, *A Life in School: What the Teacher Learned* (Addison-Wesley, 1996), p. 143.

43. This essay draws on material from Amia Srinivasan, "Sex as a Pedagogical Failure," *Yale Law Journal*, vol. 129, no. 4 (2020): 1,100–46. My thanks to the editors of the *Yale Law Journal*. For related discussion, see Sanger, "The Erotics of Torts"; Mack, "Regulating Sexual Relationships Between Faculty and Students"; Higgins, "Transference Love from the Couch to the Classroom"; and Forell, "What's Wrong with Faculty–Student Sex?"

Sex, Carceralism, Capitalism

1. Nate Berg, "Drive-thru brothels: why cities are building 'sexual infrastructure,'" *Guardian* (September 2, 2019): https://www.theguardian

.com/cities/2019/sep/02/drive-thru-brothels-why-cities-are
-building-sexual-infrastructure

2. Karen Ingala Smith (@K_IngalaSmith), *Twitter* (September 2, 2019): https://twitter.com/K_IngalaSmith/status/116847173860422 8608

3. Making Herstory (@MakeHerstory1), *Twitter* (September 2, 2019): https://twitter.com/MakeHerstory1/status/116852752818678 5794

4. See for example Claude Jaget, ed., *Prostitutes: Our Life* (Falling Wall Press, 1980); International Committee for Prostitutes' Rights, "World Charter for Prostitutes Rights: February 1985, Amsterdam," *Social Text*, no. 37 (1993): 183–5; Gail Pheterson, ed., *A Vindication of The Rights of Whores* (Seal Press, 1989); Durbar Mahila Samanwaya Committee, "Sex Workers' Manifesto: First National Conference of Sex Workers in India" [1997], *Global Network of Sex Work Projects* (2011): https://www.nswp.org/resource/sex-workers-manifesto -first-national-conference-sex-workers-india; European Conference on Sex Work, Human Rights, Labour and Migration, "Sex Workers in Europe Manifesto," *International Committee on the Rights of Sex Workers in Europe* (2005): https://www.sexworkeurope.org/resources /sex-workers-europe-manifesto; Melinda Chateauvert, *Sex Workers Unite: A History of the Movement from Stonewall to Slut Walk* (Beacon Press, 2014); Melissa Gira Grant, *Playing the Whore: The Work of Sex Work* (Verso, 2014); Chi Adanna Mgbako, *To Live Freely in This World: Sex Worker Activism in Africa* (NYU Press, 2016); Juno Mac and Molly Smith, *Revolting Prostitutes* (Verso 2018); Kay Kassirer, ed., *A Whore's Manifesto: An Anthology of Writing and Artwork by Sex Workers* (Thorntree Press 2019); and Cassandra Troyan, *Freedom & Prostitution* (The Elephants, 2020). See also Lucy Platt, Pippa Grenfell, Rebecca Meiksin, Jocelyn Elmes, Susan G. Sherman, Teela Sanders, Peninah Mwangi, and Anna-Louise Crago, "Associations between sex work laws and sex workers' health: A systematic review and meta-analysis of quantitative and qualitative studies," *PLoS Medicine*, vol. 15, no. 12 (2018): 1–54.

5. For a detailed discussion of how these different legal regimes affect sex workers, see Mac and Smith, *Revolting Prostitutes*.

6. Julie Burchill, *Damaged Gods: Cults and Heroes Reappraised* (Century, 1986), p. 9. Burchill goes on: "No wonder lesbians are so copious and vocal in the Eighties prostitution lobby; lesbians loathe

heterosexuality, and if anything is conducive to bad heterosexual relationships prostitution is" (p. 9).

7. Mac and Smith, *Revolting Prostitutes*, p. 141.

8. Max Weber, "Politics as a Vocation" [1919], in *Max Weber: The Vocation Lectures*, trans. Rodney Livingstone and ed. David Owen and Tracy B. Strong (Hackett, 2004): 32–94, p. 90.

9. Valeria Costa-Kostritsky, "The Dominique Strauss-Kahn courtroom drama has put prostitution on trial," *New Statesman* (February 20, 2015): https://www.newstatesman.com/world-affairs/2015/02/dominique-strauss-kahn-courtroom-drama-has-put-prostitution-trial

10. Gilda Sedgh, Jonathan Bearak, Susheela Singh, Akinrinola Bankole, Anna Popinchalk, Bela Ganatra, Clémentine Rossier, Caitlin Gerdts, Özge Tunçalp, Brooke Ronald Johnson Jr., Heidi Bart Johnston, and Leontine Alkema, "Abortion incidence between 1990 and 2014: global, regional, and subregional levels and trends," *The Lancet*, vol. 388, no. 10041 (2016): 258–67, p. 265.

11. Anna North, "Plenty of conservatives really do believe women should be executed for having abortions," *Vox* (April 5, 2018): https://www.vox.com/2018/4/5/17202182/the-atlantic-kevin-williamson-twitter-abortion-death-penalty

12. Examples of jurisdictions that have come closest to fully decriminalizing sex work include New South Wales, Australia (1995), and New Zealand (2003). In 2008, a formal review of the New Zealand legislation found that there had been no increase (and some signs of decrease) in the size of the sex work industry, that there was a shift from "managed" sex work to sex work being performed by women alone or in women's collectives, that sex workers were more willing to report crimes against them, that there had been no increase in sex trafficking, and that almost all sex workers felt that their labor and legal rights had been strengthened ("Report of the Prostitution Law Review Committee on the Operation of the Prostitution Reform Act 2003," *New Zealand Ministry of Justice* [2008], available at: https://prostitutescollective.net/wp-content/uploads/2016/10/report-of-the-nz-prostitution-law-committee-2008.pdf). In countries like Germany and the Netherlands, where sex work has been legalized but not fully decriminalized—that is, where part of the sex work industry has been brought within the bureaucratic control of the state, with the remainder operating as a criminalized industry—the

benefits of legalization primarily accrue to male brothel managers and clients, while many (especially "illegal") sex workers end up worse off. Rates of trafficking also increase. For discussion see Mac and Smith, *Revolting Prostitutes*, chapter 7.

13. Since the decriminalization of sex work in New Zealand, sex workers there report feeling more able to refuse clients. See "Report of the Prostitution Law Review Committee," p. 195.

14. Silvia Federici, "Wages Against Housework" [1975], in *Revolution at Point Zero: Housework, Reproduction, and Feminist Struggle* (PM Press, 2012): 15–22, p. 19. On the Wages for Housework campaign, see Wendy Edmond and Suzie Fleming, eds., *All Work and No Pay: Women, Housework, and the Wages Due* (Power of Women Collective and the Falling Wall Press, 1975); Silvia Federici and Arlen Austin, eds., *The New York Wages for Housework Committee, 1972–1977: History, Theory, and Documents* (Autonomedia, 2017); Beth Capper and Arlen Austin, "'Wages for housework means wages against heterosexuality': On the Archives of Black Women for Wages for Housework, and the Wages Due Lesbians," *GLQ: A Journal of Lesbian and Gay Studies*, vol. 24, no. 4 (2018): 445–66; Louise Toupin, *Wages for Housework: A History of an International Feminist Movement, 1972–77* (Pluto Press, 2018); and Kirsten Swinth, *Feminism's Forgotten Fight* (Harvard University Press, 2018), chapter 4.

15. Federici, "Wages Against Housework," p. 18.

16. Ibid., p. 19. On the role of "the demand" in the Wages for Housework campaign, see Kathi Weeks, *The Problem with Work: Feminism, Marxism, Antiwork Politics, and Postwork Imaginaries* (Duke University Press, 2011), chapter 3.

17. Angela Y. Davis, *Women, Race & Class* (Penguin Modern Classics, 2019 [1981]), chapter 13.

18. Ibid., p. 213.

19. Ibid., p. 218.

20. Ibid., p. 213.

21. Ibid., p. 216.

22. André Gorz, "Reform and Revolution" [1967], trans. Ben Brewster, *Socialist Register*, vol. 5 (1968): 111–43, p. 124. See also André Gorz, *A Strategy for Labor: A Radical Proposal*, trans. Martin Nicolaus and Victoria Ortiz (Beacon Press, 1967).

23. Davis, *Women, Race & Class*, p. 219, emphasis mine.

24. Gorz, "Reform and Revolution," p. 125.

25. A powerful expression of this worry comes from Sonya Aragon, an anarchist sex worker in the US: "The focus on decriminalization within the mainstream sex workers' rights movement necessitates positioning the work as a job like any other—necessitates a struggle for workers' rights, as bequeathed by a legislative body. Workers in this country are treated like shit, a reality that grows more starkly evident every day unemployment climbs and rent is not forgiven. It's not that I don't stand with the working class—of course I do—but that I don't view assimilation into state-sanctioned professionalism as our end goal. M. E. O'Brien writes, 'When refusing their imposed disposability and isolation through revolutionary activity, junkies and their friends move towards a communism not based on the dignity of work, but on the unconditional value of our lives.' I want the same to be true of whores and our friends. What would it look like to move on from the project of demanding that sex work is work? To move on to a politics of crime? I don't want to relinquish our criminal potential. I want underworld bonds, and co-conspirators, and money hidden in shoeboxes, to be redistributed to enemies of the state—the ones who will never receive a stimulus check, because they've got nothing on the books to begin with" (Sonya Aragon, "Whores at the End of the World," *n+1* (April 30, 2020): https://nplusonemag.com /online-only/online-only/whores-at-the-end-of-the-world/).

26. The Combahee River Collective, "A Black Feminist Statement" [1977], in *Home Girls: A Black Feminist Anthology*, ed. Barbara Smith (Kitchen Table: Women of Color Press, 1983): 272–92, p. 281.

27. Elizabeth Bernstein, "The Sexual Politics of the 'New Abolitionism,'" *differences*, vol. 18, no. 3 (2007): 128–51.

28. Silvia de Aquino, "Organizing to Monitor Implementation of the Maria da Penha Law in Brazil," in *Feminist Activism, Women's Rights, and Legal Reform*, ed. Mulki Al Sharmani (Zed, 2013), pp. 177–203. See also Susan Watkins, "Which Feminisms?," *New Left Review*, issue 109 (January–February 2018): 5–76, p. 51.

29. Michelle S. Jacobs, "The Violent State: Black Women's Invisible Struggle Against Police Violence," *William & Mary Journal of Race, Gender, and Social Justice*, vol. 24, no. 1 (2017): 39–100, pp. 84–7.

30. Ibid., p. 87.

31. Aya Gruber, *The Feminist War on Crime: The Unexpected Role of Women's Liberation in Mass Incarceration* (University of California Press, 2020), p. 58.

32. Sonia Bhalotra, Uma Kambhampati, Samantha Rawlings, and Zahra Siddique, "Intimate Partner Violence: The Influence of Job Opportunities for Men and Women," *The World Bank Economic Review* (2019): 1–19.

33. Jacobs, "The Violent State," pp. 88–90.

34. bell hooks, *Feminist Theory: From Margin to Center* (Routledge, 1984), p. 6.

35. Roy Walmsley, "World Female Imprisonment," 3rd edition, *World Prison Brief*: https://www.prisonstudies.org/sites/default/files/resources /downloads/world_female_imprisonment_list_third_edition_0 .pdf; and Wendy Sawyer, "The Gender Divide: Tracking Women's State Prison Growth," *Prison Policy Initiative* (2018): https://www .prisonpolicy.org/reports/women_overtime.html

36. Aleks Kajstura, "Women's Mass Incarceration: The Whole Pie 2019," *Prison Policy Initiative* (October 29, 2019): https://www.prisonpolicy .org/reports/pie2019women.html

37. Carla Boonkong and Pranee O'Connor, "Thailand jails more women than any other country in the world over pink yaba pills and ongoing drug arrests," *Thai Examiner* (January 4, 2019): https://www .thaiexaminer.com/thai-news-foreigners/2019/01/04/thai-women -prison-in-thailand-world-no1-country-drug-users-war-on-drugs/

38. "Yarl's Wood Centre: Home Office letter to protesters attacked," *BBC News* (March 6, 2018): https://www.bbc.co.uk/news/uk -england-beds-bucks-herts-43306966

39. On the relationship between poverty and crime, see John Clegg and Adaner Usmani, "The Economic Origins of Mass Incarceration," *Catalyst*, vol. 3, no. 3 (2019): https://catalyst-journal.com/vol3/no3 /the-economic-origins-of-mass-incarceration. On carceralism as a strategy of neoliberalism, see Loïc Wacquant, *Punishing the Poor: The Neoliberal Government of Social Insecurity* (Duke University Press, 2009). On the relationship between austerity policies and violence against women in Europe, see Anna Elomäki, "The Price of Austerity: The Impact on Women's Rights and Gender Equality in Europe," *European Women's Lobby* (2012): https://www.women lobby.org/IMG/pdf/the_price_of_austerity_-_web_edition.pdf, p. 10.

40. Watkins, "Which Feminisms?." For a classic account of the origins and development of Third World feminisms, see Kumari Jayawardena, *Feminism and Nationalism in the Third World* (Verso, 2016 [1986]).

41. New York Radical Feminists, *Rape: The First Sourcebook for Women*, ed. Noreen Connell and Cassandra Wilson (New American Library, 1974), p. 125.

42. Ibid., p. 250.

43. Watkins, "Which Feminisms?," p. 12.

44. Ibid., pp. 16ff.

45. For a canonical and powerful case study of the development of mass incarceration in California, where the prison population grew by 500 percent between 1982 and 2000, see Ruth Wilson Gilmore, *Golden Gulag: Prisons, Surplus, Crisis, and Opposition in Globalizing California* (University of California Press, 2007). It's important to note—as Gilmore's study makes clear—that much of the growth in prisons and incarceration rates was not led by the central government, and was not solely motivated by a project of racialized discipline. It is also important to note that while black people are disproportionately represented in the US prison system, it is not the case that most incarcerated people are black: 40 percent of the incarcerated population is black (compared with 13 percent of the total population), 39 percent white (64 percent of the total population), and 19 percent Latino (16 percent of the total population) (Wendy Sawyer and Peter Wagner, "Mass Incarceration: The Whole Pie 2020," *Prison Policy Initiative* [March 24, 2020]: https://www .prisonpolicy.org/reports/pie2020.html). The period of US mass incarceration did not see a shift in the (disproportionately high) ratio of black to white incarceration, but did see an enormous increase in the ratio of poor to middle-class incarceration.

46. On the battle for the political and economic rights of domestic workers in the US, see *National Domestic Workers Alliance* (2020): https:// www.domesticworkers.org/

47. Here for example is Federici, speaking from the tradition of Italian autonomist Marxism: "It is one thing to set up a day care center the way we want it, and then demand that the State pay for it. It is quite another to deliver our children to the State and then ask the State to control them not for five but for fifteen hours a day. It is one thing to organize communally the way we want to eat (by ourselves, in groups) and then ask the State to pay for it, and it is the opposite thing to ask the State to organize our meals. In one can we regain some control over our lives, in the other we extend the State's control over us" (Federici, "Wages Against Housework," p. 21). See also Selma James on

the "community control" of day-care centers in *Women, the Unions and Work, Or . . .What Is Not To Be Done* (Notting Hill Women's Liberation Workshop, 1972). Compare this with Angela Davis's endorsement of the state socialization of care work in *Women, Race & Class*, chapter 13.

48. Reflecting, in part, an increase in violent crime produced by large (and racialized) economic shifts in the 1960s. See Gilmore, *Golden Gulag,* and Clegg and Usmani, "The Economic Origins of Mass Incarceration."

49. Gruber, *The Feminist War on Crime,* p. 65.

50. For the carceral turn within feminism in nationalist contexts outside of the US, see for example, Don Kulick, "Sex in the New Europe: the criminalization of clients and Swedish fear of penetration," *Anthropological Theory*, vol. 3, no. 2 (2003): 199–218; Kamala Kempadoo, "Victims and Agents of Crime: The New Crusade Against Trafficking," in *Global Lockdown: Race, Gender and the Prison-Industrial Complex*, ed. Julia Sudbury (Routledge, 2005): 35–55; Christine Delphy, *Separate and Dominate: Feminism and Racism After the War on Terror*, trans. David Broder (Verso, 2015 [2008]); and Miriam Ticktin, "Sexual Violence as the Language of Border Control: Where French Feminist and Anti-Immigrant Rhetoric Meet," *Signs*, vol. 33, no. 4 (2008): 863–89.

51. This is a central theme of Gruber, *The Feminist War on Crime*. See also Kristin Bumiller, *In an Abusive State: How Neoliberalism Appropriated the Feminist Movement Against Sexual Violence* (Duke University Press, 2008).

52. Beth E. Richie, *Arrested Justice: Black Women, Violence, and America's Prison Nation* (NYU Press, 2012), chapter 3. See also Bumiller, *In an Abusive State*, chapter 4.

53. As charted in Gruber, *The Feminist War on Crime*, chapter 2.

54. See "Talking to My Students about Porn," this volume.

55. For a discussion of this history, see Richard Beck, *We Believe the Children: A Moral Panic in the 1980s* (PublicAffairs, 2015).

56. Gruber, *The Feminist War on Crime*, chapter 4.

57. See Bernstein, "The Sexual Politics of the 'New Abolitionism'"; and Mac and Smith, *Revolting Prostitutes*, chapter 3.

58. Watkins, "Which Feminisms?," pp. 35ff.

59. The Fourth World Conference on Women, "Beijing Declaration and Platform for Action," *United Nations* (1995): https://www.un.org /en/events/pastevents/pdfs/Beijing_Declaration_and_Platform _for_Action.pdf, p. 51.

60. See for example Bumiller, *In an Abusive State,* chapter 6; and Aparna Polavarapu, "Global Carceral Feminism and Domestic Violence: What the West Can Learn From Reconciliation in Uganda," *Harvard Journal of Law & Gender*, vol. 42, no. 1 (2018): 123–75. On Indian feminists' carceral response to rape, especially in the wake of the 2012 gang rape of Jyoti Singh, see Prabha Kotiswaran, "Governance Feminism in the Postcolony: Reforming India's Rape Laws," in Janet Halley, Prabha Kotiswaran, Rachel Rebouché, and Hila Shamir, *Governance Feminism: An Introduction* (University of Minnesota Press, 2018): 75–148. On Israel's carceral (and anti-immigrant) approach to trafficking, under influence from the US, see Hila Shamir, "Anti-trafficking in Israel: Neo-abolitionist Feminists, Markets, Borders, and the State," in Halley et al., *Governance Feminism*: 149–200.

61. For discussion, see Krista Hunt, "'Embedded Feminism' and the War on Terror," in *(En)Gendering the War on Terror: War Stories and Camouflaged Politics*, ed. Krista Hunt and Kim Rygiel (Ashgate, 2006): 51–71. For a classic critique of the representation of "Third World" women in western feminist writing, see Chandra Mohanty, "Under Western Eyes: Feminist Scholarship and Colonial Discourses," *boundary 2*, vol. 12, no. 3 (1984): 333–58.

62. Kim Berry, "The Symbolic Use of Afghan Women in the War On Terror," *Humboldt Journal of Social Relations*, vol. 27, no. 2 (2003): 137–60, p. 137.

63. On the history of US intervention in Afghanistan during the Cold War, see Berry, "The Symbolic Use of Afghan Women."

64. Lauren Bohn, "'We're All Handcuffed in This Country.' Why Afghanistan Is Still the Worst Place in the World to Be a Woman," *Time* (December 8, 2018): https://time.com/5472411/afghanistan-women-justice-war/

65. Steve Crabtree, "Afghans' Misery Reflected in Record-Low Well-Being Measures," *Gallup* (October 26, 2018): https://news.gallup.com/poll/244118/afghans-misery-reflected-record-low-measures.aspx

66. Bohn, "'We're All Handcuffed in This Country.'"

67. Juliet Mitchell, *Women's Estate* (Verso, 2015 [1971]), p. 61.

68. Aja Romano, "#WomenBoycottTwitter: an all-day protest inspires backlash from women of color," *Vox* (October 13, 2017): https://www.vox.com/culture/2017/10/13/16468708/womenboycott-twitter-protest-backlash-women-of-color

69. Sandra E. Garcia, "The Woman Who Created #MeToo Long Before Hashtags," *New York Times* (October 20, 2017): https://www.nytimes.com/2017/10/20/us/me-too-movement-tarana-burke.html

70. For a related critique of MeToo, see Heather Berg, "Left of #MeToo," *Feminist Studies,* vol. 46, no. 2 (2020): 259–86.

71. Most legal jurisdictions that recognize sexual harassment treat it as a civil rather than criminal offense. This marks an important distinction between the legal treatment of sexual harassment and, e.g., sexual assault. The use of the civil rather than the criminal law sidesteps some, but not all, problems associated with carceralism. It can be difficult, in practice, to keep them apart: see for example my discussion of the re-casting of the Dworkin–MacKinnon (civil) approach to pornography as an issue of criminal obscenity in "Talking to My Students about Porn" (this volume). My thanks to Susan Brison for raising this issue with me.

72. On carceralism as a technique of racial capitalism, see Jackie Wang, *Carceral Capitalism* (MIT Press, 2018).

73. Anti-carceralism does not necessarily imply an opposition to punishment as such. For there are non-carceral forms of punishment— indeed, social media shaming is a good example.

74. Gilmore, *Golden Gulag*, p. 2. See also Thomas Mathieson, *The Politics of Abolition Revisited* (Routledge, 2015 [1974]); Fay Honey Knopp, *Instead of Prisons: A Handbook for Abolitionists* (Prison Research Education Action Project, 1976); Julia Sudbury, "Transatlantic Visions: Resisting the Globalization of Mass Incarceration," *Social Justice*, vol. 27, no. 3 (2000): 133–49; Angela Y. Davis, *Are Prisons Obsolete* (Seven Stories Press, 2003); The CR10 Publications Collective, *Abolition Now! Ten Years of Strategy and Struggle Against the Prison Industrial Complex* (AK Press, 2008); Eric A. Stanley and Nat Smith, eds., *Captive Genders: Trans Embodiment and the Prison Industrial Complex* (AK Press, 2015); INCITE! Women of Color Against Violence, ed., *Color of Violence: The INCITE! Anthology* (Duke University Press, 2016); Alex S. Vitale, *The End of Policing* (Verso, 2017); Dan Berger, Mariame Kaba, and David Stein, "What Abolitionists do," *Jacobin* (August 24, 2017): https://www.jacobinmag.com/2017/08/prison-abolition-reform-mass-incarceration; Clément Petitjean and Ruth Wilson Gilmore, "Prisons and Class Warfare: An Interview with Ruth Wilson Gilmore," *Verso* (August 2, 2018): https://www.versobooks.com/blogs/3954-prisons-and-class-warfare-an-interview-with-ruth-wilson-gilmore; Liat

Ben-Moshe, *Decarcerating Disability: Deinstitutionalization and Prison Abolition* (University of Minnesota Press, 2020); and Angela Y. Davis, Gina Dent, Erica Meiners, and Beth Richie, *Abolition. Feminism. Now.* (Haymarket Books, 2021).

75. Angela Y. Davis, ed., *If They Come in the Morning . . . Voices of Resistance* (Verso, 2016 [1971]), p. xiii.

76. Rachel Kushner, "Is Prison Necessary? Ruth Wilson Gilmore Might Change Your Mind," *New York Times Magazine* (April 17, 2019): https://www.nytimes.com/2019/04/17/magazine/prison-abolition -ruth-wilson-gilmore.html. Forman is the author of *Locking Up Our Own: Crime and Punishment in Black America* (Farrar, Straus and Giroux, 2017).

77. It's important to note that violent offenses, from illegal gun possession to forcible rape and murder, account for much of the US's incarcerated population: 55 percent of all those in state prisons, and 42 percent of all those in state prisons, federal prisons and jails, and local jails combined (Wendy Sawyer and Peter Wagner, "The Whole Pie 2020"). Thus, ending incarceration for drug-related and other nonviolent offenses will not, as some proponents of carceral reform suggest, bring mass incarceration to an end.

78. Petitjean and Gilmore, "An Interview with Ruth Wilson Gilmore." For a discussion of recent attempts at police abolition in Minneapolis after the murder of George Floyd, see Charmaine Chua, "Abolition Is A Constant Struggle: Five Lessons from Minneapolis," *Theory & Event*, vol. 23, no. 4 supp. (2020): 127–47.

79. "Fred Hampton on racism and capitalism 1," *YouTube* (May 28, 2019): https://www.youtube.com/watch?v=jnlYA00Ffwo

80. For Reed's comments on the Movement for Black Lives, see Adolph Reed Jr., "Antiracism: a neoliberal alternative to a left," *Dialectical Anthropology*, vol. 42 (2018):105–15; Reed, "The Trouble with Uplift," *The Baffler*, no. 41 (September 2018): https://the-baffler.com/salvos /the-trouble-with-uplift-reed; and Adolph Reed Jr. and Walter Benn Michaels, "The Trouble with Disparity," *Common Dreams* (August 15, 2020): https://www.commondreams.org/views/2020 /08/15/trouble-disparity. See also Cedric Johnson, "The Triumph of Black Lives Matter and Neoliberal Redemption," *nonsite.org* (June 9, 2020): https://nonsite.org/the-triumph-of-black-lives-matter-and -neoliberal-redemption/

81. Reed and Michaels, "The Trouble with Disparity."

82. See for example Adolph Reed Jr., "The Limits of Anti-Racism," *Left Business Observer* (September 2009): https://www.leftbusiness observer.com/Antiracism.html; Reed, "Antiracism: a neoliberal alternative to a left"; Reed, "The Trouble with Uplift"; Daniel Denvir, Barbara J. Fields, and Karen E. Fields, "Beyond 'Race Relations': An Interview with Barbara J. Fields and Karen E. Fields," *Jacobin* (January 17, 2018): https://www.jacobinmag.com/2018/01/racecraft-racism-barbara-karen-fields; Cedric Johnson, "The Wages of Roediger: Why Three Decades of Whiteness Studies Has Not Produced the Left We Need," *nonsite.org* (September 9, 2019): https://nonsite.org/the-wages-of-roediger-why-three-decades-of-whiteness-studies-has-not-produced-the-left-we-need/; and Reed and Michaels, "The Trouble with Disparity."

83. On the historic and continued role that racism has played in thwarting the emergence of mass working-class movements, see Mike Davis, *Prisoners of the American Dream: Politics and Economy in the History of the US Working Class* (Verso, 2018 [1986]); David R. Roediger, *The Wages of Whiteness: Race and the Making of the American Working Class* (Verso, 2007 [1991]); Satnam Virdee, *Racism, Class and the Racialised Outsider* (Red Globe Press, 2014); Katherine J. Cramer, *The Politics of Resentment: Rural Consciousness in Wisconsin and the Rise of Scott Walker* (University of Chicago Press, 2016); and Michael C. Dawson, "Hidden in Plain Sight: A Note on Legitimation Crises and the Racial Order," *Critical Historical Studies*, vol. 3, no. 1 (2016): 143–61. On the class origins of race and racism, see Cedric J. Robinson, *Black Marxism: The Making of the Black Radical Tradition* (The University of North Carolina Press, 2000 [1983]); and Theodore Allen, *The Invention of the White Race,* vol. 2, *The Origins of Racial Oppression in Anglo-America* (Verso, 2012 [1997]). To say that racism emerged out of a set of shifting material conditions is not to say that it now wholly depends on them, such that "ending capitalism" would necessarily bring an end to race or racism, or that any change in racist practices or attitudes are explanatorily reducible to changes in an "underlying" class structure. Indeed, one fundamental point of collision between theorists like Adolph Reed and theorists of racial capitalism is whether race, once emergent, can be said to "take on a life of its own." On this point, see Adolph Reed Jr., "Response to Eric Arnesen," *International Labor and Working-Class History*, no. 60 (2001): 69–80; and Reed, "Unraveling the relation of race and class

in American politics," *Advance the Struggle* (June 11, 2009): https://advancethestruggle.wordpress.com/2009/06/11/how-does-race-relate-to-class-a-debate/. See also Barbara Jeanne Fields, "Slavery, Race and Ideology in the United States of America," *New Left Review,* issue I/181 (May–June 1990): 95–118, p. 101.

84. W.E.B. Du Bois, *Black Reconstruction in America: 1860–1880* (The Free Press, 1992 [1935]). It's worth noting that Adolph Reed, who has written a book on the political thought of Du Bois, nonetheless has a strong opposition to his invocation—and historical analogies more broadly—in arguments about contemporary politics. See Adolph Reed Jr., "Rejoinder," *Advance the Struggle* (June 11, 2009): https://advancethestruggle.wordpress.com/2009/06/11/how-does-race-relate-to-class-a-debate/; and Reed, "Socialism and the Argument against Race Reductionism," *New Labor Forum,* vol. 29, no. 2 (2020): 36–43.

85. On the increasing proportion of people of color and women in low-skilled, low-paying jobs in the US, see Rachel E. Dwyer and Erik Olin Wright, "Low-Wage Job Growth, Polarization, and the Limits and Opportunities of the Service Economy," *RSF: The Russell Sage Foundation Journal of the Social Sciences,* vol. 5, no. 4 (2019): 56–76.

86. As Stuart Hall famously put it: "race, and racism, [have] a practical as well as theoretical centrality to all the relations which affect black labour. The constitution of this fraction as a class, and the class relations which ascribe it, function as race relations. Race is thus, also, the modality in which class is 'lived,' the medium through which class relations are experienced, the form in which it is appropriated and 'fought through.' This has consequences for the whole class, not specifically for its 'racially defined' segment. It has consequences in terms of the internal fractioning and division within the working class which, among other ways, are articulated in part through race. This is no mere racist conspiracy from above. For racism is also one of the dominant means of ideological representation through which the white fractions of the class come to 'live' their relations to other fractions, and through them to capital Itself" (Stuart Hall, "Race, articulation and societies structured in dominance," in *Sociological theories: race and colonialism,* ed. UNESCO (UNESCO, 1980): 305–45, p. 341.

87. On the significance of so-called "identarian" movements to a successful popular socialism, see Stuart Hall, "Race, articulation and societies

structured in dominance"; Judith Butler, "Merely Cultural," *New Left Review,* issue I/227 (1998): 33–44; Michael Dawson, "Hidden in Plain Sight"; Charles W. Mills, "European Spectres," *The Journal of Ethics,* vol. 3, no. 2 (1999): 133–55; Ellen Meiksins Wood, "Class, Race, and Capitalism," *Advance the Struggle* (June 11, 2009): https://advance thestruggle.wordpress.com/2009/06/11/how-does-race-relate -to-class-a-debate/; Richard Seymour, "Cultural materialism and identity politics," *Lenin's Tomb* (November 30, 2011): http://www .leninology.co.uk/2011/11/cultural-materialism-and-identity.html; Nikhil Pal Singh, "A Note on Race and the Left," *Social Text Online* (July 31, 2015): https://socialtextjournal.org/a-note-on-race-and-the -left/; Mike Davis, *Prisoners of the American Dream*, epilogue; Keeanga -Yamahtta Taylor, *From #BlackLivesMatter to Black Liberation* (Haymarket Books, 2016); Melinda Cooper, *Family Values: Between Neoliberalism and the New Social Conservatism* (Zone Books, 2017); Paul Heideman, *Class Struggle and the Color Line: American Socialism and the Race Question, 1900–1930* (Haymarket Books, 2018); Rosa Burc, George Souvlis, and Nikhil Pal Singh, "Race and America's Long War: An Interview with Nikhil Pal Singh," *Salvage* (March 11, 2020): https://salvage .zone/articles/race-and-americas-long-war-an-interview-with -nikhil-pal-singh/; Ted Fertik and Maurice Mitchell, "Reclaiming Populism," *The Boston Review* (April 29, 2020): http://bostonreview .net/forum/reclaiming-populism/ted-fertik-maurice-mitchell-we -need-multiracial-working-class-alignment; Aziz Rana and Jedediah Britton-Purdy, "We Need an Insurgent Mass Movement," *Dissent* (Winter 2020): https://www.dissentmagazine.org/article/we-need -an-insurgent-mass-movement; and Gabriel Winant, "We Live in a Society: Organization is the entire question," *n+1* (December 12, 2020): https://nplusonemag.com/online-only/online-only/we-live -in-a-society/

88. James Baldwin, "An Open Letter to My Sister, Angela Y. Davis" [1970], in Angela Davis, ed., *If They Come in the Morning*: 19–23, p. 22.

89. Mariarosa Dalla Costa and Selma James, "Women and the Subversion of the Community" [1971], in *The Power of Women and the Subversion of the Community* (Falling Wall Press, 1975 [1972]): 21–56; Mariarosa Dalla Costa, "A General Strike" [1974], in *All Work and No Pay: Women, Housework, and the Wages Due,* ed. Wendy Edmond and Suzie Fleming (Power of Women Collective and the Falling Wall Press, 1975): 125–7; and Federici, "Wages Against Housework."

90. On this theme, see Nancy Fraser, "Contradictions of Capital and Care," *New Left Review,* issue 100 (July–August 2016): 99–117. On this process as it is playing out in the US, see Dwyer and Wright, "Low-Wage Job Growth"; and Gabriel Winant, *The Next Shift: The Fall of Industry and the Rise of Health Care in Rust Belt America* (Harvard University Press, 2021).

91. On the historical (and ongoing) relationship between the ideology of the nuclear, straight family and neoliberal capitalism, see Melinda Cooper, *Family Values.*

92. On technological development and the phenomenon of economic polarization, see David H. Autor, Frank Levy, and Richard J. Murnane, "The Skill Content of Recent Technological Change: An Empirical Exploration," *Quarterly Journal of Economics*, vol. 118, no. 4 (2003): 1,279–333; and David H. Autor and David Dorn, "The Growth of Low-Skill Service Jobs and the Polarization of the US Labor Market," *American Economic Review*, vol. 103, no. 5 (2013): 1,553–97.

93. James, *Women, the Unions and Work*, pp. 51–2.

94. Ruth D. Peterson and William C. Bailey, "Forcible Rape, Poverty, and Economic Inequality in U.S. Metropolitan Communities," *Journal of Quantitative Criminology*, vol. 4, no. 2 (1988): 99–119; Etienne G. Krug, Linda L. Dahlberg, James A. Mercy, Anthony B. Zwi, and Rafael Lozano, eds., "World report on violence and health," *World Health Organization* (2002): https://apps.who.int/iris/bitstream/handle /10665/42495/9241545615_eng.pdf, p. 159; and Ming-Jen Lin, "Does democracy increase crime? The evidence from international data," *Journal of Comparative Economics*, vol. 35, no. 3 (2007): 467–83.

95. On the importance of thinking of capitalism as a system that extends beyond economic relations, see Adolph Reed Jr., "Rejoinder," and Nancy Fraser, "Behind Marx's Hidden Abode," *New Left Review,* issue 86 (March–April 2014): 55–72.

96. Catharine A. MacKinnon, "Feminism, Marxism, Method, and the State: Toward Feminist Jurisprudence," *Signs*, vol. 8, no. 4 (1983): 635–58, p. 643.

97. Eliott C. McLaughlin, "Police officers in the US were charged with more than 400 rapes over a 9-year period," *CNN* (October 19, 2018): https://edition.cnn.com/2018/10/19/us/police-sexual -assaults-maryland-scope/index.html

98. Chaminda Jayanetti, "Scale of police sexual abuse claims revealed," *Observer* (May 18, 2019): https://www.theguardian.com/uk-news/2019/may/18/figures-reveal-true-extent-of-police-misconduct-foi

99. "Indian police 'gang-rape woman after she fails to pay bribe,'" *Guardian* (June 12, 2014): https://www.theguardian.com/world/2014/jun/12/indian-police-gang-rape-uttar-pradesh

100. A prominent example in the US is *INCITE!*, a network of radical feminists of color who are committed to the twin goals of ending state and interpersonal violence; its affiliated groups across the country run community support groups for victims of violence, conduct healthy masculinity and bystander training, create "no violence" zones, and facilitate transformative justice sessions between perpetrators and victims of violence. In 2001, *INCITE!* co-authored a statement with Critical Resistance, a US-based international abolitionist movement, entitled "Statement on Gender Violence and the Prison Industrial Complex" (reprinted in *Social Justice*, vol. 30, no. 3 (2003): 141–50). For examples and discussion of non-carceral approaches to gendered and sexual violence in North America, sometimes drawing on indigenous American practices of conflict resolution, see Natalie J. Sokoloff and Ida Dupont, "Domestic Violence at the Intersections of Race, Class, and Gender: Challenges and Contributions to Understanding Violence Against Marginalized Women in Diverse Communities," *Violence Against Women*, vol. 11, no. 1 (2005): 38–64; Donna Coker, "Restorative Justice, Navajo Peacemaking and Domestic Violence," *Theoretical Criminology*, vol. 10, no. 1 (2006): 67–85; Ching-In Chen, Jai Dulani, and Leah Lakshmi Piepzna-Samarasinha, *The Revolution Starts at Home: Confronting Intimate Violence Within Activist Communities* (South End Press, 2011); Creative Interventions, *Creative Interventions Toolkit: A Practical Guide to Stop Interpersonal Violence* (2012): https://www.creative-interventions.org/tools/toolkit/; Kristian Williams, "A Look at Feminist Forms of Justice That Don't Involve the Police," *Bitch* (August 20, 2015): https://www.bitchmedia.org/article/look-feminist-forms-justice-dont-involve-police; and Sophia Boutilier and Lana Wells, "The Case for Reparative and Transformative Justice Approaches to Sexual Violence in Canada: A proposal to pilot and test new approaches," *Shift: The Project to End Domestic Violence* (2018): https://prism.ucalgary.ca/handle/1880/109349.

For illuminating critiques of such approaches to sexual violence, see Angustia Celeste, Alex Gorrion, and Anon., *The Broken Teapot* (2014 [2012]): https://www.sproutdistro.com/catalog/zines/ac countability-consent/the-broken-teapot; and Words to Fire, ed., *Betrayal: A critical analysis of rape culture in anarchist subcultures* (Words to Fire Press, 2013). In the global context, attempts at transitional justice in post-conflict areas often use restorative rather than retributive justice models in addressing histories of political violence, including sexual violence—though these projects, as with South Africa's Truth and Reconciliation Commission, are typically state-sponsored or state-involving. Another example of a state-sponsored, non-carceral approach to gendered violence comes from Uganda, where victims of domestic violence are given the option of using a restorative rather than retributive mechanism of relief (Aparna Polavarapu, "Global Carceral Feminism and Domestic Violence"). An example of a feminist, non-state approach to gendered violence is that of the Gulabi Gang in Uttar Pradesh, India; with nearly 100,000 members, the Gang began life as a group of poor and low-caste women, dressed in pink saris and brandishing bamboo sticks, who would accost and publicly shame male perpetrators, physically defending themselves as necessary.

Bibliography

LEGAL SOURCES

Alexander v. Yale University, 459 F.Supp. 1 (D.Conn. 1979), 631 F.2d 178 (2d Cir. 1980).

Cal. Educ. Code §67386.

Complaint, *Bonsu v. University of Massachusetts—Amherst*, Civil Action No. 3:15-cv-30172-MGM (District of Massachusetts, Sept. 25, 2015).

Lanigan v. Bartlett & Co. Grain, 466 F. Supp. 1388 (W.D. Mo. 1979).

Mass. Gen. Law 265, §22.

Miller v. Bank of America, 418 F. Supp. 233 (N.D. Cal. 1976).

Munford v. James T. Barnes & Co., 441 F. Supp. 459 (E.D. Mich. 1977).

Naragon v. Wharton, 737 F.2d 1403 (5th Cir. 1984).

Okla. Stat. 21 §113.

R. v. Butler (1992) 1 S.C.R. 452.

R v. Cogan and Leak (1976) QB 217.

R. v. Scythes (1993) OJ 537.

R.A.V. v. City of St. Paul, Minnesota, 505 U.S. 377 (1992).

St. Paul Bias-Motivated Crime Ordinance, St. Paul, Minnesota, Legislative Code §292.02 (1990).

State v. Cuni, 733 A.2d 414, 159 N.J. 584 (1999).

Wis. Stat. §940.225(4).

BOOKS AND ARTICLES

"About Sexual Violence," *Rape Crisis England and Wales*: https://rape crisis.org.uk/get-informed/about-sexual-violence/

"Abstinence Education Programs: Definition, Funding, and Impact on Teen Sexual Behavior," *Kaiser Family Foundation* (June 1, 2018): https://www.kff.org/womens-health-policy/fact-sheet/abstinence-edu cation-programs-definition-funding-and-impact-on-teen-sexual -behavior/

Adams, Parveen, "Per Os(cillation)," *Camera Obscura*, vol. 6, no. 2 (1988): 7–29.

Ahmed, Sara, *Living a Feminist Life* (Duke University Press, 2017).

Alcoff, Linda Martín, *Rape and Resistance* (Polity, 2018).

Allen, Theodore, *The Invention of the White Race*, vol. 2, *The Origin of Racial Oppression in Anglo-America* (London: Verso, 2012 [1997]).

Anderson, David M., "Sexual Threat and Settler Society: 'Black Perils' in Kenya, c. 1907–30," *The Journal of Imperial and Commonwealth History*, vol. 38, no. 1 (2010): 47–74.

Celeste, Angustia, Alex Gorrion, and Anon., *The Broken Teapot* (2014 [2012]): https://www.sproutdistro.com/catalog/zines/accountability -consent/the-broken-teapot

Anon. (u/aznidentity), "Sub's Take on AF," *Reddit* (April 14, 2016): https://www.reddit.com/r/aznidentity/comments/4eu80f/the _subs_take_on_af/

Aragon, Sonya, "Whores at the End of the World," *n+1* (April 30, 2020): https://nplusonemag.com/online-only/online-only/whores-at -the-end-of-the-world/

Armstrong, Elizabeth A., Paula England, and Alison C. K. Fogarty, "Orgasm in College Hookups and Relationships," in *Families as*

They Really Are, ed. Barbara J. Risman and Virginia E. Rutter (W. W. Norton, 2015): 280–96.

"Attorney General's Commission on Pornography: Final Report," *U.S. Department of Justice* (1986).

Autor, David H. and David Dorn, "The Growth of Low-Skill Service Jobs and the Polarization of the US Labor Market," *American Economic Review*, vol. 103, no. 5 (2013): 1,553–97.

Autor, David H., Frank Levy, and Richard J. Murnane, "The Skill Content of Recent Technological Change: An Empirical Exploration," *Quarterly Journal of Economics*, vol. 118, no. 4 (2003): 1,279–333.

Baah, Nana, "This Adult Site Is Offering Ex-McDonald's Employees Camming Work," *Vice* (March 24, 2020): https://www.vice.com/en_uk/article/dygjvm/mcdonalds-workers-coronavirus-employment

Baishya, Anirban K., and Darshana S. Mini, "Translating Porn Studies: Lessons from the Vernacular," *Porn Studies*, vol. 7, no. 1 (2020): 2–12.

Baldwin, James, "An Open Letter to My Sister, Angela Y. Davis [1970]," in *If They Come in the Morning . . . Voices of Resistance*, ed. Angela Y. Davis (Verso, 2016 [1971]): 19–23.

Barale, Michèle Aina, "The Romance of Class and Queers: Academic Erotic Zones," in *Tilting the Tower*, ed. Linda Garber (Routledge, 1994): 16–24.

Barreca, Regina, "Contraband Appetites: Wit, Rage, and Romance in the Classroom," in *The Erotics of Instruction*, ed. Regina Barreca and Deborah Denenholz Morse (University Press of New England, 1997).

Bartholet, Elizabeth, Nancy Gertner, Janet Halley, and Jeannie Suk Gersen, "Fairness For All Students Under Title IX," *Digital Access to Scholarship at Harvard* (August 21, 2017): nrs.harvard.edu/urn-3:HUL.InstRepos:33789434

Bartky, Sandra Lee, *Femininity and Domination: Studies in the Phenomenology of Oppression* (Routledge, 1990).

Batty, David, and Rachel Hall, "UCL to ban intimate relationships between staff and their students," *Guardian* (February 20, 2020): https://www.theguardian.com/education/2020/feb/20/ucl-to-ban-intimate-relationships-between-staff-and-students-univesities

Bauer, Nancy, "Pornutopia," *n+1* (Winter 2007): https://nplusonemag.com/issue-5/essays/pornutopia/

Bazelon, Lara, "I'm a Democrat and a Feminist. And I Support Betsy DeVos's Title IX Reforms," *New York Times* (December 4, 2018): https://www.nytimes.com/2018/12/04/opinion/-title-ix-devos-democrat-feminist.html

Beal, Frances M., "Double Jeopardy: To Be Black and Female [1969]," in *Meridians: Feminism, Race, Transnationalism*, vol. 8, no. 2 (2008): 166–76.

Beck, Richard, *We Believe the Children: A Moral Panic in the 1980s* (PublicAffairs, 2015).

Bedi, Sonu, "Sexual Racism: Intimacy as a Matter of Justice," *The Journal of Politics*, vol. 77, no. 4 (2015): 998–1,011.

Beecher, Jonathan, "Parody and Liberation in *The New Amorous World* of Charles Fourier," *History Workshop Journal*, vol. 20, no. 1 (1985): 125–33.

——, *Charles Fourier: The Visionary and His World* (University of California Press, 1986).

Behrendt, Larissa, "Consent in a (Neo)Colonial Society: Aboriginal Women as Sexual and Legal 'Other,'" *Australian Feminist Studies*, vol. 15, no. 33 (2000): 353–67.

Ben-Moshe, Liat, *Decarcerating Disability: Deinstitutionalization and Prison Abolition* (University of Minnesota Press, 2020).

Berg, Heather, "Left of #MeToo," *Feminist Studies*, vol. 26, no. 2 (2020): 259–86.

Berg, Nate, "Drive-thru brothels: why cities are building 'sexual infrastructure,'" *Guardian* (September 2, 2019): https://www.theguardian.com/cities/2019/sep/02/drive-thru-brothels-why-cities-are-building-sexual-infrastructure

Berger, Dan, Mariame Kaba, and David Stein, "What Abolitionists Do," *Jacobin* (August 24, 2017): https://www.jacobinmag.com/2017/08/prison-abolition-reform-mass-incarceration

Bernstein, Elizabeth, "The Sexual Politics of the 'New Abolitionism,'" *differences*, vol. 18, no. 3 (2007): 128–51.

Berry, Kim, "The Symbolic Use of Afghan Women in the War On Terror," *Humboldt Journal of Social Relations*, vol. 27, no. 2 (2003): 137–60.

Bethel, Lorraine, and Barbara Smith, eds., *Conditions: Five: The Black Women's Issue* (1979).

Bhalotra, Sonia, Uma Kambhampati, Samantha Rawlings, and Zahra Siddique, "Intimate Partner Violence: The Influence of Job Opportunities for Men and Women," *The World Bank Economic Review* (2019): 1–19.

Bhonsle, Anubha, "Indian Army, Rape Us," *Outlook* (February 10, 2016): https://www.outlookindia.com/website/story/indian-army-rape-us/296634

Bird, Greta, and Pat O'Malley, "Kooris, Internal Colonialism, and Social Justice," *Social Justice*, vol. 16, no. 3 (1989): 35–50.

Blinder, Alan, "Was That Ralph Northam in Blackface? An Inquiry Ends Without Answers," *New York Times* (May 22, 2019): https://www.nytimes.com/2019/05/22/us/ralph-northam-blackface-photo.html

Blunt, Alison, "Embodying war: British women and domestic defilement in the Indian 'Mutiny,' 1857–8," *Journal of Historical Geography*, vol. 26, no. 3 (2000): 403–428.

Bohn, Lauren, "'We're All Handcuffed in This Country.' Why Afghanistan Is Still the Worst Place in the World to Be a Woman," *Time* (December 8, 2018): https://time.com/5472411/afghanistan-women-justice-war/

Boonkong, Carla, and Pranee O'Connor, "Thailand jails more women than any other country in the world over pink yaba pills and ongoing drug arrests," *Thai Examiner* (January 4, 2019): https://www.thaiexaminer.com/thai-news-foreigners/2019/01/04/thai-women-prison-in-thailand-world-no1-country-drug-users-war-on-drugs/

Bose, Adrija, "'Why Should I be Punished?': Punita Devi, Wife of Nirbhaya Convict, Fears Future of 'Shame,'" *News 18* (March 19, 2020): https://www.news18.com/news/buzz/why-should-i-be -punished-punita-devi-wife-of-nirbhaya-convict-fears-future-of -shame-delhi-gangrape-2543091.html

Bourke, Joanna, *Rape: A History from 1860 to the Present* (Virago, 2007).

Boutilier, Sophia, and Lana Wells, "The Case for Reparative and Transformative Justice Approaches to Sexual Violence in Canada: A proposal to pilot and test new approaches," *Shift: The Project to End Domestic Violence* (2018): https://prism.ucalgary.ca /handle/1880/109349

Bracewell, Lorna Norman, "Beyond Barnard: Liberalism, Antipornography Feminism, and the Sex Wars," *Signs*, vol. 42, no. 1 (2016): 23–48.

Breiding, Matthew J., Sharon G. Smith, Kathleen C. Basile, Mikel L. Walters, Jieru Chen, and Melissa T. Merrick, "Prevalence and Characteristics of Sexual Violence, Stalking, and Intimate Partner Violence Victimization—National Intimate Partner and Sexual Violence Survey, United States, 2011," *Center for Disease Control and Prevention Morbidity and Mortality Weekly Report*, vol. 63, no. 8 (2014): https://www.cdc.gov/mmwr/preview/mmwrhtml /ss6308a1.htm

"Brett Kavanaugh's Opening Statement: Full Transcript," *New York Times* (September 26, 2018): https://www.nytimes.com/2018 /09/26/us/politics/read-brett-kavanaughs-complete-opening -statement.html

Brosi, Matthew W., John D. Foubert, R. Sean Bannon, and Gabriel Yandell, "Effects of Sorority Members' Pornography Use on Bystander Intervention in a Sexual Assault Situation and Rape Myth Acceptance," *Oracle: The Research Journal of the Association of Fraternity/ Sorority Advisors*, vol. 6, no. 2 (2011): 26–35.

Bryan, Beverley, Stella Dadzie, and Suzanne Scafe, *The Heart of the Race: Black Women's Lives in Britain* (Virago, 1985).

Bumiller, Kristin, *In an Abusive State: How Neoliberalism Appropriated the Feminist Movement Against Sexual Violence* (Duke University Press, 2008).

Burc, Rosa, George Souvlis, and Nikhil Pal Singh, "Race and America's Long War: An Interview with Nikhil Pal Singh," *Salvage* (March 11, 2020): https://salvage.zone/articles/race-and-americas-long-war-an-interview-with-nikhil-pal-singh/

Burchill, Julie, *Damaged Gods: Cults and Heroes Reappraised* (Arrow Books, 1987).

Butler, Judith, *Gender Trouble: Feminism and the Subversion of Identity* (Routledge, 2010 [1990]).

——, "Merely Cultural," *New Left Review*, issue I/227 (1998): 33–44.

Cahill, Ann J., "Sexual Desire, Inequality, and the Possibility of Transformation," in *Body Aesthetics*, ed. Sherri Irvin (Oxford University Press, 2016): 281–91.

Callander, Denton, Martin Holt, and Christy E. Newman, "Just a Preference: Racialised Language in the Sex-Seeking Profiles of Gay and Bisexual Men," *Culture, Health & Sexuality*, vol. 14, no. 9 (2012): 1,049–63.

——, Christy E. Newman, and Martin Holt, "Is Sexual Racism *Really* Racism? Distinguishing Attitudes Towards Sexual Racism and Generic Racism Among Gay and Bisexual Men," *Archives of Sexual Behavior*, vol. 14, no.7 (2015): 1,991–2,000.

Canby, Vincent, "What Are We To Think of 'Deep Throat'?," *New York Times* (January 21, 1973): https://www.nytimes.com/1973/01/21/archives/what-are-we-to-think-of-deep-throat-what-to-think-of-deep-throat.html

Capper, Beth, and Arlen Austin, "'Wages for housework means wages against heterosexuality': On the Archives of Black Women for Wages for Housework, and the Wages Due Lesbians," *GLQ: A Journal of Lesbian and Gay Studies*, vol. 24, no. 4 (2018): 445–66.

Carr, Joetta L., and Karen M. VanDeusen, "Risk Factors for Male Sexual Aggression on College Campuses," *Journal of Family Violence*, vol. 19, no. 5 (2004): 279–89.

Castleman, Michael, "Surprising New Data from the World's Most Popular Porn Site," *Psychology Today* (March 15, 2018): https://www.psychologytoday.com/us/blog/all-about-sex/201803/surprising-new-data-the-world-s-most-popular-porn-site

"Chance the Rapper Apologizes for Working With R. Kelly," *NBC Chicago* (January 8, 2019): https://www.nbcchicago.com/news/local/Chance-the-Rapper-Apologizes-for-Working-With-R-Kelly-504063131.html

Chateauvert, Melinda, *Sex Workers Unite: A History of the Movement from Stonewall to SlutWalk* (Beacon Press, 2014).

Chen, Ching-In, Jai Dulani, and Leah Lakshmi Piepzna-Samarasinha, *The Revolution Starts at Home: Confronting Intimate Violence Within Activist Communities* (South End Press, 2011).

Chin, Heather J. (@HeatherJChin), *Twitter* (June 8, 2018): https://twitter.com/HeatherJChin/status/1005103359114784769.

—, *Twitter* (June 9, 2018): https://twitter.com/HeatherJChin/status/1005403920037015552

Chu, Andrea Long, "On Liking Women," *n+1* (Winter 2018): https://nplusonemag.com/issue-30/essays/on-liking-women/

—, and Anastasia Berg, "Wanting Bad Things: Andrea Long Chu Responds to Amia Srinivasan," *The Point* (July 18, 2018): https://thepointmag.com/2018/dialogue/wanting-bad-things-andrea-long-chu-responds-amia-srinivasan

Chua, Charmaine, "Abolition Is A Constant Struggle: Five Lessons from Minneapolis," *Theory & Event*, vol. 23, no. 4 supp. (2020): 127–47

Clegg, John, and Adaner Usmani, "The Economic Origins of Mass Incarceration," *Catalyst*, vol. 3, no. 3 (2019): https://catalyst-journal.com/vol3/no3/the-economic-origins-of-mass-incarceration

Coalition for a Feminist Sexuality and against Sadomasochism, [The Barnard Leaflet], reproduced in *Feminist Studies*, vol. 9, no. 1 (1983): 180–2.

Coker, Donna, "Restorative Justice, Navajo Peacemaking and Domestic Violence," *Theoretical Criminology*, vol. 10, no. 1 (2006): 67–85.

Coleman, Phyllis, "Sex in Power Dependency Relationships: Taking Unfair Advantage of the 'Fair' Sex," *Albany Law Review*, vol. 53, no. 1 (1988): 95–142.

Collins, Patricia Hill, *Black Feminist Thought* (Routledge, 1991 [1990]).

The Combahee River Collective, "A Black Feminist Statement [1977]," in *Home Girls: A Black Feminist Anthology*, ed. Barbara Smith (Kitchen Table: Women of Color Press, 1983): 272–92.

Cooper, Melinda, *Family Values: Between Neoliberalism and the New Social Conservatism* (Zone Books, 2017).

Coote, Anna, and Beatrix Campbell, *Sweet Freedom: The Struggle for Women's Liberation* (Picador, 1982).

Corbman, Rachel, "The Scholars and the Feminists: The Barnard Sex Conference and the History of the Institutionalization of Feminism," *Feminist Formations*, vol. 27, no. 3 (2015): 49–80.

Coscarelli, Joe, "R. Kelly Faces a #MeToo Reckoning as Time's Up Backs a Protest," *New York Times* (May 1, 2018): https://www.nytimes.com/2018/05/01/arts/music/r-kelly-timesup-metoo-muterkelly.html

Costa-Kostritsky, Valeria, "The Dominique Strauss-Kahn courtroom drama has put prostitution on trial," *New Statesman* (February 20, 2015): https://www.newstatesman.com/world-affairs/2015/02/dominique-strauss-kahn-courtroom-drama-has-put-prostitution-trial

Coy, Maddy, Liz Kelly, Fiona Elvines, Maria Garner, and Ava Kanyeredzi, "'Sex without consent, I suppose that is rape': How Young People in England Understand Sexual Consent," *Office of the Children's Commissioner* (2013): https://www.childrenscommissioner.gov.uk/report/sex-without-consent-i-suppose-that-is-rape/

Crabtree, Steve, "Afghans' Misery Reflected in Record-Low Well-Being Measures," *Gallup* (October 26, 2018): https://news.gallup.com/poll/244118/afghans-misery-reflected-record-low-measures.aspx

Cramer, Katherine J., *The Politics of Resentment: Rural Consciousness in Wisconsin and the Rise of Scott Walker* (University of Chicago Press, 2016).

The CR10 Publications Collective, ed., *Abolition Now! Ten Years of Strategy and Struggle Against the Prison Industrial Complex* (AK Press, 2008).

Creative Interventions, *Creative Interventions Toolkit: A Practical Guide to Stop Interpersonal Violence* (2012): https://www.creative-interventions.org/tools/toolkit

Crenshaw, Kimberlé, "Demarginalizing the Intersection of Race and Sex: A Black Feminist Critique of Antidiscrimination Doctrine, Feminist Theory and Antiracist Politics," *University of Chicago Legal Forum*, vol. 1989, no. 1 (1989): 139–67.

Crenshaw, Kimberlé Williams, "I Believe I Can Lie," *The Baffler* (January 17, 2019): https://thebaffler.com/latest/i-believe-i-can-lie-crenshaw

—, Andrea J. Ritchie, Rachel Anspach, Rachel Gilmer, and Luke Harris, "Say Her Name: Resisting Police Brutality Against Black Women," *African American Policy Forum* (2015): https://www.aapf.org/sayhername

—, Priscilla Ocen, and Jyoti Nanda, "Black Girls Matter: Pushed Out, Overpoliced and Underprotected," *African American Policy Forum* (2015): https://www.atlanticphilanthropies.org/wp-content/uploads/2015/09/BlackGirlsMatter_Report.pdf

Crewe, Tom, "The p-p-porn ban," *London Review of Books* (April 4, 2019): https://www.lrb.co.uk/the-paper/v41/n07/tom-crewe/short-cuts

Critical Resistance-INCITE!, "Statement on Gender Violence and the Prison Industrial Complex," in *Social Justice*, vol. 30, no. 3 (2003): 141–50.

Cross, Katherine (@Quinnae_Moon), *Twitter* (May 3, 2018): https://twitter.com/Quinnae_Moon/status/992216016708165632

Daggett, Cara, "Petro-masculinity: Fossil Fuels and Authoritarian Desire," *Millennium*, vol. 47, no. 1 (2018): 25–44.

Dalla Costa, Mariarosa, "A General Strike [1974]," in *All Work and No Pay: Women, Housework, and the Wages Due*, ed. Wendy Edmond and Suzie Fleming (Power of Women Collective and the Falling Wall Press, 1975): 125–7.

Dalla Costa, Mariarosa, and Selma James, "Women and the Subversion of the Community [1971]," in *The Power of Women and the Subversion of the Community* (Falling Wall Press, 1975 [1972]), 21–56.

Davis, Angela Y., ed., *If They Come in the Morning . . . Voices of Resistance* (Verso, 2016 [1971]).

—, *Women, Race & Class* (Penguin Modern Classics, 2019 [1981]).

—, *Are Prisons Obsolete* (Seven Stories Press, 2003).

—, Gina Dent, Erica Meiners, and Beth Richie, *Abolition. Feminism. Now.* (Haymarket Books, 2021).

Davis, Mike, *Prisoners of the American Dream: Politics and Economy in the History of the US Working Class* (Verso, 2018 [1986]).

—, "Trench Warfare: Notes on the 2020 Election," *New Left Review*, no. 126 (Nov/Dec 2020): https://newleftreview.org/issues/ii126/articles/mike-davis-trench-warfare

Dawson, Michael C., "Hidden in Plain Sight: A Note on Legitimation Crises and the Racial Order," *Critical Historical Studies*, vol. 3, no. 1 (2016): 143–61.

de Aquino, Silvia, "Organizing to Monitor Implementation of the Maria da Penha Law in Brazil," in *Feminist Activism, Women's Rights, and Legal Reform*, ed. Mulki Al Sharmani (Zed, 2013): 177–203.

de Beauvoir, Simone, *The Second Sex*, trans. Constance Borde and Sheila Malovany-Chevallier (Vintage, 2011 [1949]).

DeChiara, Peter, "The need for universities to have rules on consensual sexual relationships between faculty members and students," *Columbia Journal of Law and Social Problems*, vol. 21, no. 2 (1988): 137–62.

Dedeo, Simon, "Hypergamy, Incels, and Reality," *Axiom of Chance* (November 15, 2018): http://simondedeo.com/?p=221

Delphy, Christine, *Separate and Dominate: Feminism and Racism After the War on Terror*, trans. David Broder (Verso, 2015 [2008]).

Denvir, Daniel, Barbara J. Fields, and Karen E. Fields, "Beyond 'Race Relations': An Interview with Barbara J. Fields and Karen E. Fields," *Jacobin* (January 17, 2019): https://www.jacobinmag.com/2018/01/racecraft-racism-barbara-karen-fields

Deresiewicz, William, "Love on Campus," *The American Scholar* (June 1, 2007): https://theamericanscholar.org/love-on-campus/

Diary of a Conference on Sexuality (1982), available at: http://www.darkmatterarchives.net/wp-content/uploads/2011/12/Diary-of-a-Conference-on-Sexuality.pdf

Douthat, Ross, "The Redistribution of Sex," *New York Times* (May 2, 2018): https://www.nytimes.com/2018/05/02/opinion/incels-sex-robots-redistribution.html

Drolet, Gabrielle, "The Year Sex Work Came Home," *New York Times* (April 10, 2020): https://www.nytimes.com/2020/04/10/style/camsoda-onlyfans-streaming-sex-coronavirus.html

Du Bois, W.E.B., *Black Reconstruction in America: 1860–1880* (The Free Press, 1992 [1935]).

Dullea, Georgia, "In Feminists' Antipornography Drive, 42d Street Is the Target," *New York Times* (July 6, 1979): https://www.nytimes.com/1979/07/06/archives/in-feminists-antipornography-drive-42d-street-is-the-target.html

Du Mez, Kristin Kobes, *Jesus and John Wayne: How White Evangelicals Corrupted a Faith and Fractured a Nation* (Liveright, 2020).

Durbar Mahila Samanwaya Committee, "Sex Workers' Manifesto: First National Conference of Sex Workers in India [1997]," *Global Network of Sex Work Projects* (2011): https://www.nswp.org/resource/sex-workers-manifesto-first-national-conference-sex-workers-india

Dworkin, Andrea, *Intercourse* (Basic Books, 2007 [1987]).

——, "Suffering and Speech," in *In Harm's Way: The Pornography Civil Rights Hearings*, ed. Catharine A. MacKinnon and Andrea Dworkin (Harvard University Press, 1997): 25–36.

Dwyer, Rachel E., and Erik Olin Wright, "Low-Wage Job Growth, Polarization, and the Limits and Opportunities of the Service

Economy," *RSF:The Russell Sage Foundation Journal of the Social Sciences*, vol. 5, no. 4 (2019): 56–76.

Dziech, Billie Wright, and Linda Weiner, *The Lecherous Professor: Sexual Harassment On Campus* (University of Illinois Press, 1990 [1984]).

Echols, Alice, *Daring to Be Bad: Radical Feminism in America 1967–1975* (University of Minnesota Press, 2011 [1989]).

—, "Retrospective: Tangled Up in Pleasure and Danger," *Signs*, vol. 42, no. 1 (2016): 11–22.

Edmond, Wendy, and Suzie Fleming, eds., *All Work and No Pay: Women, Housework, and the Wages Due* (Power of Women Collective and the Falling Wall Press, 1975).

Edwards, Frank, Hedwig Lee, and Michael Esposito, "Risk of being killed by police use of force in the United States by age, race–ethnicity, and sex," *Proceedings of the National Academy of the Sciences of the United States of America*, vol. 116, no. 34 (2019): 16,793–8.

Elomäki, Anna, "The Price of Austerity: The Impact on Women's Rights and Gender Equality in Europe," *European Women's Lobby* (2012): https://www.womenlobby.org/IMG/pdf/the_price_of _austerity_-_web_edition.pdf

Epstein, Rebecca, Jamilia J. Blake, and Thalia González, "Girlhood Interrupted: The Erasure of Black Girls' Childhood," *Georgetown Center on Poverty and Inequality* (2017): https://ssrn.com/abstract=3000695

Erens, Bob, Andrew Phelps, Soazig Clifton, David Hussey, Catherine H. Mercer, Clare Tanton, Pam Sonnenberg, Wendy Macdowall, Andrew J. Copas, Nigel Field, Kirstin Mitchell, Jessica Datta, Victoria Hawkins, Catherine Ison, Simon Beddows, Kate Soldan, Filomeno Coelho da Silva, Sarah Alexander, Kaye Wellings, and Anne M. Johnson, "National Survey of Sexual Attitudes and Lifestyles 3," *Natsal* (2013): https://www.natsal.ac.uk/natsal-3.aspx

Etherington, Norman, "Natal's Black Rape Scare of the 1870s," *Journal of Southern African Studies*, vol. 15, no. 1 (1988): 36–53.

European Conference on Sex Work, Human Rights, Labour and Migration, "Sex Workers in Europe Manifesto," *International*

Committee on the Rights of Sex Workers in Europe (2005): https://www
.sexworkeurope.org/resources/sex-workers-europe-manifesto

Farai, Sekai (@SekaiFarai), *Twitter* (March 17, 2018): https://twitter
.com/SekaiFarai/status/975026817550770177

Farley, Lin, *Sexual Shakedown: The Sexual Harassment of Women on the Job*
(McGraw-Hill, 1978).

Federal Bureau of Investigation, *Crime in the United States 1996, Section
II: Crime Index Offenses Reported* (1997): https://ucr.fbi.gov/crime
-in-the-u.s/1996/96sec2.pdf

Federici, Silvia, "Wages Against Housework" [1975], in *Revolution at Point
Zero: Housework, Reproduction, and Feminist Struggle* (PM Press, 2012): 15–22.

——, and Arlen Austin, eds., *The New York Wages for Housework Committee,
1972–1977: History, Theory, and Documents* (Autonomedia, 2017).

Fertik, Ted, and Maurice Mitchell, "Reclaiming Populism," *The Boston
Review* (April 29, 2020): http://bostonreview.net/forum/reclaiming
-populism/ted-fertik-maurice-mitchell-we-need-multiracial
-working-class-alignment

Fields, Barbara Jeanne, "Slavery, Race and Ideology in the United States
of America," *New Left Review*, issue I/181 (May–June 1990): 95–118.

Filipovic, Jill, "Is the US the only country where more men are
raped than women?," *Guardian* (February 21, 2012): https://www
.theguardian.com/commentisfree/cifamerica/2012/feb/21/us
-more-men-raped-than-women).

Firestone, Shulamith, *The Dialectic of Sex* (Verso, 2015 [1970]).

Fischel, Joseph J., *Screw Consent: A Better Politics of Sexual Justice*
(University of California Press, 2019).

Forell, Caroline, "What's Wrong with Faculty-Student Sex? The Law
School Context," *Journal of Legal Education*, vol. 47, no. 1 (1997): 47–72.

Forman, James, Jr., *Locking Up Our Own: Crime and Punishment in Black
America* (Farrar, Straus and Giroux, 2017).

The Fourth World Conference on Women, "Beijing Declaration and
Platform for Action," *United Nations* (1995): https://www.un.org
/en/events/pastevents/pdfs/Beijing_Declaration_and_Platform
_for_Action.pdf

Fraser, Nancy, "Behind Marx's Hidden Abode," *New Left Review*, issue 86 (March–April 2014): 55–72.

—, "Contradictions of Capital and Care," *New Left Review*, issue 100 (July–August 2016): 99–117.

"Fred Hampton on racism and capitalism 1," *YouTube* (May 28, 2019): https://www.youtube.com/watch?v=jnlYA00Ffwo

Freud, Sigmund, *An Autobiographical Study*, trans. James Strachey (Hogarth Press and The Institute of Psycho-Analysis, 1950 [1925]).

—, "Further Recommendations in the Technique of Psycho-Analysis: Observations on Transference-Love [1915]," in *Freud's Technique Papers*, trans. Joan Riviere and ed. Stephen Ellman (Other Press, 2002): 65–80.

Gago, Verónica, *Feminist International: How to Change Everything*, trans. Liz Mason-Deese (Verso, 2020).

Gallop, Jane, *Feminist Accused of Sexual Harassment* (Duke University Press, 1997).

Garcia, Sandra E., "The Woman Who Created #MeToo Long Before Hashtags," *New York Times* (October 20, 2017): https://www.nytimes.com/2017/10/20/us/me-too-movement-tarana-burke.html

Gersen, Jacob, and Jeannie Suk, "The Sex Bureaucracy," *California Law Review*, vol. 104, no. 4 (2016): 881–948.

Ghomeshi, Jian, "Reflections from a Hashtag," *New York Review of Books* (October 11, 2018): https://www.nybooks.com/articles/2018/10/11/reflections-hashtag/

Gilmore, Ruth Wilson, *Golden Gulag: Prisons, Surplus, Crisis, and Opposition in Globalizing California* (University of California Press, 2007).

"Give parents the right to opt their child out of Relationship and Sex Education," *Petitions: UK Government and Parliament* (December 18, 2018): https://petition.parliament.uk/petitions/235053

Glazek, Christopher, "Raise the Crime Rate," *n+1* (Winter 2012): https://nplusonemag.com/issue-13/politics/raise-the-crime-rate/

Goldberg, Michelle, "The Shame of the MeToo Men," *New York Times* (September 14, 2018): https://www.nytimes.com/2018/09/14/opinion/columnists/metoo-movement-franken-hockenberry-macdonald.html

Gorz, André, "Reform and Revolution [1967]," trans. Ben Brewster, *Socialist Register* vol. 5 (1968): 111–43.

——, *A Strategy for Labor: A Radical Proposal*, trans. Martin Nicolaus and Victoria Ortiz (Beacon Press 1967).

Gould, Jon B., and Richard A. Leo, "One Hundred Years Later: Wrongful Convictions After a Century of Research," *The Journal of Criminal Law and Criminology*, vol. 100, no. 3 (2010): 825–68.

Gqola, Pumla Dineo, *Rape: A South African Nightmare* (MF Books Joburg, 2015).

Graff, Agniezska, Ratna Kapur, and Suzanna Danuta Walters, eds., *Signs*, vol. 44, no. 3, "Gender and the Rise of the Global Right" (2019).

Grant, Melissa Gira, *Playing the Whore: The Work of Sex Work* (Verso, 2014).

Green, Leslie, "Pornographies," *The Journal of Political Philosophy*, vol. 8, no. 1 (2000): 27–52.

Gross, Bruce, "False Rape Allegations: An Assault on Justice," *The Forensic Examiner*, vol. 18, no. 1 (2009): 66–70.

Gross, Samuel R., Maurice Possley, and Klara Stephens, "Race and Wrongful Convictions in the United States," *National Registry of Exonerations* (2017): http://www.law.umich.edu/special/exoneration/Documents/Race_and_Wrongful_Convictions.pdf

Gruber, Aya, *The Feminist War on Crime: The Unexpected Role of Women's Liberation in Mass Incarceration* (University of California Press, 2020).

Hald, Gert Martin, Neil M. Malamuth, and Carlin Yuen, "Pornography and Attitudes Supporting Violence Against Women: Revisiting the Relationship in Nonexperimental Studies," *Aggressive Behavior*, vol. 36, no. 1 (2010): 14–20.

Hall, Stuart, "Race, articulation and societies structured in dominance," in *Sociological theories: race and colonialism*, ed. UNESCO (UNESCO, 1980): 305–45.

Halley, Janet, "Trading the Megaphone for the Gavel in Title IX Enforcement," *Harvard Law Review Forum*, vol. 128 (2015): 103–17.

—, "The Move to Affirmative Consent," *Signs*, vol. 42, no. 1 (2016): 257–79.

Hambleton, Alexandra, "When Women Watch: The Subversive Potential of Female-Friendly Pornography in Japan," *Porn Studies*, vol. 3, no. 4 (2016): 427–42.

"Hathras case: A woman repeatedly reported rape. Why are police denying it?," *BBC News* (October 10, 2020): https://www.bbc.co.uk/news/world-asia-india-54444939

Heideman, Paul, *Class Struggle and the Color Line: American Socialism and the Race Question, 1900–1930* (Haymarket Books, 2018).

Heller, Zoë, "'Hot' Sex & Young Girls," *New York Review of Books* (August 18, 2016): https://www.nybooks.com/articles/2016/08/18/hot-sex-young-girls/

Helman, Rebecca, "Mapping the unrapeability of white and black womxn," *Agenda: Empowering women for gender equality*, vol. 32, no. 4 (2018): 10–21.

Hemingway, Mollie, and Carrie Severino, "Christine Blasey Ford's Father Supported Brett Kavanaugh's Confirmation," *The Federalist* (September 12, 2019): https://thefederalist.com/2019/09/12/christine-blasey-fords-father-supported-brett-kavanaughs-confirmation/

Higgins, Chris, "Transference Love from the Couch to the Classroom: A Psychoanalytic Perspective on the Ethics of Teacher-Student Romance," in *Philosophy of Education* (Philosophy of Education Society, 1998): 357–65.

Hill, Jemele, "What the Black Men Who Identify With Brett Kavanaugh Are Missing," *The Atlantic* (October 12, 2018): https://www.theatlantic.com/ideas/archive/2018/10/why-black-men-relate-brett-kavanaugh/572776/

Hitt, Jack, Joan Blythe, John Boswell, Leon Botstein, and William Kerrigan, "New Rules About Sex on Campus," *Harper's Magazine* (September 1993): 33–42.

Hockenberry, John, "Exile," *Harper's* (October 2018): https://harpers.org/archive/2018/10/exile-4/

Home Office and the Office for National Statistics, "An Overview of Sexual Offending in England and Wales" (2013): https://www.gov.uk/government/statistics/an-overview-of-sexual-offending-in-england-and-wales

Honig, Bonnie, "The Trump Doctrine and the Gender Politics of Power," *Boston Review* (July 17, 2018): http://bostonreview.net/politics/bonnie-honig-trump-doctrine-and-gender-politics-power

hooks, bell, *Ain't I a Woman? Black women and feminism* (South End Press, 1981).

——, *Feminist Theory: From Margin to Center* (Routledge, 1984).

——, "Eros, Eroticism and the Pedagogical Process," *Cultural Studies*, vol. 7, no. 1 (1993): 58–64.

——, "Embracing Freedom: Spirituality and Liberation," in *The Heart of Learning: Spirituality in Education*, ed. Steven Glazer (Tarcher/Putnam, 1999).

Hooton, Christopher, "A long list of sex acts just got banned in UK porn," *Independent* (December 2, 2014): https://www.independent.co.uk/news/uk/a-long-list-of-sex-acts-just-got-banned-in-uk-porn-9897174.html

Hunt, Krista, "'Embedded Feminism' and the War on Terror," in *(En)Gendering the War on Terror: War Stories and Camouflaged Politics*, ed. Krista Hunt and Kim Rygiel (Ashgate, 2006): 51–71.

INCITE! Women of Color Against Violence, ed., *Color of Violence: The INCITE! Anthology* (Duke University Press, 2016).

Indian Ministry of Health and Family Welfare, "National Family Health Survey (NFHS-4)" (2015–2016): https://dhsprogram.com/pubs/pdf/FR339/FR339.pdf

"Indian police 'gang-rape woman after she fails to pay bribe,'" *Guardian* (June 12, 2014): https://www.theguardian.com/world/2014/jun/12/indian-police-gang-rape-uttar-pradesh

Ingala Smith, Karen (@K_IngalaSmith), *Twitter* (September 2, 2019): https://twitter.com/K_IngalaSmith/status/1168471738604228608

Inglis, Amirah, *The White Women's Protection Ordinance: Sexual Anxiety and Politics in Papua* (Chatto and Windus, 1975).

International Committee for Prostitutes' Rights, "World Charter for Prostitutes Rights: February 1985, Amsterdam," in *Social Text*, no. 37 (1993): 183–5.

"International technical guidance on sexuality education," *United National Educational, Scientific and Cultural Organization (UNESCO)*, rev. ed. (2018): https://www.unaids.org/sites/default/files/media_asset/ITGSE_en.pdf

Jacobs, Katrien, "Internationalizing Porn Studies," *Porn Studies*, vol. 1, no. 1–2 (2014): 114–19.

Jacobs, Michelle S., "The Violent State: Black Women's Invisible Struggle Against Police Violence," *William & Mary Journal of Race, Gender, and Social Justice*, vol. 24, no. 1 (2017): 39–100.

Jaget, Claude, ed., *Prostitutes: Our Life* (Falling Wall Press, 1980).

Jain, Uday, "White Marxism: A Critique of Jacobin Magazine," *New Socialist* (August 11, 2017): https://newsocialist.org.uk/white-marxism-critique/

James, Selma, *Women, the Unions and Work, Or . . . What Is Not To Be Done* (Notting Hill Women's Liberation Workshop, 1972).

—, *Sex, Race and Class* (Falling Wall Press, 1975).

Jayanetti, Chaminda, "Scale of police sexual abuse claims revealed," *Guardian* (May 18, 2019): https://www.theguardian.com/uk-news/2019/may/18/figures-reveal-true-extent-of-police-misconduct-foi

Jayawardena, Kumari, *Feminism and Nationalism in the Third World* (Verso, 2016 [1986]).

Jeffreys, Sheila, "The Need for Revolutionary Feminism," *Scarlet Woman*, issue 5 (1977): 10–12.

—, "Let us be free to debate transgenderism without being accused of 'hate speech,'" *Guardian* (May 29, 2012): https://www.theguardian.com/commentisfree/2012/may/29/transgenderism-hate-speech

Johnson, Cedric, "The Wages of Roediger: Why Three Decades of Whiteness Studies Has Not Produced the Left We Need," *nonsite.org* (September 9, 2019): https://nonsite.org/the-wages

-of-roediger-why-three-decades-of-whiteness-studies-has-not
-produced-the-left-we-need/

—, "The Triumph of Black Lives Matter and Neoliberal Redemption," *nonsite.org* (June 9, 2020): https://nonsite.org /the-triumph-of-black-lives-matter-and-neoliberal-redemption/

Jolly, Joanna, "Does India have a problem with false rape claims?," *BBC News* (February 8, 2017): https://www.bbc.co.uk/news /magazine-38796457

Jolly, Margaretta, *Sisterhood and After: An Oral History of the UK Women's Liberation Movement, 1968–present* (Oxford University Press, 2019).

Jones, Claudia, "An End to the Neglect of the Problems of the Negro Woman! [1949]," in *Claudia Jones: Beyond Containment*, ed. Carole Boyce Davies (Ayebia Clarke Publishing, 2011): 74–86.

Julian, Kate, "Why Are Young People Having So Little Sex?," *The Atlantic* (December 2018): https://www.theatlantic.com/magazine /archive/2018/12/the-sex-recession/573949/

Kajstura, Aleks, "Women's Mass Incarceration: The Whole Pie 2019," *Prison Policy Initiative* (October 29, 2019): https://www.prisonpolicy .org/reports/pie2019women.html

Kassirer, Kay, ed., *A Whore's Manifesto: An Anthology of Writing and Artwork by Sex Workers* (Thorntree Press 2019).

Kelly, Kate, and David Enrich, "Kavanaugh's Yearbook Page Is 'Horrible, Hurtful' to a Woman It Named," *New York Times* (September 24, 2018): https://www.nytimes.com/2018/09/24/business/brett-kava naugh-yearbook-renate.html

Kelly, Liz, Jo Lovett, and Linda Regan, "A gap or a chasm?: Attrition in reported rape cases," *Home Office Research Study* 293 (2005): http:// webarchive.nationalarchives.gov.uk/20100418065544/homeoffice .gov.uk/rds/pdfs05/hors293.pdf

Kempadoo, Kamala, "Victims and Agents of Crime: The New Crusade Against Trafficking," in *Global Lockdown: Race, Gender and the Prison-Industrial Complex*, ed. Julia Sudbury (Routledge, 2005): 35–55.

Kimmel, Michael, *Angry White Men: American Masculinity at the End of an Era* (Nation Books, 2013).

Kincaid, James R., "*Pouvoir, Félicité, Jane, et Moi* (Power, Bliss, Jane, and Me)," *Critical Inquiry*, vol. 25, no. 3 (1999): 610–16.

Kipnis, Laura, *Unwanted Advances: Sexual Paranoia Comes to Campus* (HarperCollins, 2017).

Klein, Ezra, "'Yes Means Yes' is a terrible law, and I completely support it," *Vox* (October 13, 2014): https://www.vox.com/2014/10/13/6966847/yes-means-yes-is-a-terrible-bill-and-i-completely-support-it

Knopp, Fay Honey, *Instead of Prisons: A Handbook for Abolitionists* (Prison Research Education Action Project, 1976).

Kollontai, Alexandra, "Love and the New Morality," in *Sexual Relations and the Class Struggle/Love and the New Morality*, trans. Alix Holt (Falling Wall Press, 1972).

Kotiswaran, Prabha, "Governance Feminism in the Postcolony: Reforming India's Rape Laws," in Janet Halley, Prabha Kotiswaran, Rachel Rebouché, and Hila Shamir, *Governance Feminism: An Introduction* (University of Minnesota Press, 2018): 75–148.

Krug, Etienne G., Linda L. Dahlberg, James A. Mercy, Anthony B. Zwi, and Rafael Lozano, eds., "World report on violence and health," *World Health Organization* (2002): https://apps.who.int/iris/bitstream/handle/10665/42495/9241545615_eng.pdf

Kulick, Don, "Sex in the New Europe: the criminalization of clients and Swedish fear of penetration," *Anthropological Theory*, vol. 3, no. 2 (2003): 199–218.

Kushner, Rachel, "Is Prison Necessary? Ruth Wilson Gilmore Might Change Your Mind," *New York Times Magazine* (April 17, 2019): https://www.nytimes.com/2019/04/17/magazine/prison-abolition-ruth-wilson-gilmore.html.

Langton, Rae, "Speech Acts and Unspeakable Acts," *Philosophy and Public Affairs*, vol. 22, no. 4 (1993): 293–330.

——, "Is Pornography Like The Law?," in *Beyond Speech: Pornography and Analytic Feminist Philosophy*, ed. Mari Mikkola (Oxford University Press, 2017): 23–38.

Lavin, Talia, *Culture Warlords: My Journey Into the Dark Web of White Supremacy* (Hachette, 2020).

Le Dœuff, Michèle, *Hipparchia's Choice: An Essay Concerning Women, Philosophy, etc.*, trans. Trista Selous (Columbia University Press, 2007 [1989]).

Lewis, Sophie, *Full Surrogacy Now: Feminism Against Family* (Verso, 2019).

Lim, Audrea, "The Alt-Right's Asian Fetish," *New York Times* (January 6, 2018): https://www.nytimes.com/2018/01/06/opinion/sunday/alt-right-asian-fetish.html

Lin, Ming-Jen, "Does democracy increase crime? The evidence from international data," *Journal of Comparative Economics*, vol. 35, no. 3 (2007): 467–83.

Longeaux y Vásquez, Enriqueta, "The Mexican-American Woman," in *Sisterhood is Powerful: An Anthology of Writings from the Women's Liberation Movement*, ed. Robin Morgan (Vintage, 1970): 379–84.

Lorde, Audre, "Uses of the Erotic: The Erotic as Power [1978]," in *Sister Outsider* (Crossing Press, 1984): 53–9.

Lyons, Matthew N., *Insurgent Supremacists: The U.S. Far Right's Challenge to State and Empire* (PM Press and Kersplebedeb, 2018).

Mac, Juno, and Molly Smith, *Revolting Prostitutes* (Verso, 2018).

Mack, Margaret H., "Regulating Sexual Relationships Between Faculty and Students," *Michigan Journal of Gender & Law*, vol. 6, no. 1 (1999): 79–112.

MacKinnon, Catharine A., *Sexual Harassment of Working Women: A Case of Sex Discrimination* (Yale University Press, 1979).

—, "Feminism, Marxism, Method, and the State: Toward Feminist Jurisprudence," *Signs*, vol. 8, no. 4 (1983): 635–58.

—, "Sexuality, Pornography, and Method: 'Pleasure under Patriarchy,'" *Ethics*, vol. 99, no. 2 (1989): 314–46.

—, *Toward a Feminist Theory of the State* (Harvard University Press, 1991 [1989]).

—, *Only Words* (Harvard University Press, 1996 [1993]).

—, "Rape Redefined," *Harvard Law & Policy Review*, vol. 10, no. 2 (2016): 431–77.

Making Herstory (@MakeHerstory1), *Twitter* (September 2, 2019): https://twitter.com/MakeHerstory1/status/1168527528186785794

Malamuth, Neil M., Tamara Addison, and Mary Koss, "Pornography and Sexual Aggression: Are There Reliable Effects and Can We Understand Them?," *Annual Review of Sex Research*, vol. 11, no. 1 (2000): 26–91.

Manne, Kate (@kate_manne), *Twitter* (August 25, 2018): https://twitter.com/kate_manne/status/1033420304830349314

Manson, Marianna, and Erika Lust, "Feminist Porn Pioneer Erika Lust on the Cultural Cornerstones of Her Career," *Phoenix* (May 31, 2018): https://www.phoenixmag.co.uk/article/feminist-porn-pioneer-erika-lust-on-the-cultural-cornerstones-of-her-career/

Mathieson, Thomas, *The Politics of Abolition Revisited* (Routledge, 2015 [1974]).

Mattheis, Ashley, "Understanding Digital Hate Culture," *CARR: Centre for the Analysis of the Radical Right* (August 19, 2019): https://www.radicalrightanalysis.com/2019/08/19/understanding-digital-hate-culture/

McGrath, Ann, "'Black Velvet': Aboriginal women and their relations with white men in the Northern Territory, 1910–40," in *So Much Hard Work: Women and Prostitution in Australian History*, ed. Kay Daniels (Fontana Books, 1984): 233–97.

McLaughlin, Eliott C., "Police officers in the US were charged with more than 400 rapes over a 9-year period," *CNN* (October 19, 2018): https://edition.cnn.com/2018/10/19/us/police-sexual-assaults-maryland-scope/index.html

McVeigh, Tracy, "Can Iceland lead the way towards a ban on violent online pornography?," *Observer* (February 16, 2013): https://www.theguardian.com/world/2013/feb/16/iceland-online-pornography

Mesch, Gustavo S., "Social bonds and Internet Pornographic Exposure Among Adolescents," *Journal of Adolescence*, vol. 32, no. 3 (2009): 601–18.

Mgbako, Chi Adanna, *To Live Freely in This World: Sex Worker Activism in Africa* (NYU Press, 2016).

Mill, John Stuart, "On Liberty," in *On Liberty, Utilitarianism, and Other Essays*, ed. Mark Philp and Frederick Rosen (Oxford World Classics, 2015 [1859]): 1–112.

Mills, Charles W., "European Spectres," *The Journal of Ethics*, vol. 3, no. 2 (1999): 133–55.

Millward, Jon, "Deep Inside: A Study of 10,000 Porn Stars and Their Careers," *Jon Millward: Data Journalist* (February 14, 2013): https://jonmillward.com/blog/studies/deep-inside-a-study-of-10000-porn-stars/

Miren, Frankie, "British BDSM Enthusiasts Say Goodbye to Their Favorite Homegrown Porn," *Vice* (December 1, 2014): https://www.vice.com/en_uk/article/nnqybz/the-end-of-uk-bdsm-282

Mitchell, Juliet, *Women's Estate* (Verso, 2015 [1971]).

Mitra, Durba, *Indian Sex Life: Sexuality and the Colonial Origins of Modern Social Thought* (Princeton University Press, 2020).

Mohanty, Chandra, "Under Western Eyes: Feminist Scholarship and Colonial Discourses," *boundary 2*, vol. 12, no. 3 (1984): 333–58.

Montgomery, Blake (@blakersdozen), *Twitter* (March 31, 2020): https://twitter.com/blakersdozen/status/1245072167689060353

Moraga, Cherríe, and Gloria E. Anzaldúa, eds., *This Bridge Called My Back: Writings by Radical Women of Color* (Persephone Press, 1981).

Morgan, Robin, "Goodbye to All That [1970]," in *The Sixties Papers: Documents of a Rebellious Decade*, ed. Judith Clavir Albert and Stewart Edward Albert (Praeger, 1984): 509–16.

—, "Theory and Practice: Pornography and Rape [1974]," in *Take Back the Night: Women on Pornography*, ed. Laura Lederer (William Morrow and Company, 1980): 134–47.

Mulvey, Laura, "Visual Pleasure and Narrative Cinema," *Screen*, vol. 16, no. 3 (1975): 6–18.

Murphy, Meghan, "Ross Douthat revealed the hypocrisy in liberal feminist ideology, and they're pissed," *Feminist Currents* (May 4, 2018): https://www.feministcurrent.com/2018/05/04/ross-douthat-revealed-hypocrisy-liberal-feminist-ideology-theyre-pissed/

Nash, Jennifer C., "Strange Bedfellows: Black Feminism and Antipornography Feminism," *Social Text*, vol. 26, no. 4 (2008): 51–76.

—, *The Black Body in Ecstasy: Reading Race, Reading Pornography* (Duke University Press, 2014).

National Domestic Workers Alliance (2020): https://www.domestic workers.org/

"The National Registry of Exonerations," *The National Registry of Exonerations:* https://www.law.umich.edu/special/exoneration/Pages /about.aspx

New York Radical Feminists, *Rape: The First Sourcebook for Women*, ed. Noreen Connell and Cassandra Wilson (New American Library, 1974).

Newman, Sandra, "What kind of person makes false rape accusations?," *Quartz* (May 11, 2017): https://qz.com/980766/the-truth -about-false-rape-accusations/

Ng, Celeste (@pronounced_ing), *Twitter* (June 2, 2015): https:// twitter.com/pronounced_ing/status/605922260298264576

—, (@pronounced_ing), *Twitter* (March 17, 2018): https://twitter .com/pronounced_ing/status/975043293242421254

—, "When Asian Women Are Harassed for Marrying Non-Asian Men," *The Cut* (October 12, 2018): https://www.thecut.com/2018/10 /when-asian-women-are-harassed-for-marrying-non-asian-men .html

North, Anna, "Plenty of conservatives really do believe women should be executed for having abortions," *Vox* (April 5, 2018): https://www.vox.com/2018/4/5/17202182/the-atlantic-kevin -williamson-twitter-abortion-death-penalty

Oddone-Paolucci, Elizabeth, Mark Genius, and Claudio Violato, "A Meta-Analysis of the Published Research on the Effects of Pornography," in *The Changing Family and Child Development* (Ashgate, 2000): 48–59.

Orenstein, Peggy, *Girls & Sex: Navigating the Complicated New Landscape* (One World, 2016).

Palazzolo, Joe, "Racial Gap in Men's Sentencing," *Wall Street Journal* (February 14, 2013): https://www.wsj.com/articles/SB100014241 27887324432004578304463789858002

Pape, John, "Black and White: The 'Perils of Sex' in Colonial Zimbabwe," *Journal of Southern African Studies*, vol. 16, no. 4 (1990): 699–720.

Park, Madison, "Kevin Spacey apologizes for alleged sex assault with a minor," *CNN* (October 31, 2017): https://www.cnn.com/2017 /10/30/entertainment/kevin-spacey-allegations-anthony-rapp /index.html

"Perpetrators of Sexual Violence: Statistics," *RAINN:* https://www .rainn.org/statistics/perpetrators-sexual-violence

Peterson, Jordan, "Biblical Series IV: Adam and Eve: Self-Consciousness, Evil, and Death," *The Jordan B. Peterson Podcast* (2017): https://www .jordanbpeterson.com/transcripts/biblical-series-iv/

Peterson, Ruth D., and William C. Bailey, "Forcible Rape, Poverty, and Economic Inequality in U.S. Metropolitan Communities," *Journal of Quantitative Criminology*, vol. 4, no. 2 (1988): 99–119.

Petitjean, Clément, and Ruth Wilson Gilmore, "Prisons and Class Warfare: An Interview with Ruth Wilson Gilmore," *Verso* (August 2, 2018): https://www.versobooks.com/blogs/3954-prisons-and-class -warfare-an-interview-with-ruth-wilson-gilmore

Petrosky, Emiko, Janet M. Blair, Carter J. Betz, Katherine A. Fowler, Shane P.D. Jack, and Bridget H. Lyons, "Racial and Ethnic Differences in Homicides of Adult Women and the Role of Intimate Partner Violence—United States, 2003–2014," *Morbidity and Mortality Weekly Report*, vol. 66, no. 28 (2017): 741–6.

Pheterson, Gail, ed., *A Vindication of the Rights of Whores* (Seal Press, 1989).

Pinsker, Joe, "The Hidden Economics of Porn," *The Atlantic* (April 4, 2016): https://www.theatlantic.com/business/archive/2016/04 /pornography-industry-economics-tarrant/476580/

Plato, *Republic*, trans. G.M.A. Grube and ed. C.D.C. Reeve (Hackett, 1991).

Platt, Lucy, Pippa Grenfell, Rebecca Meiksin, Jocelyn Elmes, Susan G. Sherman, Teela Sanders, Peninah Mwangi, and Anna-Louise Crago, "Associations between sex work laws and sex workers' health: A systematic review and meta-analysis of quantitative and qualitative studies," *PLoS Medicine*, vol. 15, no. 12 (2018): 1–54.

Polavarapu, Aparna, "Global Carceral Feminism and Domestic Violence: What the West Can Learn From Reconciliation in Uganda," *Harvard Journal of Law & Gender*, vol. 42, no. 1 (2018): 123–75.

Pornhub Insights, "2017 Year in Review," *Pornhub* (January 9, 2018): https://www.pornhub.com/insights/2017-year-in-review

——, "2019 Year in Review," *Pornhub* (December 11, 2019): www.pornhub.com/insights/2019-year-in-review

Pugh, Martin, *Women and the Women's Movement in Britain since 1914* (Palgrave, 2015 [1992]).

Purves, Libby, "Indian women need a cultural earthquake," *The Times* (December 31, 2012): https://www.thetimes.co.uk/article/indian-women-need-a-cultural-earthquake-mtgbgxd3mvd

Rabuy, Bernadette, and Daniel Kopf, "Prisons of Poverty: Uncovering the pre-incarceration incomes of the imprisoned," *Prison Policy Initiative* (July 9, 2015): https://www.prisonpolicy.org/reports/income.html

Rana, Aziz, and Jedediah Britton-Purdy, "We Need an Insurgent Mass Movement," *Dissent* (Winter 2020): https://www.dissentmagazine.org/article/we-need-an-insurgent-mass-movement

Rand, Jacki Thompson, *Kiowa Humanity and the Invasion of the State* (University of Nebraska Press, 2008).

Reagon, Bernice Johnson, "Coalitional Politics: Turning the Century [1981]," in *Home Girls: A Black Feminist Anthology*, ed. Barbara Smith (Kitchen Table: Women of Color Press, 1983): 356–68.

"The Reckoning: Women and Power in the Workplace," *New York Times Magazine* (December 13, 2017): https://www.nytimes.com/interactive/2017/12/13/magazine/the-reckoning-women-and-power-in-the-workplace.html

"Redstockings Manifesto [1969]," in *Sisterhood is Powerful: An Anthology of Writings from the Women's Liberation Movement*, ed. Robin Morgan (Vintage, 1970): 533–6.

Reed, Adolph, Jr., "Response to Eric Arnesen," *International Labor and Working-Class History*, no. 60 (2001): 69–80.

—, "Unraveling the relation of race and class in American politics," *Advance the Struggle* (June 11, 2009): https://advancethestruggle.word press.com/2009/06/11/how-does-race-relate-to-class-a-debate/

—, "Rejoinder," *Advance the Struggle* (June 11, 2009): https://advance thestruggle.wordpress.com/2009/06/11/how-does-race-relate-to -class-a-debate/

—, "The Limits of Anti-Racism," *Left Business Observer* (September 2009): https://www.leftbusinessobserver.com/Antiracism .html

—, "Antiracism: a neoliberal alternative to a left," *Dialectical Anthropology*, vol. 42 (2018): 105–15.

—, "The Trouble with Uplift," *The Baffler*, no. 41 (September 2018): https://thebaffler.com/salvos/the-trouble-with-uplift-reed

—, "Socialism and the Argument against Race Reductionism," *New Labor Forum*, vol. 29, no. 2 (2020): 36–43.

—, and Walter Benn Michaels, "The Trouble with Disparity," *Common Dreams* (August 15, 2020): https://www.commondreams.org/views /2020/08/15/trouble-disparity

Rees, Jeska, "A Look Back at Anger: the Women's Liberation Movement in 1978," *Women's History Review*, vol. 19, no. 3 (2010): 337–56.

"Report of the Prostitution Law Review Committee on the Operation of the Prostitution Reform Act 2003," *New Zealand Ministry of Justice* (2008): https://prostitutescollective.net/wp-content/uploads /2016/10/report-of-the-nz-prostitution-law-committee-2008 .pdf

Rich, Adrienne, "Taking Women Students Seriously [1978]," in *On Lies, Secrets, and Silence: Selected Prose, 1966–1978* (Virago, 1984 [1980]): 237–45.

—, "Compulsory Heterosexuality and Lesbian Existence [1980]," in *Journal of Women's History*, vol. 15, no. 3 (2003): 11–48.

Richards, Tara N., Courtney Crittenden, Tammy S. Garland, and Karen McGuffee, "An Exploration of Policies Governing Faculty-to-Student Consensual Sexual Relationships on University Campuses: Current Strategies and Future Directions," *Journal of College Student Development*, vol. 55, no. 4 (2014): 337–52.

Richie, Beth E., *Arrested Justice: Black Women, Violence, and America's Prison Nation* (NYU Press, 2012).

Robin, Corey, "The Erotic Professor," *The Chronicle of Higher Education* (May 13, 2018): https://www.chronicle.com/article/the-erotic-professor/

Robinson, Cedric J., *Black Marxism: The Making of the Black Radical Tradition* (University of North Carolina Press, 2000 [1983]).

Robinson, Russell K., and David M. Frost, "LGBT Equality and Sexual Racism," *Fordham Law Review*, vol. 86, issue 6 (2018): 2,739–54.

Roediger, David R., *Wages of Whiteness: Race and the Making of the American Working Class* (Verso, 2007 [1991]).

Romano, Aja, "#WomenBoycottTwitter: an all-day protest inspires backlash from women of color," *Vox* (October 13, 2017): https://www.vox.com/culture/2017/10/13/16468708/womenboycott twitter-protest-backlash-women-of-color

—, "How the alt-right's sexism lures men into white supremacy," *Vox* (April 26, 2018): https://www.vox.com/culture/2016/12/14/13576192/alt-right-sexism-recruitment

Ronson, Jon, "The Butterfly Effect," *Audible* (2017): www.jonronson.com/butterfly.html

Rosen, Jeffrey, "Ruth Bader Ginsburg Opens Up About #MeToo, Voting Rights, and Millennials," *The Atlantic* (February 15, 2018): https://www.theatlantic.com/politics/archive/2018/02/ruth-bader-gins burg-opens-up-about-metoo-voting-rights-and-millenials/553409/

Roser, Max, Hannah Ritchie, and Esteban Ortiz-Ospina, "Internet," *Our World in Data* (2017): https://ourworldindata.org/internet

Ross, Becki L., "'It's Merely Designed for Sexual Arousal': Interrogating the Indefensibility of Lesbian Smut [1997]," in *Feminism and Pornography*, ed. Drucilla Cornell (Oxford University Press, 2007 [2000]): 264–317.

Royalle, Candida, "Porn in the USA [1993]," in *Feminism and Pornography*, ed. Drucilla Cornell (Oxford University Press, 2007 [2000]): 540–50.

Rubin, Gayle, "Blood Under the Bridge: Reflections on 'Thinking Sex,'" *GLQ: A Journal of Lesbian and Gay Studies*, vol. 17, no. 1 (2011): 15–48.

Russell, Polly, "Unfinished Business," *The British Library* (2020): https://www.bl.uk/podcasts

Ryan, Lisa, "Hockenberry Accusers Speak Out After *Harper's* Publishes Essay," *The Cut* (September 12, 2018): https://www.thecut.com/2018/09/john-hockenberry-accusers-harpers-essay.html

Ryzik, Melena, Cara Buckley, and Jodi Kantor, "Louis C.K. Is Accused by 5 Women of Sexual Misconduct," *New York Times* (November 9, 2017): https://www.nytimes.com/2017/11/09/arts/television/louis-ck-sexual-misconduct.html

Sanger, Carol, "The Erotics of Torts," *Michigan Law Review*, vol. 96, no. 6 (1998): 1,852–83.

Sawyer, Wendy, "The Gender Divide: Tracking Women's State Prison Growth," *Prison Policy Initiative* (January 9, 2018): https://www.prisonpolicy.org/reports/women_overtime.html

—, and Peter Wagner, "Mass Incarceration: The Whole Pie 2020," *Prison Policy Initiative* (March 24, 2020): https://www.prisonpolicy.org/reports/pie2020.html

Scales, Ann, "Avoiding Constitutional Depression: Bad Attitudes and the Fate of *Butler* [1994]," in *Feminism and Pornography*, ed. Drucilla Cornell (Oxford University Press, 2007 [2000]): 318–44.

Scully, Pamela, "Rape, Race, and Colonial Culture: The Sexual Politics of Identity in the Nineteenth-Century Cape Colony, South Africa," *American Historical Review*, vol. 100, no. 2 (1995): 335–59.

Sedgh, Gilda, Jonathan Bearak, Susheela Singh, Akinrinola Bankole, Anna Popinchalk, Bela Ganatra, Clémentine Rossier, Caitlin

Gerdts, Özge Tunçalp, Brooke Ronald Johnson Jr., Heidi Bart Johnston, and Leontine Alkema, "Abortion incidence between 1990 and 2014: global, regional, and subregional levels and trends," *The Lancet*, vol. 388, no. 10041 (2016): 258–67.

Seshia, Maya, "Naming Systemic Violence in Winnipeg's Street Sex Trade," *Canadian Journal of Urban Research*, vol. 19, no. 1 (2010): 1–17.

"Sex and HIV Education," *Guttmacher Institute* (January 1, 2021): https://www.guttmacher.org/state-policy/explore/sex-and -hiv-education

Seymour, Richard, "Cultural materialism and identity politics," *Lenin's Tomb* (November 30, 2011): http://www.leninology.co.uk/2011/11 /cultural-materialism-and-identity.html

Shamir, Hila, "Anti-trafficking in Israel: Neo-abolitionist Feminists, Markets, Borders, and the State," in Janet Halley, Prabha Kotiswaran, Rachel Rebouché, and Hila Shamir, *Governance Feminism: An Introduction* (University of Minnesota Press, 2018): 149–200.

Sharpe, Jenny, *Allegories of Empire: The Figure of Woman in the Colonial Text* (University of Minnesota Press, 1993).

Shaw, Yowei (u/believetheunit), "NPR reporter looking to speak with asian women about internalized racism in dating," *Reddit* (June 6, 2018): https://www.reddit.com/r/asiantwoX/comments/8p3p7t /npr_reporter_looking_to_speak_with_asian_women/

—, and Kia Miakka Natisse, "A Very Offensive Rom-Com (2019)," NPR's *Invisibilia*: https://www.npr.org/programs/invisibilia /710046991/a-very-offensive-rom-com

Sheen, David, "Israel weaponizes rape culture against Palestinians," *Electronic Intifada* (January 31, 2017): https://electronicintifada.net /content/israel-weaponizes-rape-culture-against-palestinians /19386

Shklar, Judith N., "The Liberalism of Fear," in *Liberalism and the Moral Life*, ed. Nancy L. Rosenblum (Harvard University Press, 1989): 21–38.

Siegel, Reva B., "Introduction: A Short History of Sexual Harassment," in *Directions in Sexual Harassment Law*, ed. Catharine A. MacKinnon and Reva B. Siegel (Yale University Press, 2004): 1–39.

Singh, Nikhil Pal, "A Note on Race and the Left," *Social Text Online* (July 31, 2015): https://socialtextjournal.org/a-note-on-race-and-the-left/

Smith, Andrea, *Conquest: Sexual Violence and American Indian Genocide* (South End Press, 2005).

Smith, Patrick, and Amber Jamieson, "Louis C.K. Mocks Parkland Shooting Survivors, Asian Men, And Nonbinary Teens In Leaked Audio," *BuzzFeed News* (December 31, 2018): https://www.buzz feednews.com/article/patricksmith/louis-ck-mocks-parkland -shooting-survivors-asian-men-and

Snitow, Ann, Christine Stansell, and Sharon Thompson, eds., *Powers of Desire: The Politics of Sexuality* (Monthly Review Press, 1983).

Sokoloff, Natalie J., and Ida Dupont, "Domestic Violence at the Intersections of Race, Class, and Gender: Challenges and Contributions to Understanding Violence Against Marginalized Women in Diverse Communities," *Violence Against Women*, vol. 11, no. 1 (2005): 38–64.

Solanas, Valerie, *SCUM Manifesto* (Verso, 2015 [1967]).

Solnit, Rebecca, "A broken idea of sex is flourishing. Blame capitalism," *Guardian* (May 12, 2018): www.theguardian.com/com mentisfree/2018/may/12/sex-capitalism-incel-movement-misogyny -feminism

—, "Men Explain *Lolita* to Me," *Literary Hub* (December 17, 2015): https://lithub.com/men-explain-lolita-to-me/

Spacey, Kevin, "Let Me Be Frank," *YouTube* (December 24, 2018): www .youtube.com/watch?v=JZveA-NAIDI

"SRE—the evidence," *Sex Education Forum* (January 1, 2015): http://www .sexeducationforum.org.uk/resources/evidence/sre-evidence

Srinivasan, Amia, "Sex as a Pedagogical Failure," *Yale Law Journal*, vol. 129, no. 4 (2020): 1,100–46.

Stanley, Eric A., and Nat Smith, eds., *Captive Genders: Trans Embodiment and the Prison Industrial Complex* (AK Press, 2015).

"Statutory RSE: Are teachers in England prepared?," *Sex Education Forum* (2018): https://www.sexeducationforum.org.uk/resources /evidence/statutory-rse-are-teachers-england-prepared

Stedman, Patrick (@Pat_Stedman), *Twitter* (October 30, 2020): https://twitter.com/Pat_Stedman/status/1322359911871819778.

Stern, Alexandra Minna, *Proud Boys and the White Ethnostate: How the Alt-Right Is Warping the American Imagination* (Beacon Press, 2019).

Stoya, "Feminism and Me," *Vice* (August 15, 2013): https://www.vice.com/en/article/bn5gmz/stoya-feminism-and-me

—, "Can There Be Good Porn?," *New York Times* (March 4, 2018): https://www.nytimes.com/2018/03/04/opinion/stoya-good-porn.html

"Study exposes secret world of porn addiction," *University of Sydney* (May 10, 2012): http://sydney.edu.au/news/84.html?newscategoryid=1&newsstoryid=9176

Sudbury, Julia, "Transatlantic Visions: Resisting the Globalization of Mass Incarceration," *Social Justice*, vol. 27, no. 3 (2000): 133–49.

Sullivan, Corrinne Tayce, "Indigenous Australian women's colonial sexual intimacies: positioning indigenous women's agency," *Culture, Health & Sexuality*, vol. 20, no. 4 (2018): 397–410.

Sullivan, Eileen, "Perceptions of Consensual Amorous Relationship Policies (CARPs)," *Journal of College and Character*, vol. 5, no. 8 (2004).

Swinth, Kirsten, *Feminism's Forgotten Fight* (Harvard University Press, 2018).

Tarrant, Shira, *The Pornography Industry: What Everyone Needs to Know* (Oxford University Press, 2016).

Taylor, Keeanga-Yamahtta, *From #BlackLivesMatter to Black Liberation* (Haymarket Books, 2016).

Taylor, Stuart, Jr., "Pornography Foes Lose New Weapon in Supreme Court," *New York Times* (February 25, 1986): https://www.nytimes.com/1986/02/25/us/pornography-foes-lose-new-weapon-in-supreme-court.html

"Technology And Female Hypergamy, And The Inegalitarian Consequences," *Château Heartiste* (January 4, 2018): https://heartiste.org/2018/01/04/technology-and-female-hypergamy-and-the-inegalitarian-consequences/

Thorneycroft, Ryan, "If not a fist, then what about a stump? Ableism and heteronormativity within Australia's porn regulations," *Porn Studies*, vol. 7, no. 2 (2020): 152–67.

Threadcraft, Shatema, "North American Necropolitics and Gender: On #BlackLivesMatter and Black Femicide," *South Atlantic Quarterly*, vol. 116, no. 3 (2017): 553–79.

Ticktin, Miriam, "Sexual Violence as the Language of Border Control: Where French Feminist and Anti-Immigrant Rhetoric Meet," *Signs*, vol. 33, no. 4 (2008): 863–89.

Tolentino, Jia, "Jian Ghomeshi, John Hockenberry, and the Laws of Patriarchal Physics," *New Yorker* (September 17, 2018): https://www.newyorker.com/culture/cultural-comment/jian-ghomeshi-john-hockenberry-and-the-laws-of-patriarchal-physics

Tompkins, Jane, *A Life in School: What the Teacher Learned* (Addison-Wesley, 1996).

Toobin, Jeffrey, "X-Rated," *New Yorker* (October 3, 1994): 70–8.

—, "The Trouble with Sex," *New Yorker* (February 9, 1998): 48–55.

Tooming, Uku, "Active Desire," *Philosophical Psychology*, vol. 32, no. 6 (2019): 945–68.

Toupin, Louise, *Wages for Housework: A History of an International Feminist Movement, 1972–77* (Pluto Press, 2018).

Troyan, Cassandra, *Freedom & Prostitution* (The Elephants, 2020).

Turner, Dan A., "Letter from Brock Turner's Father" (2016), available at: https://www.stanforddaily.com/2016/06/08/the-full-letter-read-by-brock-turners-father-at-his-sentencing-hearing/

"UK's controversial 'porn blocker' plan dropped," *BBC News* (October 16, 2019): https://www.bbc.co.uk/news/technology-50073102

Virdee, Satnam, *Racism, Class and the Racialised Outsider* (Red Globe Press, 2014).

"Virginia's Justin Fairfax Compared Himself To Lynching Victims In An Impromptu Address," *YouTube* (February 25, 2019): https://www.youtube.com/watch?v=ZTaTssa2d8E

Vitale, Alex S., *The End of Policing* (Verso 2017).

Wacquant, Loïc, *Punishing the Poor: The Neoliberal Government of Social Insecurity* (Duke University Press, 2009).

Wagner, Kyle, "The Future Of The Culture Wars Is Here, And It's Gamergate," *Deadspin* (October 14, 2014): https://deadspin .com/the-future-of-the-culture-wars-is-here-and-its-gamerga -1646145844

Walmsley, Roy, "World Female Imprisonment," 3rd edition, *World Prison Brief*: https://www.prisonstudies.org/sites/default/files /resources/downloads/world_female_imprisonment_list_third _edition_0.pdf

Walsh, Kelly, Jeanette Hussemann, Abigail Flynn, Jennifer Yahner, and Laura Golian, "Estimating the Prevalence of Wrongful Convictions," *Office of Justice Programs' National Criminal Justice Reference Service* (2017): https://www.ncjrs.gov/pdffiles1/nij/grants/251115.pdf

Wandor, Michelene, *Once a Feminist: Stories of a Generation* (Virago, 1990).

Wang, Jackie, *Carceral Capitalism* (MIT Press, 2018).

Ware, Vron, *Beyond the Pale: White Women, Racism and History* (Verso, 1992).

Watkins, Susan, "Which Feminisms?," *New Left Review*, issue 109 (January–February 2018): 5–76.

Weber, Max, "Politics as a Vocation [1919]," in *Max Weber: The Vocation Lectures*, trans. Rodney Livingstone and ed. David Owen and Tracy B. Strong (Hackett, 2004): 32–94.

Weeks, Kathi, *The Problem with Work: Feminism, Marxism, Antiwork Politics, and Postwork Imaginaries* (Duke University Press, 2011).

Wells, Ida B., "Southern Horrors: Lynch Law in All Its Phases [1892]," in *Southern Horrors and Other Writings: The Anti-Lynching Campaign of Ida B. Wells, 1892–1900*, ed. Jacqueline Jones Royster (Bedford Books, 1997): 49–72.

—, "A Red Record. Tabulated Statistics and Alleged Causes of Lynchings in the United States, 1892-1893-1894 [1895]," in *The Light of Truth: Writings of an Anti-Lynching Crusader*, ed. Mia Bay (Penguin Classics, 2014): 220–312.

Weller, Sheila, "How Author Timothy Tyson Found the Woman at the Center of the Emmett Till Case," *Vanity Fair* (January 26,

2017): https://www.vanityfair.com/news/2017/01/how-author
-timothy-tyson-found-the-woman-at-the-center-of-the-emmett
-till-case

West, Carolyn M., and Kalimah Johnson, "Sexual Violence in the Lives of African American Women," *National Online Resource Center on Violence Against Women* (2013): https://vawnet.org/sites/default/files/materials/files/2016-09/AR_SVAAWomenRevised.pdf

West, Lindy, *Shrill: Notes from a Loud Woman* (Quercus, 2016).

"What's the State of Sex Education In the U.S.?," *Planned Parenthood*: https://www.plannedparenthood.org/learn/for-educators/whats-state-sex-education-us

Whipp, Glen, "A year after #MeToo upended the status quo, the accused are attempting comebacks—but not offering apologies," *Los Angeles Times* (October 5, 2018): https://www.latimes.com/entertainment/la-ca-mn-me-too-men-apology-20181005-story.html

Wilkerson, William S., *Ambiguity and Sexuality: A Theory of Sexual Identity* (Palgrave Macmillan, 2007).

Williams, Cristan, and Catharine A. MacKinnon, "Sex, Gender, and Sexuality: The TransAdvocate interviews Catharine A. MacKinnon," *TransAdvocate* (April 7, 2015): https://www.transadvocate.com/sex-gender-and-sexuality-the-transadvocate-interviews-catharine-a-mackinnon_n_15037.htm

Williams, Kristian, "A Look at Feminist Forms of Justice That Don't Involve the Police," *Bitch* (August 20, 2015): https://www.bitchmedia.org/article/look-feminist-forms-justice-dont-involve-police

Williams, Linda, *Hard Core: Power, Pleasure, and the "Frenzy of the Visible"* (University of California Press, 1999 [1989]).

Willis, Ellen, "Feminism, Moralism, and Pornography" [1979], in *Powers of Desire: The Politics of Sexuality*, ed. Ann Snitow, Christine Stansell, and Sharon Thompson (Monthly Review Press, 1983): 460–7.

——, "Lust Horizons: Is the Women's Movement Pro-Sex?" [1981], in *No More Nice Girls: Countercultural Essays* (University of Minnesota Press, 2012 [1992]): 3–14.

Wilson, Elizabeth, "The Context of 'Between Pleasure and Danger': The Barnard Conference on Sexuality," *Feminist Review*, vol. 13, no. 1 (1983): 35–41.

Winant, Gabriel, "We Live in a Society: Organization is the entire question," *n+1* (December 12, 2020): https://nplusonemag.com /online-only/online-only/we-live-in-a-society/

——, *The Next Shift: The Fall of Industry and the Rise of Health Care in Rust Belt America* (Harvard University Press, 2021).

Wood, Ellen Meiksins, "Class, Race, and Capitalism," *Advance the Struggle* (June 11, 2009): https://advancethestruggle.wordpress .com/2009/06/11/how-does-race-relate-to-class-a-debate/

Words to Fire, ed., *Betrayal: A critical analysis of rape culture in anarchist subcultures* (Words to Fire Press, 2013).

Wright, Paul J., and Michelle Funk, "Pornography Consumption and Opposition to Affirmative Action for Women: A Prospective Study," *Psychology of Women Quarterly*, vol. 38, no. 2 (2014): 208–21.

Wypijewski, JoAnn, "What We Don't Talk About When We Talk About #MeToo," *The Nation* (February 22, 2018): https:// www.thenation.com/article/archive/what-we-dont-talk-about -when-we-talk-about-metoo/

Yang, Wesley, "The Face of Seung-Hui Cho," *n+1* (Winter 2008): https://nplusonemag.com/issue-6/essays/face-seung-hui-cho/

——, "The Passion of Jordan Peterson," *Esquire* (May 1, 2018): https://www.esquire.com/news-politics/a19834137/jordan -peterson-interview/

——, "The Revolt of the Feminist Law Profs: Jeannie Suk Gersen and the fight to save Title IX from itself," *Chronicle of Higher Education* (August 7, 2019): https://www.chronicle.com/article /the-revolt-of-the-feminist-law-profs/

"Yarl's Wood Centre: Home Office letter to protesters attacked," *BBC News* (March 6, 2018): https://www.bbc.co.uk/news/uk -england-beds-bucks-herts-43306966

Yoffe, Emily, "The Uncomfortable Truth about Campus Rape Policy," *The Atlantic* (September 6, 2017): https://www.theatlantic.com

/education/archive/2017/09/the-uncomfortable-truth-about-campus-rape-policy/538974/

Zheng, Robin, "Why Yellow Fever Isn't Flattering: A Case Against Racial Fetishes," *Journal of the American Philosophical Association*, vol. 2, no. 3 (2016): 400–19.

Index

A NOTE ABOUT THE AUTHOR

Amia Srinivasan was born in 1984 in Bahrain and was raised in London, New York, Singapore, and Taiwan. She is currently the Chichele Professor of Social and Political Theory at All Souls College, Oxford University. She has written on subjects as diverse as sex, death, octopuses, anger, surfing, and the politics of pronouns for publications including the *London Review of Books*, where she is a contributing editor; *The Times Literary Supplement*; *The New Yorker*; and *The New York Times*. She lives in Oxford.